MYTHS OF HISTORY: A HACKETT SERIES

Seven Myths of the American Revolution

Edited, with an Introduction, by Jim Piecuch

Series Editors
Alfred J. Andrea and Andrew Holt

Hackett Publishing Company, Inc.
Indianapolis/Cambridge

For further information, please address
   Hackett Publishing Company, Inc.
   P.O. Box 44937
   Indianapolis, Indiana 46244-0937

   www.hackettpublishing.com

Cover design by Rick Todhunter and Brian Rak
Interior design by E. L. Wilson
Composition by Aptara, Inc.

Library of Congress Control Number: 2023932072

ISBN-13: 978-1-64792-134-7 (pbk.)
ISBN-13: 978-1-64792-135-4 (PDF ebook)

The paper used in this publication meets the minimum requirements of American
National Standard for Information Sciences—Permanence of Paper for Printed Library
Materials, ANSI Z39.48–1984.

∞

CONTENTS

About this Series

The Myths of History series is dedicated to exposing and correcting some of the misconceptions, misjudgments, distortions, exaggerations, outdated interpretations, fallacies, seductive canards, and blatant lies that stick like super-glued sticky notes to so many of history's most significant events and actors.

The editors and authors involved in this work do not believe they are presenting pure *truth* or claim they are rendering the final word on any issue under examination. The craft of history does not allow its practitioners to speak with the voice of unquestionable authority, and the study of history does not produce immutable laws and timeless narratives that will never be revised in the light of further investigation. Rather, each historian involved in this series offers a counter-narrative reflecting the best, most up-to-date scholarship on some important element of the past that has become encrusted with misconceptions that wither when tested against the available evidence and the general consensus of the profession.

The reason for engaging such "myths" is simple. The past is neither dead nor forgotten. Carefully honed knowledge of our shared past informs our understanding of who we are and our place in the here and now, and it also allows us to place our current concerns into a broad perspective. This never-ending dialogue between the present and the past is vital to our lives, our societies, our cultures, our world, and it is incumbent upon us to understand that past as correctly as the evidence and our fallible intellects allow.

Because of the value inherent in such an investigation and understanding of the past, each book in this series speaks to a general readership, namely students and the larger reading public. For that reason, no matter how complex a topic might be, the editors and authors are committed to presenting it clearly and without recourse to technical gymnastics and jargon. This is possible without sacrificing nuance and without any dumbing down.

Many readers will note our debt to Matthew Restall's groundbreaking *Seven Myths of the Spanish Conquest*, which serves as a model for the series. Indeed, this series—to which Restall has granted his imprimatur—is a homage to his pioneering work.

Alfred J. Andrea
Andrew Holt

When we created the Myths of History series in 2015, everyone involved acknowledged that our list of desired titles had to include a book on the many myths and misunderstandings that surround the American Revolution. After many false starts, we found the right person to undertake the task, Jim Piecuch. He and his colleagues have put together a book that meets our highest hopes and standards as it explores and explodes some of the major misbegotten notions and ill-conceived interpretations surrounding "the shot heard round the world" and all that preceded and followed. It was worth the wait.

As we, the editors, worked with Jim and his team of scholars on this book, we had ample time to reflect on the myths we had grown up with, which were part of our vision of the American Revolution. We would like to share a few with you.

Ah, the stately homes of Colonial New England, how they can inspire so many historical myths. A case in point is the manor-like Vassall-Longfellow House and six other grand homes along Brattle Street in Cambridge, Massachusetts. Named after Major General William Brattle, whose house was one of the seven, Brattle Street earned the popular appellation "Tory Row" in the late eighteenth century. The nickname was still common when one of the editors of this series walked that street almost

Vassall-Longfellow House, 105 Brattle Street, Cambridge, MA. Photo by A. J. Andrea.

daily as a youth. Gazing at these seven homes, each built by a wealthy Loyalist, who retreated to the safety of British-occupied Boston to escape the wrath of local Patriots and later sailed in exile to Halifax, Nova Scotia, and beyond, that young man naturally assumed that all, or most Loyalists, also known as Tories, were members of the colonies' wealthy, Anglo-Saxon elite. In his imagination, Tories were propertied, well-educated pillars of the Anglican Church and were tied profitably into Great Britain's imperial networks.

All of that was true of Lieutenant Colonel John Vassall Jr., a Harvard College alumnus and militia officer who owned a vast slave-operated sugar plantation in Jamaica. He also housed enslaved African Americans at his ninety-acre estate on Brattle Street (then known as the Watertown Road), having overseen construction of its massive house in 1759. Baptized in Boston's Old North Church, he was a founder and warden of Cambridge's Christ Church. In 1774, this member of the establishment fled, along with his family, to Boston, then on to Halifax, and from there to England, where he died in 1797. The Patriots took over the home, along with other Tory houses along the road, and General George Washington appropriated it for his headquarters in July 1775. From there, he directed the siege of Boston, which ended with an orderly British retreat by sea on March 17, 1776. And here, we have already confronted several myths.

As Jim Piecuch convincingly demonstrates in his highly nuanced chapter, "The Loyalists," although "royal officials, merchants, lawyers, and clergy of the Church of England comprised a significant percentage of Loyalists" (p. 166), the origins, occupations, religious affiliations, relative wealth, and social classes of Tories were far more varied than that youth ever imagined.

And then there is the siege of Boston. Every schoolchild in Vermont learns how cannon and mortars captured at Fort Ticonderoga by Ethan Allen's Green Mountain Boys and trekked laboriously through winter snows to Boston turned the tide when set up on Dorchester Heights. Faced with imminent disaster, General Sir William Howe was forced to evacuate all British forces. Well, not quite right. First, of the fifty-nine pieces of artillery that Colonel Henry Knox's soldiers transported from Lake Champlain to Boston, thirty came from the fort at Crown Point, captured by a force commanded by Ethan Allen's cousin Seth Warner two days after Ticonderoga fell. Somehow Crown Point is lost in the popular story. Perhaps it is because reconstructed, privately owned, and visitor-rich Fort Ticonderoga has a better public relations department than the small New York state-park team that oversees and interprets the ruins at Crown Point. Then again, Ethan Allen, a shameless self-promoter, is to this day a larger-than-life folk hero in Vermont, Seth Warner undeservedly less so, despite his critical role in the Battle of Bennington (fought largely by New Hampshire and Massachusetts militia in present-day New York state but celebrated as a Vermont state holiday. Go figure).

Regardless, were not those artillery pieces crucial in forcing the British regulars and their Loyalist allies out of Boston? After all, the National Park Service memorial on Dorchester Heights claims: "Under the leadership of General John Thomas,

3,000 soldiers fortified these heights in March 1776, forcing the evacuation of British troops from Boston." Well, maybe not. The cannon and mortars were old and ill-cared-for by the skeleton British forces at the two captured forts. Adding to that was the inexperience of the Patriots manning the guns. At least three blew up, causing multiple casualties. Could Washington's army have sustained an effective barrage? It is questionable. Still, the fortification on Dorchester Heights likely hastened the British evacuation by a few weeks. Evidence indicates that as early as the summer of 1775, the British command had decided to quit Boston for strategic reasons, but bureaucratic inertia delayed the withdrawal. There was no initial rush to leave because the siege was not really a siege. With command of the sea and Boston Harbor, the Royal Navy was able to adequately support and provision the troops and citizens of the city. But the tale of a siege brought to a victorious conclusion by the heroic and harrowing actions of the volunteers under Ethan Allen and Henry Knox makes a more satisfying story.

And speaking of satisfying stories, there is the oft-told tale of Paul Revere. In 1843, Henry Wadsworth Longfellow and his wife, Fanny Appleton, received the former Vassall House as a wedding present from Fanny's father. An internationally recognized poet and professor at Harvard, Longfellow published in mid-December 1860 "Paul Revere's Ride" as a way of stirring patriotic fervor in the hearts of New Englanders on the eve of the Civil War. As with his world-acclaimed epic poems, he played fast and loose with historical fact, but Calliope, the muse of epic poetry, is not the handmaiden of Clio.

Because the poem is so memorable (in days past, generations of schoolchildren were forced to memorize and recite it) and the story so stirring, the myths embedded in it have become an integral part of the popular narrative of the Revolution's first days. Today the restored Paul Revere House, a National Historic Landmark along Boston's Freedom Trail, is one of the most visited tourist attractions in a city filled with sites to satisfy all interests. Undoubtedly many who tour the house have accepted Longfellow's poetic fictions as fact.

Without going into a detailed deconstruction of the poem, it suffices to note that the poet's portrayal of Revere as a solitary hero is simply wrong; a fair number of Sons of Liberty spread the word throughout the countryside that the "regulars are coming." One of the most important messengers was the overlooked William Dawes. But Dawes did not have a latter-day Homer. And those two lanterns in the steeple of the Old North Church? They were not there to inform Revere that the soldiers (not the British—even Patriots at this time saw themselves as British) were coming by sea—across Boston Harbor. Revere had ordered the lanterns set out to inform others who were also spreading the word. And he did not row himself across the harbor to Charlestown. Others rowed him across (and today, a plaque marks the approximate spot of his landing). Finally, despite what the poem says, he never reached Concord. He was detained by an army patrol, and his horse was confiscated. From there he walked to Lexington.

Enough of this. We cannot hope to equal the scholarship that informs the pages that follow. In addition to the already-cited essay on the Loyalists by Jim Piecuch, you will read his chapters on the endlessly repeated myth that oppressive British taxation was a major factor in precipitating the Revolution and the equally unfounded accusation that the British army was guilty of numerous atrocities during the war. Further, Jeff W. Dennis and Jim have combined to produce an eye-opening chapter on the Revolution's "invisible participants," women and religious minorities. Along similar lines, Jeff explodes the myths of merciless Indians guilty of innumerable savageries and well-satisfied African American slaves who supposedly sat out the war. Two other scholars present us with revealing chapters on the competing armies. Mark Edward Lender studies the relative merits and battle-effectiveness of the citizen-soldiers of the various militias vis-à-vis the qualities and military value of the regulars enrolled in the ranks of the Continental Army. Finally, putting to rest, we hope, the myth of aristocratic twits leading the brutish rabble of Great Britain's gin lanes, Don N. Hagist explores the professionalism of the British army.

Taken individually and collectively, these chapters will force many readers to rethink in a radical way their long-held notions regarding the American War for Independence. We could not be happier.

Alfred J. Andrea
Andrew Holt

When I was invited to edit this volume addressing myths of the American Revolution, I welcomed the opportunity. After many years of research in eighteenth-century primary sources, I discovered that much of what we think we "know" about the Revolutionary era is incomplete, inaccurate, or often simply wrong. It took me some time to come to grips with that fact because, like most Americans, I was and am a product of these myths. I acquired my knowledge of the Revolution in grade school during the 1960s and 1970s, supplemented by television dramas, documentaries, and the occasional cartoon (the most memorable featuring Mr. Magoo), along with books from the school and city library. In high school, our required American history course covered the period after the Civil War. My only exposure to the Revolution came from reading *Johnny Tremain* in an English class, plus some outside reading. Nonetheless, I thought I knew a fair amount about the subject.

That changed when I entered college as an adult, exploring a possible career change. Having chosen to major in history, I took a course on the Revolution, during which I realized how little I really knew about the topic. However, throughout my undergraduate and graduate coursework, I continued to believe that I possessed insufficient knowledge, not inaccurate information, while appreciating the fresh perspectives provided by my professors.

When I began researching my doctoral dissertation, I finally realized the extent to which I was still a prisoner of myths. My topic, those who supported the British in the southern colonies, forced me to reconsider many long-held beliefs. First, I recognized that my perception of the Revolution was still based on a simplistic dichotomy of good Revolutionaries versus the evil, oppressive British. The more sources I read, the more I understood that the British were not evil; from their perspective, they were attempting to suppress a treasonous rebellion. Moreover, those African Americans and Native Americans who allied themselves with the British had done so not to support oppression but to protect their own interests—interests that were not likely to receive much consideration or sympathy from the Revolutionaries.

The last domino to fall was my dislike of the Loyalists. Again, this was based on my opinion that if the Revolution was good, those Americans who opposed it were of course bad. Initially, my reading of secondary sources seemed to confirm this view. Several highly regarded historians recounted how selfish Loyalists had abandoned their support for the Revolution because the Revolutionaries had seized a prized horse or denied someone a promotion in the military. Later, when I began reading the Loyalist claims, my initial reaction was that Loyalists were indeed foolish. After all, who would sacrifice a home, hundreds of acres of land, and livestock just because someone took their horse? The more claims I read, however, the more I began to doubt the secondary accounts. The majority of claimants were clearly intelligent, some well-educated and successful. Their alleged motives did not make sense. So I went back to the secondary sources, found the citations that supported the demeaning accusations, and discovered that the allegations came not from Loyalists but from their enemies. Furthermore, most of the charges leveled against Loyalists did not even come from their contemporaries; they originated in the reminiscences of people recorded many decades after the Revolution, people who claimed to have heard the stories from their ancestors, usually grandparents. Such testimony hardly seemed credible without confirmation from other sources.

Having put aside my personal biases, I completed my dissertation. While I did not abandon my respect for the Revolutionaries or my admiration for their achievements, I succeeded in treating both sides with the fairness the subjects of our research deserve. However, when the work was later published, someone who reviewed the book for a newspaper mistakenly accused me not only of advocating for the treacherous Loyalists but also of being angry that they ended up on the losing side. Such is the power of myth that an even-handed treatment of the Loyalists was somehow considered biased in their favor.

The misunderstanding and misrepresentation of Loyalists are frequently the results of oversight by some historians. Many neglect to consult British sources and incorporate that material into their work. In part, this results from difficulty accessing such documents. Whereas most college and university libraries contain the published writings of George Washington, Thomas Jefferson, John Adams, Benjamin Franklin, and other prominent Revolutionaries, which are also easily accessible from the National Archives' Founders Online website (https://founders.archives.gov), similar collections by British participants in the struggle are harder to obtain. Only a handful of British officers, such as General Sir Henry Clinton and Lieutenant Colonel Banastre Tarleton, published memoirs of their experiences, and the papers of General Charles, Earl Cornwallis, were not published until 2010. Other essential collections, such as the British Headquarters (Sir Guy Carleton) Papers, are available only on microfilm in the United States at a few research libraries. Important collections like the Thomas Gage Papers, Henry Clinton Papers, and Lord George Germain Papers are held in a single library, and researchers must travel there to study the original manuscripts. With limited time and funds available for research, numerous academic historians rely mainly on easily accessible American materials, so publications on the Revolution often have an inadvertent bias.

Occasionally the bias is deliberate, a situation I have noticed in the work of several popular historians. Free from the academic checks and balances provided by peer reviewers, they often simply reinforce existing myths to appeal to readers who prefer a simplified account of the Revolution where heroic Americans triumph over the villainous British. Several years ago, I moderated a roundtable discussion where one of the participants, the author of four books on the Revolution, vigorously defended some well-known myths. Afterward, I called his attention to documents that contradicted one of his positions. He replied that he was unfamiliar with them and asked me to send him the citations. When I emailed the information, he responded that the materials were useless because the documents were written by British officers. His reaction was testimony both to the power of myths and the reluctance of some people to have their existing beliefs challenged.

The purpose of this volume is to address many of the myths involving the American Revolution so that readers may gain a more complete understanding of the struggle that produced the independent United States. While it is impossible to cover every myth from this era, we examine the most important and influential ones, correcting longstanding inaccuracies and omissions in histories of the Revolution. Readers will find that this history is far richer, more complex, and different from how it is frequently portrayed, and perhaps gain the desire to study further the fascinating era of America's founding.

This book is the result of much effort by many historians. I would like to thank Alfred J. Andrea and Andrew Holt, series editors, for their valuable editorial contributions, and the authors who contributed excellent essays—Jeff W. Dennis, Don N. Hagist, and Mark Edward Lender. I also want to include a special word of gratitude to my wife, Lori, for her patience in allowing me to fill the house with stacks of books and research materials during my work on this volume.

Jim Piecuch

INTRODUCTION

> The History of our Revolution will be one continued Lye from one End to the other. The Essence of the whole will be *that Dr Franklins electrical Rod, Smote the Earth and out Sprung General Washington. That Franklin electrifed him with his Rod—and thence forward these two conducted all the Policy Negotiations Legislation and War.* These underscored Lines contain the whole Fable Plot and Catastrophy.[1]
>
> —*John Adams, 1790*

So wrote John Adams to his friend Benjamin Rush in the spring of 1790. Adams was aware that the record of the American Revolution was being written, or in his opinion, rewritten, even as he penned his letter. While Adams exaggerated the extent of the falsehoods that would become part of the Revolution's history, he correctly observed that the account of the Revolution and the actions of its key participants would be deliberately contrived. The resulting narrative would not be as catastrophic as Adams feared. Still, his prediction proved accurate insofar as the history of America's battle for independence that became prevalent in the following years would be neither complete nor wholly accurate. This was largely an unfortunate necessity, as the founding generation struggled to find a means to strengthen national unity by promoting a common identity for the people of the United States.[2]

Unifying the inhabitants of thirteen disparate states was a daunting task, given the ethnic, religious, and economic differences that existed within the new nation. From their founding as colonies, one historian noted, the states had developed "fundamentally different economic, social, and political systems and widely varying cultural values and beliefs. The holy experiments of New England and Pennsylvania rested uneasily on the same continent with the openly materialistic, exploitative colonies to the south."[3] Robert G. Parkinson agreed that "the catalog of forces acting against American unity was impressive" at the start of the Revolution, and noted that earlier attempts to convince the colonies to act together, such as the 1754 Albany Plan of

---

1. John Adams to Benjamin Rush, 4 April 1790, *Founders Online*, National Archives, https://founders. archives.gov/documents/Adams/06-20-02-0181. [Original source: *The Adams Papers*, Papers of John Adams, vol. 20, *June 1789–February 1791*, ed. Sara Georgini, Sara Martin, R. M. Barlow, Gwen Fries, Amanda M. Norton, Neal E. Millikan, and Hobson Woodward (Cambridge, MA: Harvard University Press, 2020), 304–8.] (accessed Aug. 11, 2019).

2. Eve Kornfeld, *Creating an American Culture, 1775–1800: A Brief History with Documents* (Boston, MA: Bedford/St. Martin's, 2001), 3.

3. Kornfeld, *Creating an American Culture*, 3.

Union, had failed.[4] A British observer asserted in 1775 that "fire and water are not more heterogeneous than the different colonies in North America . . . such is the difference of character, of manners, of religion, of interest" between them that without British control they were likely to plunge into civil war.[5]

The variations among the colonies were the product of their individual development over the previous 150 years. Ethnic diversity reflected the different origins of the colonies and the effects of immigration from various parts of Europe. In addition to the majority of the Euro-American population who were of English ancestry, the thirteen colonies that became the United States included descendants of the Dutch who had originally colonized the region that became New York; Swedes and Finns in Delaware (the former New Sweden); German-speaking people from central Europe who settled largely in Pennsylvania, with substantial numbers in New Jersey, Maryland, the Carolinas, and Georgia; Scots-Irish in most of the states; Highland Scots who were most numerous in North Carolina; Irish scattered throughout the states; and Jews who primarily lived in seaport towns.[6]

Religious diversity followed ethnic differences to some extent, though not completely, and the vast majority of Americans professed some form of Protestantism. The Church of England, or Anglican Church, was present in each of the thirteen colonies and was the established, taxpayer-supported denomination in Maryland, Virginia, the Carolinas, Georgia, and some New York counties; in terms of members it was the second-largest denomination in America. The Congregational Church, almost exclusively located in New England, claimed the largest membership, tracing its origins to the Puritan founders of Massachusetts. The Dutch Reformed Church retained adherents in New York. Quakers remained numerous if no longer a majority in Pennsylvania, where various smaller sects such as the Mennonites and Moravians had sought toleration for their beliefs. A considerable number of Lutherans also resided in the state and neighboring Delaware. Presbyterianism, the third-largest denomination in America, also had significant numbers in Pennsylvania, New Jersey, and along the southern frontier. Religious differences had been exacerbated by the series of religious revivals that began in the 1720s and continued into the 1760s, known collectively as the Great Awakening. The revivalists, with their emphasis on conversion experiences in place of formal theological training, created fractures within Congregational and Presbyterian churches while also spurring the growth of Methodist and Baptist groups. Finally, about 25,000 Roman Catholics and 1,500–2,000 Jews lived in the thirteen colonies, where they were denied political rights and often faced persecution. There were also

---

4. Robert G. Parkinson, *The Common Cause: Creating Race and Nation in the American Revolution* (Chapel Hill: University of North Carolina Press, 2016), 2.

5. Parkinson, *Common Cause*, 3–4.

6. Jerome R. Reich, *Colonial America* (Englewood Cliffs, NJ: Prentice Hall, 1994), 137–41.

several hundred Indians who had converted to Christianity, Congregationalists in Massachusetts and Moravians in Pennsylvania.[7]

Ethnic and religious differences between and within the states were compounded by stark economic differences that influenced political and social conditions. Most residents of New England engaged in subsistence farming, with significant numbers making their living from fishing, timbering, and as seafarers. At the same time, ship-building thrived in port towns where merchants engaged in overseas trade. Agriculture was also the chief occupation in New York, Pennsylvania, and New Jersey, and the region's warmer climate and more fertile soil enabled farmers to export crops such as wheat and livestock through the prosperous ports of New York City and Philadelphia. Farther south, agriculture remained dominant, though its character changed dramatically. Virginia, Maryland, and North Carolina produced tobacco for export, with the bulk of the crop grown on large plantations with enslaved Africans providing the labor. South Carolina and Georgia plantations also utilized slaves to raise and export rice. People who lived in the interior of the southern states were generally subsistence farmers who owned few or no slaves. Although slavery existed in every state, the large number of slaves in the southern states—40 percent of Virginia's population and 60 percent of South Carolina's—was reflected in every aspect of their society, from the legal system to religious beliefs that asserted a biblical justification for slavery, creating a deep division between the southern states and those in the north, where Massachusetts and New Hampshire abolished slavery during the Revolution and other northern states would eventually, if in some cases slowly, do the same.[8]

A further obstacle to unity was that, before joining together in opposition to British policy in the decade before the Revolution, the residents of the various colonies had only minimal contact with their neighbors, and the little interaction that did occur was often unfriendly, involving issues such as boundary disputes. The only consistent link between the colonies had been through their shared ties to Britain, a link that the Revolution had severed. The Revolution had forged bonds between those Americans who had worked together in the Continental Congress and Continental Army and who hoped to create stronger bonds of union between the newly independent states, in contrast to many Americans who returned their focus to local and regional affairs at the end of the war.[9]

Those Americans who wished to promote unity after independence had been achieved turned to a variation of a method that had worked adequately during the war. Revolutionary leaders, realizing that their success depended on unifying as many of the colonists as possible, had, from the beginning of the conflict, worked "to craft an appeal that . . . overcame some of those inherited fault lines and jealousies" between

---

7. Reich, *Colonial America*, 210–11, 212, 213, 217, 218–19, 221, 222–23.

8. Reich, 126, 150–53, 169, 184.

9. Kornfeld, *Creating an American Culture*, 4, 6–7; Parkinson, *Common Cause*, 2.

the colonies and their inhabitants, in order "to make what they called 'the cause' common."[10] To do so, "patriot publicists had to discover and disseminate stories with clear, compelling heroes and villains if they wanted the rebellion to have broad, popular support."[11] These stories, published in newspapers in every colony, were in effect the first histories of the Revolution. They emphasized the shared political values that had inspired colonial opposition to British policy while linking the British to Indians and African Americans, who were both depicted as dangerous foes, to take advantage of the fact that most colonists viewed these two marginalized groups with suspicion, at the least, or more often, with outright hostility.[12]

The step to be taken next was to create a comprehensive history of the Revolution. Such a history would have a variety of uses. It would educate Americans in politics and morality while providing an accurate account of the creation of the United States. At the same time, it would counter unflattering accounts of the new nation and the Revolution that had already begun to emerge in Britain.[13] If American writers could create a national history, advocates of a stronger union hoped, it was possible that a greater "sense of national identity and unity would follow."[14]

Several authors had already undertaken the task of researching and writing local and regional histories, but these tended to reinforce rather than weaken localism. Because the task was so difficult, only two writers succeeded in publishing national histories in the first three decades after the Revolution: David Ramsay's *History of the American Revolution* in 1789 and Mercy Otis Warren's *History of the Rise, Progress and Termination of the American Revolution* in 1805. While striving for accuracy, both works nevertheless contributed to the growth of myths. Ramsay, attempting to trace the history of the colonies to show the development of a common American identity, struggled to deal with issues such as slavery and religious persecution; in the end, he resolved his dilemma by creating a prototype American colonist who was white, male, courageous, independent, and cherished liberty, equality, the common good, and other republican political values, untainted by slave ownership, greed, or other negative characteristics. Warren's Revolutionary shared the same political beliefs as Ramsay's colonist, though given her Massachusetts origins, she placed more emphasis on New England's role in the struggle. She also drew a starker contrast between heroes and villains and was among the first Revolutionary historians to portray prominent patriots as untarnished heroes, beginning the process that would make George Washington, Benjamin Franklin, and other founders into legendary figures.[15]

---

10. Parkinson, *Common Cause*, 4.

11. Parkinson, 9.

12. Parkinson, 9, 10, 20.

13. Kornfeld, *Creating an American Culture*, 39–40.

14. Kornfeld, 40.

15. Kornfeld, 40, 43–44, 47–48.

The next and most successful writer to mythologize the Revolution, or at least its arguably most important figure, was Mason Locke Weems. Hoping to take advantage of Washington's death in 1799 to promote national unity while profiting from selling a biographical account of the first president, Weems published the first edition of his *Life of George Washington* in 1800. The book became a bestseller, and he continually revised it, producing nine editions. He covered various aspects of Washington's life to teach moral lessons as well as history, thus helping cement Washington's position as the first national hero of the United States. Weems employed religious stories and political material to appeal to as many readers as possible. Since he was not above using his imagination to improve the story, Weems embellished and exaggerated elements of Washington's life and went so far as to create wholly fictitious material, such as the famous account of a youthful Washington admitting to cutting down a prized cherry tree, which did not appear until the fifth edition of the book.[16]

Using myth to promote unity during a war and strengthen national bonds afterward was not harmful in itself, except when people were vilified to achieve those goals or were omitted from historical accounts because they did not fit into the prevailing image of white, male, Protestant republicans. A more dangerous use of myth was to revise history to serve political ends. This process began in the 1790s. With France convulsed by revolution and many Americans urging the United States to support the fledgling republic in Europe, Alexander Hamilton strongly objected. Horrified by the violence of the French revolutionaries and angry with his political rival Thomas Jefferson, who was sympathetic to France, Hamilton recast the account of the American Revolution to draw a contrast between the two struggles. "The cause of France is compared with that of America during its late revolution," Hamilton wrote. "Would to heaven that the comparison were just. Would to heaven we could discern in the mirror of French affairs the same humanity, the same decorum, the same gravity, the same order, the same dignity, the same solemnity, which distinguished the cause of the American Revolution."[17] Hamilton, of course, knew better. He had witnessed much of the violence of the United States' War for Independence, with houses and towns burned, enemies executed without trial, and numerous other cruelties. Yet it was more important for Hamilton to shape a myth that served his political goal, nonintervention in the French Revolutionary Wars, than to tell the truth about the American Revolution. He succeeded to the extent that his view of the Revolution became, according to historian Bradford Perkins, a "prism" through which Americans subsequently viewed and judged revolutions in other nations.[18]

---

16. Kornfeld, 48–49.

17. Alexander Hamilton, c. 1793, Studylib.net, https://studylib.net/doc/8055898 (accessed Nov. 16, 2021).

18. Bradford Perkins, *The Creation of a Republican Empire, 1776–1865* (New York: Cambridge University Press, 1995), 12–15.

Following in the path of Ramsay, Warren, Weems, and Hamilton, their successors continued to produce histories of the Revolution that sanitized American actions, enhanced the reputations of the founders, demonized the British and their supporters, and omitted mention of those who did not match the ideal of the white, male, Protestant, virtuous republican citizen. Thus the story of the American Revolution, from the outset, became more than mere history; as historian Jane Kamensky noted, it "functioned . . . as an origins story for the United States," the American equivalent of the biblical Book of Genesis, "the rock upon which we would build a sovereign people." The standard accounts emphasized the birth of the United States, the triumphs of its people and institutions, and the virtues of Americans with "a distinct bias toward individual heroes," laying the foundation for what became known as "American exceptionalism."[19] This secular scripture, like its religious counterparts, has proven difficult to challenge and attempts to do so often produce a backlash. Yet, it has been altered when influential Americans believed doing so was necessary. When Robert Goldstein released his patriotic film *The Spirit of '76* in 1917, its dramatization of the 1778 Wyoming Valley "massacre" enraged many Americans, the United States having recently entered World War I on the side of Great Britain. The federal government agreed and charged Goldstein with violating the recently passed Espionage Act. Goldstein was convicted; the judge denounced him for his anti-British film and sentenced him to ten years in prison. A century later, the pendulum had swung once again, and Mel Gibson's 2000 Revolutionary War film *The Patriot* contained several scenes of British soldiers killing wounded American soldiers and unarmed civilians, with the protests of historians against such inaccuracy largely ignored.[20]

The Patriot fit perfectly within the triumphalist and heroic historical views of the Revolution. Nor were the objections of historians to the film unusual. As Kamensky noted, "scholars have long recognized that this triumphalist understanding of the American Revolution is historically inaccurate, professionally untenable, and politically destructive." However, she observed, "historians tend to be much better at tearing things down than at building them up."[21] The result has been a conflict between those who, for example, wish to make known the full story of Revolutionary heroes like Washington, going beyond his role as commander of the Continental Army and president to examine his actions as a slave owner and his hostility toward Indians, and other historians who present generally favorable depictions of Washington and other founders in books that reach larger numbers of readers than do scholarly works. The dispute over how the story of the Revolution should be told was a major point of contention during the 1990s when scholars put forth proposed national standards for

---

19. Jane Kamensky, "Two Cheers for the Nation: An American Revolution for the Revolting United States," *Reviews in American History* 47, no. 3 (September 2019): 310.

20. Thomas Fleming, *The Illusion of Victory: America in World War I* (New York: Basic Books, 2003), 189–90; *The Patriot*, directed by Roland Emmerich (Columbia Pictures, 2000).

21. Kamensky, "Two Cheers for the Nation," 311.

teaching history in American schools that sparked a backlash from those committed to the traditional accounts.[22]

The most recent controversy over how the American Revolution should be remembered and taught centered on the 1619 Project, produced by the *New York Times* under the direction of journalist Nikole Hannah-Jones. The project experienced great initial success, being adopted in over 3,500 classrooms, in every state, within six months of its August 2019 publication, primarily for use as a supplement to the existing curriculum. The project placed slavery at the center of American history, even claiming that the founding of the United States should be dated to 1619, when the first Africans arrived in Virginia, rather than 1776, when the Declaration of Independence was adopted. Numerous educators have praised the project for helping students understand the powerful, lingering impact of slavery in America. The project won a George Polk Award for journalism in February 2020. However, many scholars have questioned the accuracy of the material and taken issue with Hannah-Jones's assertion that the American Revolution was undertaken to preserve slavery. Critics pointed out that the relationship between the Revolution and slavery was complex, with some Revolutionaries urging the abolition of slavery while others vigorously defended it.[23]

Among the critics were several prominent historians. James McPherson stated that he "was disturbed by what seemed like a very unbalanced, one-sided account, which lacked context and perspective on the complexity of slavery."[24] Gordon Wood declared that he "just couldn't believe" Hannah-Jones's assertion that the preservation of slavery was the primary motive for the Revolution, insisting that she had exaggerated British opposition to slavery in the 1770s. He also noted that many leaders of the Revolutionary movement, such as John Adams, never owned slaves and were, in fact, opponents of slavery and that the Revolution brought positive changes to the United States, including the assurance that a society of hereditary and inherently unequal classes would not exist in America.[25]

Another challenge to the 1619 Project came from Robert L. Woodson Sr., founder of the Woodson Center, who, with other African Americans, created the 1776 Unites project to publish scholarly essays and furnish curriculum materials and other

---

22. Kamensky, 312.

23. John Murawski, "Disputed *NY Times* '1619 Project' Already Shaping Schoolkids' Minds on Race," Real Clear Investigations, January 31, 2020, https://www.realclearinvestigations.com (accessed Nov. 18, 2021); Cathy Young, "A Story of 1619, 1776 and 2020: Telling the Whole Truth about America and Slavery," *New York Daily News*, February 24, 2020, https://www.nydailynews.com (accessed Nov. 18, 2021).

24. Tom Mackaman, "An Interview with Historian James McPherson on the *New York Times*' 1619 Project," World Socialist Web Site, November 14, 2019, https://www.wsws.org (accessed Nov. 19, 2021).

25. Tom Mackaman, "An Interview with Historian Gordon Wood on the *New York Times*' 1619 Project," World Socialist Web Site, November 27, 2019, https://www.wsws.org (accessed Nov. 19, 2021).

resources that provide "perspectives that celebrate the progress America has made on delivering its promise of equal opportunity." Woodson asserted that the 1619 Project promotes "diabolical, self-destructive" views of white Americans as oppressors and blacks as victims, portrayals that he considers false.[26]

In September 2020, then-president Donald Trump entered the fray when he created the 1776 Commission to counter the 1619 Project and what he perceived as other threats to the proper version of American history and the Revolution. The commission released a report in January 2021 that the administration described as "a rebuttal of reckless 're-education' attempts that seek to reframe American history around the idea that the United States is not an exceptional country but an evil one."[27] Yet, just as the 1619 Project met opposition, so too did the 1776 Commission. One scholar noted that the eighteen-member commission consisted "of mostly male conservative educators," none of whom was a historian, and that the report was "an attempt to rewrite American history, focusing on our founding ideologies and mythologizing a very specific version of our origin story" to promote a political agenda. The report ignored the issue of slavery in the colonial and post-Revolutionary eras and made no mention at all of Native Americans. The Biden administration shelved the report in January 2021, and the commission is no longer active.[28] Meanwhile, Hannah-Jones made revisions to the 1619 Project's content, including a complete rewrite of the section on the American Revolution that removed the statement that the Revolution's purpose had been to preserve slavery, and the new version, which many scholars applaud for its value in addressing the issue of slavery in the United States, was released as a book in November 2021.[29]

Surely, as John Adams feared, the overall tendency has been to oversimplify the history of the American Revolution, to focus only on certain heroic figures, and to tell only certain dramatic stories. Perhaps, though, a more complete account can be provided, one that does not sacrifice accuracy, or ignore American flaws, while still serving the purpose of a national history that can unify rather than divide Americans. Former president of the United States, Theodore Roosevelt, believed that was possible. While serving as president of the American Historical Association in 1912, Roosevelt, himself an advocate of a triumphalist history filled with accounts of heroes, nevertheless pointed out the importance of studying the everyday lives of ordinary Americans as

26. Mike Sabo, "'1776' Is Helping Turn Civics Education Around," RealClear Education, August 26, 2020, https://www.realcleareducation.com (accessed Nov. 18, 2021).

27. "1776 Commission Takes Historic and Scholarly Step to Restore Understanding of the Greatness of the American Founding," WhiteHouse.gov, January 18, 2021, https://trumpwhitehouse.archives.gov (accessed Nov. 18, 2021).

28. Robyn Autry, "Trump's '1776 Commission' Tried to Rewrite U.S. History. Biden Had Other Ideas," NBC News, January 21, 2021, https://www.nbcnews.com (accessed Nov. 19, 2021).

29. Claretta Bellamy, "Nikole Hannah-Jones on the 1619 Project Book, Harsh Truths of the Black Experience," NBC News, November 18, 2021, https://www.nbcnews.com (accessed Jan. 6, 2022).

essential to understanding history and the necessity of addressing the negative as well as the positive in America's past. "Those who tell the Americans of the future what the Americans of to-day and of yesterday have done," Roosevelt remarked, "will perforce tell much that is unpleasant. This is but saying that they will describe the archtypical civilization of this age . . . when the tale is finally told, I believe that it will show that the forces working for good in our national life outweigh the forces working for evil, and that, with many blunders and shortcomings, with much halting and turning aside from the path, we shall yet in the end prove our faith by our works."[30] That is a point on which, perhaps, both the advocates and opponents of the 1619 Project could agree.

This volume cannot correct every one of the many myths surrounding the American Revolution, but it does provide perspective on the most important and widely accepted ones. The first chapter examines the traditional view that British officials drove the colonists to revolt by burdening them with heavy taxes, while Chapter 2 addresses the myth that the British army consisted of ignorant, unmotivated soldiers led by arrogant aristocrats. The third chapter discusses the debate over whether the Revolution was won by the professional soldiers of the Continental Army or the armed citizens of the militia, and the fourth assesses the accuracy of the numerous atrocities allegedly committed by the British. Chapter 5 describes the significant roles played by people long overlooked in traditional histories of the war: women and religious minorities, while Chapter 6 examines the participation of two groups often relegated to the margins of Revolutionary history, Indians and African Americans. Finally, Chapter 7 focuses on another group of participants frequently neglected or marginalized, the American Loyalists who supported Britain during the conflict.

Replacing the myths of the Revolution with factual accounts does not diminish the story of America's founding. On the contrary, the true history of the American Revolution, with its complexities, forgotten incidents, overlooked individuals and groups of people, and occasional contradictions, is just as dramatic, fascinating, and rich as any of the mythical versions, with the added benefit that it is an accurate retelling of the creation of the United States.

---

30. Theodore Roosevelt, "History as Literature," Annual Address of the President of the American Historical Association, December 27, 1912, https://www.historians.org (accessed Nov. 20, 2021).

1. Oppressive British Taxation

Jim Piecuch

> No modern revolution was deeper rooted in taxation than the revolt of the Thirteen Colonies in British North America. British taxation not only caused the revolution, but perhaps most important, it acted as a unifying force in the colonies. . . . You could justifiably say that the American Revolution occurred, not because we objected to taxes without representation, but because we objected to taxes, period.[1]
>
> —*Charles Adams, specialist in international taxation, 2006*

Many Americans can easily identify the cause of the American Revolution: oppressive British taxation. This simplistic explanation has been promulgated for decades and has gained additional credibility in recent years. For example, ABC Television's popular *Schoolhouse Rock!* series of educational animated short films with accompanying songs included an episode entitled "No More Kings" that addressed Americans' fight for independence. In the episode, British soldiers collect bags of tax money from the colonists and deposit the heaps of gold at the feet of King George III, who laughs uproariously as the colonists are forced to cover themselves with wooden barrels because the taxes have taken all their possessions, including the clothes from their backs. The film originally aired from 1975 to 1984, usually on Saturday mornings, and was rebroadcast from 1993 to 1996, shaping the views of countless schoolchildren. The episode remains popular and is still shown in schools and used in homeschooling.[2] Numerous other online educational materials advance similar views; a practice U.S. history quiz describes the Sugar Act of 1764 as "economically oppressive, in that it required [colonists] to pay a heavy tariff on raw materials and manufactured products imported from foreign countries."[3] The myth of crushing British taxation also influenced American politics, helping to fuel the growth of the TEA (Taxed Enough Already) Party in 2009. Tea Party members often wore colonial attire at their rallies, adopted the Revolutionary-era Gadsden flag with its rattlesnake and "Don't Tread On Me" motto as their emblem, and claimed to be following in the

---

1. Charles Adams, "The Rocky Road of American Taxation," Mises Institute, April 15, 2006, https://mises.org (accessed March 31, 2020).

2. *Schoolhouse Rock!*, season 4, episode 1, "No More Kings," written by Lynn Ahern, aired September 20, 1975, on ABC, https://www.youtube.com/watch?v=p8BwWBc571k (accessed March 31, 2020).

3. Chapter 2 Quiz, Quizlet, https://quizlet.com (accessed March 31, 2020).

footsteps of the American colonists in the fight against oppressive taxes.[4] Historian Benjamin L. Carp attended a Tea Party rally in New York on April 15, 2009, where he observed signs reading "Welcome to the Second American Revolution," and participants stated that they, like their eighteenth-century predecessors, were protesting high taxes. Carp noted some similarities between the two movements, such as the fact that the contemporary United States government and its British counterpart two centuries earlier had sparked anger by attempting to "bail out companies that were deemed too big to fail." He added that "in both cases, taxes . . . were not the immediate source of the problem," while pointing out a crucial difference in circumstances: in 1773, American colonists were not represented in Parliament and thus had no influence in shaping policy, whereas the twenty-first-century protesters could elect representatives to Congress.[5]

Attributing the Revolution to high taxes provides an easily understood motive for the colonial rebellion and meshes nicely with certain political viewpoints. Yet it overlooks more important and complex political and economic factors in the American colonies as well as the motivations of British leaders, whose actions, when presented within a larger context, were neither unjustified nor oppressive. In addition, the common depiction of George III as a tyrant, as in the *Schoolhouse Rock!* episode, and supported by a lengthy list of grievances in the Declaration of Independence, incorrectly blamed the king for the colonists' hardships.

Britain's Imperial Difficulties

Great Britain's victory in the French and Indian War in North America (1754–1763) and the concurrent Seven Years' War (1756–1763), fought primarily in Europe, brought problems as well as benefits to the triumphant nation. The British Empire gained vast new territories, including Canada (ceded by France), Spanish Florida, and Caribbean islands, along with acquisitions in Africa and India. These new colonies, however, had to be secured for the home country to reap benefits from them. On the North American mainland, previously hostile populations of "60,000 French Canadians, 3000 Spanish subjects in Florida, and perhaps 150,000 western Indians," most of whom were former allies of France and Spain, meant that "a standing army was imperative" if Britain was to uphold its authority and keep order in a region stretching from north of Quebec along the Appalachian frontier to the Gulf of Mexico.[6] British

---

4. "Thousands of Anti-Tax 'Tea Party' Protesters Turn Out in U.S. Cities," Fox News, April 15, 2009, https://www.foxnews.com (accessed March 31, 2020).

5. Benjamin L. Carp, "Nice Party, But Not So Revolutionary," *Washington Post*, April 19, 2009, https://www.washingtonpost.com (accessed Nov. 14, 2022).

6. Keith Mason, "Britain and the Administration of the American Colonies," in *Britain and the American Revolution*, ed. H. T. Dickinson (London: Addison Wesley Longman, 1998), 41.

officials calculated that 10,000 troops were necessary to garrison the new possessions and guard the frontier, at a cost estimated at £225,000 per year for the soldiers' pay alone, plus additional expenses to maintain a larger naval force in American waters.[7]

The financial burden promised to worsen an already strained government budget. British officials had begun voicing concern over the growing national debt early in the war, with some fearing that it might be impossible to continue to raise funds and that the government might default on payments. The shortfall was made up in part by tax increases; Britain's annual prewar tax revenue amounted to £8.4 million, which increased to £9.8 million by 1762. Taxes consumed about 9 percent of national income and "could not be permitted to rise any more for fear of unrest in Parliament and on the streets." A new tax on cider had led to public protests.[8] At the same time, the cost of government borrowing nearly doubled as a result of higher interest rates. Even with increased taxes, revenue fell far short of the amount needed to finance the war, and the national debt of Britain nearly doubled to £132,716,000 in 1763. In an effort to lower costs, with the coming of peace, the British government cut military expenditures by reducing the size of the army and navy.[9] This was insufficient to remedy the country's debt problem, however, and in their search for new sources of revenue, officials in London turned their gaze toward North America.

The Situation in the American Colonies

While the British government struggled to meet its financial obligations and assert control over its enlarged empire, American colonists continued to enjoy unrivaled prosperity. American economic growth had far surpassed that of Britain. Although statistics for the colonial era can only be estimated, the economic output of the thirteen colonies probably grew at an average annual rate of 3.5 percent from 1650 to 1770, an increase that historians John J. McCusker and Russell R. Menard described as "a remarkable performance by any standard." On the other hand, Britain's economic output for the same period increased by less than 0.5 percent per year.[10] While wealth was not evenly distributed in the colonies, varying by region, occupation, and an individual's social standing, "the colonies experienced little if any of the abject

7. John L. Bullion, *A Great and Necessary Measure: George Grenville and the Genesis of the Stamp Act, 1763–1765* (Columbia: University of Missouri Press, 1982), 22.

8. Nick Bunker, *An Empire on the Edge: How Britain Came to Fight America* (New York: Alfred A. Knopf, 2014), 17–18.

9. Bullion, *Great and Necessary Measure*, 16, 18, 21–22; John Derry, "Government Policy and the American Crisis, 1760–1776," in Dickinson, *Britain and the Revolution*, 45.

10. John J. McCusker and Russell R. Menard, *The Economy of British North America, 1607–1789* (Chapel Hill: University of North Carolina Press, 1991), 57.

poverty found in contemporary Europe." The income of wealthy colonists increased faster than that of other groups, but "the poor prospered as well," albeit more slowly.[11]

The primary reason for the colonists' prosperity was the widespread availability of land at a low cost. With about 80 percent of the colonial population employed in agriculture, there was a continual shortage of wage laborers, so that demand pushed wages higher. Most wage workers lived in the coastal cities, and the majority of those who labored for wages, wherever they resided, "did so only briefly, when they were young and before they married. High wages, ample occasions for employment, and cheap land guaranteed diligent and frugal workers a quick accumulation of the capital required to set up as independent farmers."[12] The best opportunity to succeed in agriculture was found in the middle colonies (New York, New Jersey, and Pennsylvania), where the most important product was wheat; by 1750, farm yields in that region were so productive that about 40 percent of the crop could be exported and the proceeds used to purchase goods. Many products, particularly luxury items, were imported from Britain. Still, American artisans, who made up about 18 percent of the population, produced a large variety of goods, including furniture, shoes, clothing, bread, beer, coaches, and silverware. Like laborers, artisans enjoyed high wages, and a steady stream emigrated from the British Isles, drawn by the better income they could earn in the colonies.[13]

New Customs Regulations

Political leaders in London were aware of the colonists' prosperity and knew that the colonists paid only a small amount in taxes to support the British government. Military officers and civilian officials who served in America during the war were amazed by the colonists' wealth in the form of land, livestock, farm buildings, and agricultural produce.[14] One Briton wrote that "the very lowest orders . . . there are really better fed, clothed, and every way accommodated" than were the hardest working artisans in London.[15] Reports of the Americans' bountiful farms and the high wages earned by laborers circulated among the people in Britain, some of whom expressed jealousy at the Americans' wealth.[16] Some Americans, however, believed that Britons had an exaggerated idea of the colonists' affluence, a false impression created by the colonists themselves. In 1765, John Dickinson asserted "that an opinion has been

---

11. McCusker and Menard, *Economy of British North America*, 59.

12. McCusker and Menard, 245.

13. Jerome R. Reich, *Colonial America* (Englewood Cliffs, NJ: Prentice Hall, 1994), 151, 174.

14. Mason, "Britain and the Colonies," 41; Oliver M. Dickerson, *The Navigation Acts and the American Revolution* (Philadelphia: University of Pennsylvania Press, 1951), 55.

15. Bullion, *Great and Necessary Measure*, 67.

16. Dickerson, *Navigation Acts*, 52.

industriously propagated in *Great-Britain* that the colonies are wallowing in wealth and luxury." Dickinson denied this, insisting that British army officers and other Britons who had been in the colonies during the recently concluded war had seen an artificial prosperity fueled by temporary wartime military spending. Furthermore, when entertaining these visitors, the colonists, motivated by an "imprudent excess of kindness," had "indulged themselves in many uncommon expenses" to impress their British guests.[17]

The way in which some Americans prospered likewise aroused discontent in the parent country. Imperial trade was regulated by the Navigation Acts, a series of laws passed by Parliament beginning in 1651. Historian Keith Mason described the original Navigation Act as "the first substantive effort to define the economic relationship between England and the colonies." Under that law, "all goods imported into England or the colonies" had to be carried in English or colonial vessels. "The aim was clearly to create a self-contained economic system," Mason observed.[18] The American colonists showed no outward signs of opposition to the Navigation Acts, and in fact, New England's fishing and shipbuilding industries and colonial trade as a whole was protected by and dependent on the Navigation Acts. "Instead of being oppressive the shipping clauses of the Navigation Act had become an important source of colonial prosperity which was shared by every colony," historian Oliver M. Dickerson noted.[19]

Despite the benefits they received and their apparent compliance, the colonists had been violating a key provision of the law. To protect the valuable sugar production of the British West Indies, Parliament had passed the Molasses Act in 1733, placing high duties on sugar, molasses (a byproduct of sugar refining), and rum imported from foreign sources. Although colonists on the North American mainland could have imported these products duty-free from the British Caribbean islands, the higher quality sugar and molasses produced there made these items more expensive. Therefore, Americans preferred to smuggle the goods (except rum, which the colonists produced themselves) from foreign colonies because the potential profits were greater than the relatively low risks involved in smuggling. Even the impropriety of aiding enemies in wartime did not stop the illegal trade. During the Anglo-Spanish War (1739–1748) and the War of the Austrian Succession (1744–1748) against France, and throughout the French and Indian War, the colonists continued to export goods to the Spanish and French colonies in the Caribbean in exchange for sugar and especially molasses.[20]

The British government knew that smuggling was rampant in the colonies, and in 1748, political leaders realized that they could no longer ignore the Americans'

---

17. T. H. Breen, "Narrative of Commercial Life: Consumption, Ideology, and Community on the Eve of the American Revolution," *William and Mary Quarterly* 50, no. 3 (1993): 473.

18. Mason, "Britain and the Colonies," 23.

19. Dickerson, *Navigation Acts*, 31, 32.

20. McCusker and Menard, *Economy of British North America*, 48–49.

violations of the law; if the empire were to function effectively, officials in London had to exert greater authority over the colonies by means of a uniform imperial policy. British leaders took advantage of domestic political stability and the successful conclusion of the War of the Austrian Succession to adjust colonial policy. George Dunk, the Earl of Halifax, led the effort as head of the Board of Trade, which advised the government on colonial matters. In 1752, Halifax convinced the government to strengthen the board's authority in the colonies, and he also tried to increase the power of the colonial governors. However, the colonial legislatures resisted what they perceived as a threat to their dominance in domestic affairs, so Halifax achieved little in the way of reform before the effort was put aside two years later with the outbreak of war in North America.[21]

Although the conflict required collaboration between the British government and the North American colonists, so far as British officials were concerned, the war only seemed to demonstrate the Americans' refusal to cooperate fully for the common cause. "Throughout the war," Mason wrote, "the colonial assemblies exploited the government's need for defence requisitions to wrest even more authority away from the [royal governors]; colonial merchants flagrantly violated the Navigation Acts" by "trading with the French and Spanish Caribbean; and many lower houses" of the colonial legislatures "refused to come forward with men and material for the war effort. Actions such as these left many members of the British political establishment feeling bitter and hostile towards the colonists and ever more determined to put them in their place."[22]

The circumstances of the war and the subsequent peace treaty reinforced these views. The colonists had started the conflict by challenging French claims to the Ohio River Valley. Virginia also claimed that territory under its original royal charter, and in 1745 a group of wealthy land speculators formed what later became known as the Ohio Company and obtained a land grant in the area from the provincial legislature. The company planned to profit from selling the land to settlers and took the first step in 1749, establishing a fort at the site of present-day Cumberland, Maryland. In 1753, the French governor of Quebec, the Marquis de Duquesne, responded by constructing forts near the Allegheny River. The following year, Virginia dispatched troops under militia colonel George Washington to challenge the French, only to see Washington forced to surrender at Fort Necessity on July 4, 1754, in the first significant battle of the war.[23] The eventual British victory produced important benefits for the Americans. France had lost its colonial possessions on the North American mainland, Spain had been ousted from Florida, both nations' Indian allies had been deprived of direct support, and British garrisons in Canada, Florida, and along the

---

21. Mason, "Britain and the Colonies," 36, 37, 38–39.

22. Mason, 40.

23. Fred Anderson, *Crucible of War: The Seven Years' War and the Fate of Empire in British North America, 1754–1766* (New York: Alfred A. Knopf, 2000), 23, 27, 32, 64.

colonies' western frontier provided a level of security the colonists had not known since their founding. Political leaders in London and many Britons, however, believed that the Americans' safety had been achieved at the expense of the British people, who had borne almost the entire financial burden of the war while the colonists had contributed relatively little.[24]

Statistics demonstrate that Britons' resentment at their far higher tax burden was well founded. In Britain, with a population of eight million, annual tax revenues amounted to ten million pounds, an average of 25 shillings per person, while in the colonies, three million people paid a total of only £75,000 per year in imperial taxes, an average of 6 pence, or 0.5 shillings, each, and lower in relation to taxpayers' income since the colonists' wages were three times higher than those of British workers, and living expenses in America were lower than in Britain.[25] "These considerations," Mason contended, "led the government in London to conclude that imperial reform was essential."[26]

In 1763, British leaders took the first step with the decision to reform the collection of customs duties in America. With the national debt increasing, that appeared to be the obvious place to start because, incredibly, the customs service in North America operated at a loss. Customs officials collected between £1,000 and £2,000 per year in revenue against expenses that ranged from £7,000 to £8,000 per year, so that under the best circumstances, the government lost £5,000 in some years and up to £7,000 in others. These losses could not be sustained if the empire were to remain economically viable. To promote the enforcement of the revenue laws, in July 1763, the government ordered all customs officers to America, threatening that they would lose their appointments if they had not departed Britain by August 31. They were to receive assistance in the performance of their duties from other royal authorities; in the fall, colonial governors and army and naval officers were ordered to cooperate with customs agents to halt smuggling.[27]

George Grenville, who headed King George III's cabinet (a position equivalent to the present-day prime minister), was concerned with Britain's growing debt and eager to restore financial stability. He knew that the mainland colonists ignored the Navigation Acts to the detriment of the government's revenue and the trade of other colonies. Britain's dominance of the European sugar trade was considered essential to the country's financial security; however, the colonists continued to smuggle foreign sugar and molasses rather than trade within the empire. British officials estimated that the Americans imported over 43,000 hogsheads of foreign molasses each year,

---

24. Mason, "Britain and the Colonies," 41; H. T. Dickinson, "Britain's Imperial Sovereignty: The Ideological Case Against the American Colonists," in Dickinson, *Britain and the Revolution*, 69; Derry, "Government Policy," 45–46.

25. Dickerson, *Navigation Acts*, 53, 54.

26. Mason, "Britain and the Colonies," 41.

27. Bullion, *Great and Necessary Measure*, 40, 64, 71, 72, 73.

each hogshead containing one hundred gallons. Altogether, seventy-three large distilleries in America produced nearly 25,000 tons of rum annually, almost all made from smuggled molasses. Experts at the Treasury believed that customs officials were bribed at a rate of about 1.25 pence per gallon to overlook the smuggling and that the total amount of goods smuggled into the colonies each year amounted to £500,000. Sugar planters in the British West Indies also knew that they were losing molasses sales to foreign competition and demanded that Parliament take action to protect their interests and put an end to the smuggling.[28]

Grenville needed to devise a measure to reduce smuggling and bring badly needed revenue into the British treasury while addressing the concerns of the sugar planters, who exerted influence in Parliament through the so-called "West India lobby." Any reform measure, Grenville knew, should not harm trade between the American colonies and the home country, which "contributed significantly to Britain's burgeoning economic prosperity. If Britain were to retain its control over this trade and maximize the benefits to be gained from it," historian H. T. Dickinson observed, "then the long-standing commercial regulations governing this trade, which had so often been evaded by the colonists in the past, had to be tightened and made more effective."[29] In addition, Grenville had to consider the political implications of taxing the colonies, including the need to assert the government's authority.[30]

The resulting legislation, the Sugar Act of 1764, reduced the duty of 6 pence per gallon on foreign molasses imposed by the Molasses Act to 3 pence per gallon while further strengthening the enforcement of customs laws. At the same time, the duty on foreign sugar was increased by over 500 percent, the colonies were forbidden to import rum, and heavy customs duties were placed on linens, indigo, coffee, pimento, and wine. Government officials believed the colonists could easily afford to pay these taxes, especially the lower molasses duty.[31] Grenville expected the act to benefit the imperial economy's overall trade and encourage the colonial distilleries by allowing them to import foreign molasses legally at the cost of less than 2 pence per gallon more than they had previously paid once the cost of bribes was factored into the price. Historians disagree over how much revenue Grenville expected to raise under the new law. John Derry put the figure at £45,000 per year,[32] John L. Bullion at as much as £77,775,[33] and Dickerson at a more conservative £30,000 annually. The tax burden would not be evenly distributed among the colonial populace but would have the greatest effect on the five port towns where most smuggling occurred: Boston and

---

28. Bullion, 3, 17, 19, 39, 67, 82, 85, 86.

29. Dickinson, "Britain's Imperial Sovereignty," 66.

30. Bullion, *Great and Necessary Measure*, 4.

31. Reich, *Colonial America*, 282; Derry, "Government Policy," 49; Bullion, *Great and Necessary Measure*, 24–25.

32. Derry, "Government Policy," 50.

33. Bullion, *Great and Necessary Measure*, 91.

Salem, Massachusetts; New York; Philadelphia; and Charleston, South Carolina.[34] An amendment to the act strengthened enforcement by granting jurisdiction over smuggling cases to the courts of admiralty, a reform that customs officials had long desired. Accused smugglers brought to trial in their home ports were rarely convicted by local judges and juries who saw nothing wrong with evading customs duties. By transferring those cases to admiralty courts, where royally appointed civilian judges sat without juries, smugglers would be far less likely to escape punishment.[35]

The Americans challenged the Sugar Act on economic grounds, in part because the colonies were suffering from an economic depression when the measure took effect. The Rhode Island legislature appealed to the Board of Trade, and the New York and Massachusetts legislatures composed official appeals to Parliament, asserting that the colonies' purchases of £120,000 worth of British goods each year were largely paid for by profits from the molasses trade, and the new law would cause imperial commerce to suffer. None of the legislatures challenged Parliament's authority to enact the new law until October 1764, when Massachusetts legislators shifted from an economic to a political argument, declaring that the customs duties imposed by the Sugar Act were, in reality, a tax, and thus could not be imposed without the approval of the colonists' elected representatives.[36] The colonists also devoted much attention to a resolution included in the act that did not have an immediate effect. Because Grenville did not expect the new customs duties to produce enough revenue to relieve the government's financial difficulties, he included a clause stating that "towards further defraying the said Expences, it may be proper to charge certain Stamp Duties in the said Colonies and Plantations."[37] When Rhode Island and New York legislators followed the lead of Massachusetts and similarly argued that the Sugar Act was an unconstitutional tax, they emphasized that their chief concern was the proposed stamp duties.[38]

The Stamp Act

Grenville did not wait to see how much new revenue the Sugar Act would generate. He remained focused on financial matters and the debt, studying precedent thoroughly before deciding to propose stamp duties for the colonies. Even then, he "gave the colonists a year in which they could make suggestions for other means of raising revenue or propose amendments to the Stamp Bill to make the collection of the duties simpler and more amenable." Derry observed that "Grenville's motives for doing so

---

34. Dickerson, *Navigation Acts*, 185–86.

35. Edmund S. Morgan and Helen M. Morgan, *The Stamp Act Crisis: Prologue to Revolution* (Chapel Hill: University of North Carolina Press, 1995), 24–25, 27.

36. Morgan and Morgan, *Stamp Act Crisis*, 28, 31, 35–36.

37. Morgan and Morgan, 26.

38. Morgan and Morgan, 37.

are still a matter of debate. Possibly he thought that the failure of the Americans to come forward with viable proposals of their own would make them accept the stamp duties as unavoidable, or he may have been seeking to earn a reputation for open-mindedness while remaining convinced that his stamp tax would prove to be the only option."[39] Edmund S. and Helen M. Morgan offered a variation of Derry's argument: that Grenville "managed to maneuver the colonists into a position where a stamp act would appear to be the result of their own failure to come to the assistance of the mother country in an hour of need." The colonists were familiar with stamp duties, as the New York and Massachusetts legislatures had already enacted domestic stamp taxes to raise revenue for the provincial governments.[40]

When the colonial legislatures did not respond to Grenville's request to produce their own tax plans, he went ahead with his legislation in Parliament. He believed that the Stamp Act was a fair method of taxation, and this opinion was widely shared. Its effect would be proportional to all the colonies in mainland North America and the West Indies. The wealthiest colonies would pay a greater share than the less prosperous colonies, and if, in practice, this turned out not to be the case, the rates could be easily adjusted. This was reflected in the initial allocation of stamped paper shipped to America after the passage of the act. The West Indies colonies received 52.5 percent of the stamped paper, while only 47.5 percent was sent to the mainland colonies, including Nova Scotia, Quebec, and East and West Florida. Some Americans agreed that a stamp tax was an appropriate means of raising revenue, including Benjamin Franklin, who was in London at the time and consulted before Grenville introduced the bill. Only after Franklin learned of American opposition to the Stamp Act did he change his opinion. To make the tax more palatable to the colonists, the law specified that all the proceeds from the stamp duties would be applied to the cost of maintaining British military garrisons in America. Grenville also appointed colonists to serve as stamp tax collectors to avoid accusations that Americans would be forced to pay the salaries of British officials. Stamp distributors were appointed in each colony, as a major advantage of the duty was that it was easy and inexpensive to administer. Grenville expected the proceeds to cover one-third of the cost of the troops in America, and Britain would pay the balance.[41]

A few members of Parliament objected to the Stamp Act, although they did not question Parliament's authority to tax the colonies. Grenville responded to some skepticism concerning the colonists' ability to pay with diligently compiled figures showing that the combined debt of all the North American colonies totaled approximately £900,000, a fraction of Britain's national debt. While no one could say with certainty when the latter might be paid, the last of the colonial debts were scheduled to be paid

---

39. Derry, "Government Policy," 49–50.

40. Morgan and Morgan, *Stamp Act Crisis*, 55.

41. Derry, "Government Policy," 50–51; Dickerson, *Navigation Acts*, 192; Bullion, *Great and Necessary Measure*, 105–6.

by 1769. The act was passed in March 1765 to take effect on November 1. All shipping documents, legal papers, licenses, diplomas, newspapers, and almanacs had to be written or printed on paper embossed with a stamp of the value specified for each, purchased from the stamp distributor. Playing cards and dice were also taxed. The law required the buyer to pay for the paper in coinage rather than the paper currency often circulated in the colonies. Because such "hard money" was scarce in America and Grenville did not want to deprive the colonists of it, the provision that it be used for the expenses of the troops in America would prevent such a drain from occurring; no money would actually be transferred from America to Britain, and the amounts to be collected were in general small, though some professions, such as attorneys and merchants, would bear a disproportionately large share of the tax.[42] Despite its being considered an internal tax by the colonists, the "main burden of the tax would have fallen upon, and was intended to fall upon, trade and shipping."[43]

Nevertheless, the colonists based their opposition to the Stamp Act on the argument that it was an internal tax and therefore violated the principles of the British constitution since such taxes could only be levied by their own provincial legislatures, the colonies not being represented in Parliament. British officials and most members of Parliament rejected that claim, insisting that the colonists were "virtually represented" in Parliament, whose members acted for the empire as a whole and not individual constituencies. The concept of virtual representation was generally accepted in Britain but not America, where "it was repugnant to [the colonists'] whole conception of representative government."[44] In an essay in the *New York Gazette* that was later reprinted in Pennsylvania and Maryland, a writer using the pseudonym "Freeman" laid out the Americans' position, asserting that Grenville "grounds his Pretence of the Parliament's Right to Tax the Colonies, entirely upon this, *that they are* virtually *represented in Parliament:* If therefore he fails in the Proof of their being so Represented, he must, by his own Argument, give up the Point, and allow that the Parliament has not Manner of Right to tax the Colonies."[45] The colonists could find no such proof; the voters of Maryland's Anne Arundel County denounced the idea of virtual representation as "fantastical and frivolous," a description with which most Americans agreed.[46]

American opponents of the Stamp Act did not completely reject the authority of Parliament. The colonists' primary concern was to define the boundaries between the power of Parliament and that of their own legislatures.[47] As the legislatures gathered to debate the new law, Virginia's House of Burgesses took the lead in defining colonial

---

42. Morgan and Morgan, *Stamp Act Crisis*, 70, 72–73.
43. Dickerson, *Navigation Acts*, 191.
44. Morgan and Morgan, *Stamp Act Crisis*, 82.
45. Morgan and Morgan, 82.
46. Morgan and Morgan, 82–83.
47. Morgan and Morgan, 86.

opposition. One of four resolutions the representatives approved in May 1765 stated clearly "That the Taxation of the People by themselves, or by Persons chosen by themselves to represent them, who can only know what Taxes the People are able to bear, or the easiest Method of raising them . . . is the only Security against a burthensome Taxation . . . without which the ancient Constitution cannot exist."[48] Most of the other colonial legislatures subsequently approved similar declarations, with several adding their objection to Parliament's authority "to extend the jurisdiction of the admiralty courts," an issue first raised by the Sugar Act.[49]

In response to a proposal by the Massachusetts legislature, representatives of nine colonies (New Hampshire, Virginia, North Carolina, and Georgia did not participate) met in New York as the "Stamp Act Congress" from October 7 through October 25.[50] The delegates approved a series of resolutions explaining their opposition to the act. They first addressed the political issues, declaring that they could only be taxed by their own representatives, that they were "not, and from their local Circumstances cannot be, Represented in the House of Commons" in Britain, thus rejecting the concept of virtual representation, and that only their own elected legislatures had the right to tax them, any other form of taxation was a violation of "the Principles and Spirit of the *British* Constitution." Two other resolutions defended the colonists' right to trial by jury and stated that the extension of the jurisdiction of admiralty courts threatened that right. The next group of resolutions focused on economic issues. The taxes would be "extremely Burthensome and Grievous; and from the scarcity of Specie, the Payment of them absolutely impracticable." Furthermore, Americans already contributed to the empire's prosperity by purchasing goods manufactured in Britain, but the stamp tax and other duties and "Restrictions imposed by several late Acts of Parliament" would "render them unable to purchase" those goods. The Congress concluded the document with a request that the Stamp Act be repealed along with all legislation increasing the jurisdiction of the admiralty courts.[51]

The delegates found the most difficult issue to be whether they should petition to repeal all the recent taxes, including those imposed by the Sugar Act, or the Stamp Act alone. They unanimously agreed that the British government had the right to regulate colonial trade and that those laws should be obeyed, but disagreed over explicitly acknowledging that right in the petition. Some delegates believed that without such a statement, Parliament would never repeal the Stamp Act; however, the majority opted to remain silent on the issue.[52]

---

48. Morgan and Morgan, 95.

49. Morgan and Morgan, 103.

50. Morgan and Morgan, 108.

51. Morgan and Morgan, 110–12.

52. Morgan and Morgan, 112–13.

News that the British Parliament had imposed a stamp tax in the colonies sparked protests and riots in 1765, with the most violent resistance in Boston. Colonists protested what they perceived to be Parliament's unconstitutional usurpation of the power of the colonial legislatures rather than the tax itself, which was small. *The Stamp Act Riots at Boston*, woodcut engraving, 1886. Library of Congress.

Although the colonial legislatures and the Stamp Act Congress conducted themselves with decorum and affirmations of their loyalty to Great Britain, some Americans took a more radical approach. On August 14, a crowd in Boston destroyed a building owned by stamp distributor Andrew Oliver that they erroneously believed was intended for use as the stamp office and ransacked Oliver's home for good measure. He and Governor Francis Bernard fled to the safety of a fort in Boston harbor. The next targets were Lieutenant Governor Thomas Hutchinson, customs collector Benjamin Hallowell, and suspected Stamp Act supporter William Story, whose homes were ransacked by mobs two days later. New York City was also the scene of vigorous protests, and harassment and intimidation eventually led the stamp distributors in most colonies to resign.[53]

Meanwhile, the situation across the Atlantic changed. Grenville fell out of favor with the king, and in July, the Marquis of Rockingham, who sympathized with the colonists, replaced him as head of the ministry. To protest the Stamp Act, in many colonies, the Sons of Liberty had organized nonimportation agreements (boycotts) of British goods, and merchants in Britain pressed Rockingham to repeal the act so trade could resume. Rockingham and his supporters were willing to do so; however,

---

53. Morgan and Morgan, 130–31, 132–33, 159–63.

they encountered opposition from members of Parliament who were angered by the colonial protests and demanded that the government assert its authority in America. Rockingham finally resolved the problem in January 1766 by coupling the repeal of the Stamp Act with a second piece of legislation, the Declaratory Act, which asserted Parliament's sovereignty over the colonies. Before introducing the bills, Rockingham's supporters summoned Franklin to present rehearsed testimony before Parliament. Asked whether Pennsylvania's legislature meant customs duties as well as the stamp tax when they expressed their opposition to "all taxes" in their resolutions, Franklin replied that they referred only to internal taxes. The House of Commons voted to repeal the act in February. Americans celebrated news of the repeal, paying little attention to the Declaratory Act or its implications for future British policy.[54]

Just as the petition of the Stamp Act Congress combined a protest over constitutional issues with complaints about burdensome taxes, historians have also disagreed over the question of political versus economic motives for American resistance to British taxation. Bernard Bailyn, in his highly influential study, *The Ideological Origins of the American Revolution*, argued that political considerations were paramount in the colonists' reaction to the Stamp Act and subsequent British tax legislation. According to Bailyn, who reached his conclusions after studying American pamphlets, the colonists' reaction was based on a "distinctive ideological strain" that originated in seventeenth-century England and was "modified and enlarged" in the early eighteenth century by British political radicals, most notably John Trenchard and Thomas Gordon.[55] These writers "decried the corruption of the age and warned of the dangers of incipient autocracy."[56] By the 1720s, Bailyn asserted, these ideas were "central to American political expression."[57] The radical writers warned that corrupt ministers would manipulate Parliament in pursuit of personal power, in the process destroying British liberty and enforcing their will through a "standing army," a military force that would crush any opposition as they reduced the people to the status of slaves.[58] Bailyn described the effects of these ideas in America as "an intellectual switchboard wired so that certain combinations of events would activate a distinct set of signals—danger signals, indicating hidden impulses and the likely trajectory of events."[59] The Stamp Act, a putatively unconstitutional tax, triggered the alarm and impelled the colonists to act in defense of their liberty.[60] In Bailyn's view, the American Revolution and the controversies that preceded it were "an ideological, constitutional, political

---

54. Morgan and Morgan, 272, 274, 278–79, 287, 291, 300.

55. Bernard Bailyn, *The Ideological Origins of the American Revolution* (Cambridge, MA: Belknap Press, 1992), 34–35.

56. Bailyn, *Ideological Origins*, 39.

57. Bailyn, 43.

58. Bailyn, 62–63, 86.

59. Bailyn, 22–23.

60. Bailyn, 94.

struggle" rather than a contest "to force changes in the organization of the society or the economy."[61]

Other historians, such as Gary B. Nash, countered that economic issues did play a role in American opposition to British policy. In his study of the northern seaports of Boston, New York, and Philadelphia, Nash found that in the decades preceding passage of the Stamp Act, wealth in the three cities became increasingly concentrated in the hands of a small group of people. At the same time, those at the lower end of the economic spectrum suffered from declining incomes and growing poverty, producing class conflict in all three communities.[62] "Only the economic buffeting suffered by the seaport towns after 1760 and the buildup of antagonisms on local issues can fully explain the extraordinary response to the Stamp Act," Nash wrote.[63] He conceded that political ideology played a role in the dispute between the colonies and Britain, though he found "no strict correspondence between occupation or wealth and ideological outlook."[64] Nash did not explore the motives of colonists who dwelt in small towns, rural areas, or southern port cities such as Charleston.

The Stamp Act may have increased the financial burden on the urban poor, but the cost would not have been high, for they did not need shipping documents or many other taxed items. Regardless of who paid the duties, the colonists were aware that "the sums involved were in fact quite small," leading some Americans to believe that the British government had deliberately kept the tax low so that people "may be inclined to acquiesce under it."[65] Franklin knew as much and understood that even those who would have been required to make the most use of stamped paper would not have found the cost a hardship. Some of the opinions expressed by members of the House of Lords who opposed repeal of the act were published in a pamphlet entitled *Protest Against the Bill to Repeal the American Stamp Act, of Last Session.* Franklin acquired a copy and made notes on the various points, one of which was that the colonists could easily afford to pay the stamp duty, as the average annual cost per colonist amounted to only one-third of the wages earned by a laborer in a single day. In the margin, Franklin wrote that "Ship Money might have been easily paid," implying that, like the earlier levy imposed by Charles I without the approval of Parliament, the issue was not the amount of the tax but its constitutionality.[66]

---

61. Bailyn, x.

62. Gary B. Nash, *The Urban Crucible: The Northern Seaports and the Origins of the American Revolution* (Cambridge, MA: Harvard University Press, 1986), 99–101, 246–47.

63. Nash, *Urban Crucible*, 184.

64. Nash, 217–18.

65. Bailyn, *Ideological Origins*, 100.

66. "Marginalia in Protests of the Lords against Repeal of the Stamp Act," 1766, in *The Papers of Benjamin Franklin*, ed. Leonard W. Labaree (New Haven, CT: Yale University Press, 1969), 13:215.

The Townshend Act

Repeal of the Stamp Act irked many British politicians. Some disliked the colonists' challenge to the concept of virtual representation, while others, among them Charles Townshend, did not share the belief of their colleagues that Americans had been truthful when they said they opposed internal but not external taxes. Townshend was certain that "the distinction between external duties and internal taxes was intellectually fraudulent, a mere trick to avoid accepting legitimate authority."[67] As head of the ministry in 1767, Townshend faced the same problem that had vexed Grenville: how to shore up Britain's finances by securing revenue from the colonies. He also wished to deal with another problem; several colonial legislatures were using their power to raise and allocate funds to gain leverage over governors and judges, in some cases even refusing to pay the salaries of those who refused to accede to the legislature's policies. The British government wanted to ensure the independence of the governors and the impartiality of the courts in America by preventing these officials from becoming dependent on the legislatures. Townshend hoped to beat the Americans at their own game of semantics "by exploiting the distinction between taxation for the purposes of revenue and taxation for the control of trade to which many Americans had referred during the controversy over the Stamp Act." He would use customs duties "to pay the salaries of governors, judges and other colonial officials. If the Americans really believed in the distinction between the two types of taxation, they could hardly object," and as with the Stamp Act, the funds raised would be spent in the colonies, an effort to blunt arguments that the colonists' money was being drawn to Britain.[68] The Townshend Act of 1767 placed import duties on paper, glass, tea, lead, and the coloring used in paint, with the expectation of raising £40,000 per year.[69]

To the surprise of many Britons, Americans objected to the taxes. Some colonists said the duties did not meet the distinction between external and internal taxes, while others abandoned the arguments against the Stamp Act and denied the validity of the distinction. The most articulate and effective proponent of the latter view, John Dickinson, argued in the second of his *Letters from a Farmer in Pennsylvania* that "parliament unquestionably possesses a legal authority to *regulate* the trade of *Great-Britain* and all her colonies."[70] However, Dickinson claimed that when Parliament previously imposed customs duties, "raising a revenue thereby was never intended."[71] He warned of the consequences of accepting the Townshend duties, telling his readers

---

67. Derry, "Government Policy," 51.

68. Derry, 55.

69. Dickerson, *Navigation Acts*, 197.

70. John Dickinson, *Letters from a Farmer in Pennsylvania*, Letter II, in *The American Revolution: Writings from the Pamphlet Debate*, 2 vols., ed. Gordon S. Wood (New York: Library of America, 2015), 1:413.

71. Dickinson, *Letters from a Farmer*, Letter II, 1:414.

that "if you ONCE admit, that *Great-Britain* may lay duties upon her exportations to us, *for the purpose of levying money on us only*, she then will have nothing to do, but to lay those duties on the articles which she prohibits us to manufacture—and the tragedy of *American* liberty is finished."[72] Dickinson's argument amounted to legal hairsplitting, for by their nature, customs duties raised revenue as well as regulated trade. Nevertheless, he convinced numerous colonists to protest the act. Townshend's plan to use the proceeds from the new taxes to pay colonial governors and judges also fueled American opposition because the colonists feared that the British government was attempting to reduce the power of their legislatures.[73]

The amount to be raised by the Townshend Act certainly did not motivate American opposition because it was relatively insignificant, as the colonists themselves admitted. In his seventh letter, Dickinson conceded as much. "Some persons may think this act of no consequence, because the duties are so *small*," he wrote. "A fatal error. *That* is the very circumstance most alarming to me. For I am convinced, that the authors of this law would never have obtained an act to raise so trifling a sum as it must do, had they not intended by *it* to establish a *precedent* for future use. To console ourselves with the *smallness* of the duties, is to walk deliberately into the snare that is set for us." The trap, Dickinson explained, was the "destruction of this constitutional security" of taxation by one's own representatives.[74] Charles Thomson of Philadelphia shared this opinion, writing Benjamin Franklin in November 1769 to complain that the British intended to subjugate the colonies by denying Americans their right to be taxed only by their elected legislatures. Thomson observed that the Townshend duties "were not very grievous" in terms of their financial cost. "But if the principle is established," he declared, echoing Dickinson, "and the authority by which they are laid is admitted, there is no security for what remains."[75]

The vigorous American opposition to the Townshend duties surprised British officials. The colonists adopted the same tactics they had used to protest the Stamp Act, refusing to purchase British goods and harassing merchants who imported and sold them. In 1770, the new head of the ministry, Lord North, gave up the effort to collect the taxes and asked Parliament to repeal all the Townshend duties except for the one on tea. The Townshend duties had raised £21,842 pounds from 1768 through 1770, barely half the amount expected to have been collected in one year. Approximately three-quarters of the revenue came from the tea duty.[76] By repealing most of the duties, North "hoped to show that the British had no intention of tyrannizing over the Americans. The retention of the duty [on tea] upheld the principle of

---

72. Dickinson, *Letters from a Farmer*, Letter II, 1:420.

73. Derry, "Government Policy," 56.

74. Dickinson, *Letters from a Farmer*, Letter VII, in Wood, *American Revolution*, 1:449.

75. Charles Thomson to Franklin, November 26, 1769, in *Papers of Franklin*, ed. William B. Willcox (New Haven, CT: Yale University Press, 1972), 16:238–239.

76. Dickinson, "Britain's Imperial Sovereignty," 83; Dickerson, *Navigation Acts*, 198.

British troops had been sent to Boston in 1768 to quell opposition to the Townshend Act, and their presence angered colonists. On March 5, 1770, Bostonians' harassment of British soldiers resulted in a bloody confrontation that became known as "The Boston Massacre." Paul Revere's portrayal of the event, based on an earlier engraving by Henry Pelham, was intended to serve as pro-American propaganda. By depicting the British troops formed in a line with an officer commanding them, Revere created the impression that the British attacked the colonists, when in fact, the opposite was true. He also showed the colonists as well-dressed, respectable Bostonians when the majority were actually laborers, apprentices, and sailors. Although it was later claimed that the Americans had been protesting the Townshend Act, in reality, the unrest was primarily due to economic reasons, such as off-duty British soldiers taking jobs formerly done by colonists. *The Bloody Massacre Perpetrated in King Street Boston on March 5th 1770 by a Party of the 29th Regt.*, engraving with watercolor by Paul Revere, 1770. Library of Congress.

parliamentary sovereignty."[77] Even the king wished to retain one tax on the colonies to demonstrate Parliament's right to tax them.[78]

The Tea Act

After most of the Townshend duties were repealed, the colonists resumed their purchases of British goods. However, many Americans still refused to purchase the taxed tea, preferring to drink tea smuggled from the Dutch East Indies. One of the most successful tea smugglers, John Hancock of Boston, earned much of his fortune by importing and selling contraband tea. Nevertheless, many Americans, including Bostonians, bought tea from Britain and paid the tax without complaint.[79]

American purchases of taxed tea and the genesis of the Tea Act demonstrate that the protests that culminated in the Boston Tea Party of December 16, 1773, had no grounding in economic concerns. At the time of the act's passage, the East India Company had been in financial difficulty for several years. The company, in addition to its monopoly on the tea trade in the British Empire, controlled British colonial possessions in India, where France threatened its position. At the same time, its finances were jeopardized by poor management and corruption. Since mid-1771, it had been importing more tea than the British market could absorb. Over the next year, the company accumulated such a large quantity of tea in its warehouses that officials feared the price might collapse. These worries proved justified when the wholesale price of tea dropped by 20 percent in the fall of 1772, leaving the company with insufficient funds to pay its debts and unable to borrow additional money to meet the demands of creditors. Complicating the company's financial dilemma was the legal requirement that its tea could only be sold at wholesale price to merchants, who then offered it for sale on the retail market. This meant that the tea could not be sold profitably in Britain.[80]

The East India Company's difficulties were serious enough in their own right, yet conditions in Britain made the situation worse. In June 1772, banks began to fail, precipitating an economic crash. Aware that the collapse of the East India Company would only aggravate the already severe recession, British leaders found themselves with little choice but to assist the company. However, the king and Lord North were reluctant to do so. In addition to North's concern for Britain's economy, his reasons

---

77. Derry, "Government Policy," 56.

78. Dickinson, "Britain's Imperial Sovereignty," 83.

79. Bunker, *Empire on the Edge*, 49; "John Hancock—Smuggling Powerhouse," Boston Tea Party Historical Society, http://www.boston-tea-party.org/smuggling/John-Hancock.html (accessed May 29, 2020); Dickerson, *Navigation Acts*, 91.

80. Derek W. Beck, *Igniting the American Revolution, 1773–1775* (Naperville, IL: Sourcebooks, 2015), 4; Bunker, *Empire on the Edge*, 24, 42, 131.

Americans throwing the Cargoes of the Tea Ships into the River, at Boston

Recent opponents of taxation policy in the United States have claimed to draw inspiration from the Boston Tea Party of 1773. However, the Tea Act passed that year did not increase the tax on imported tea but instead lowered its overall cost. Colonists protested because they believed that Parliament was trying to deceive them into paying unconstitutional taxes. They demonstrated their hostility to the law by dumping cargoes of tea into the harbor on December 16. *Americans Throwing the Cargoes of the Tea Ships into the River, at Boston*, engraving by W. D. Cooper in Richard Johnson, *The History of North America* (London: E. Newbery, 1789).

for acting included a desire to force the company to make reforms and worry that the company's continued instability or collapse would jeopardize control of its territories in India, leaving an opening for European rivals to make inroads into the company's possessions there.[81]

Negotiations between political leaders and company officials continued for several months before an agreement was reached. Despite its own financial problems, the British government would loan the company £1.4 million to allow it to remain solvent until tea sales improved. Tea imported into Britain would be exempted from duties that made the tea more than twice as expensive as in Continental Europe. To further reduce the price of tea and thus increase consumption, the company would be permitted to sell directly to retailers. Some officials proposed repealing the duty of three pence per pound (weight) on tea sold in America in the belief that this would increase sales. However, North rejected the suggestion as the treasury needed additional revenue. Neither politicians nor company officials worried about tea sales in the colonies because Americans purchased substantial quantities of tea, even though the duty remained in place. The Tea Act was finalized and became law on May 10, 1773.[82] In the government's view, the act "would bring down the price of tea in America and

81. Bunker, *Empire on the Edge*, 81, 82, 91, 135, 136.
82. Bunker, 137, 138, 153, 155, 156; Beck, *Igniting the Revolution*, 4.

North was convinced that what he had done was in the interests of the company, while being beneficial to the Americans."[83]

Evidently, no one in Britain anticipated the effect the Tea Act produced in the colonies. At the time of its passage, Franklin made no mention of it in his correspondence, and neither did Edmund Burke, who had long advocated for the colonists in Parliament. Colonial resistance to the act developed slowly; the first opposition arose in New York among smugglers and their merchant partners who feared that enforcement of the act would reduce their profits. Unable to state this publicly, they complained that the East India Company would gain a monopoly over American trade to the detriment of small merchants and shippers. Philadelphians soon joined the protests, and "slowly, the American resistance grew and reshaped itself into a defensible and legitimate argument: the Tea Act was a renewed effort by the British Ministry to force-feed America a tax it had never consented to."[84] Public opposition then increased significantly, culminating in the Boston Tea Party in December. Most of the participants may have been acting on political principles. However, with the cost of East India Company tea lower than that of smuggled tea, John Hancock stood to lose a substantial portion of his income. His close friend and political collaborator Samuel Adams played a major role in organizing the Tea Party and may have been defending both the colonists' position on taxation and his colleague's financial interests.[85] After the Tea Party, "there was almost universal agreement among British politicians . . . that the perpetrators of a wanton and monstrous affront should be punished," resulting in the passage of the Coercive Acts to chastise Massachusetts. These included: the Boston Port Act, which closed the city's port to all shipping except essential goods such as fuel and firewood until the East India Company was reimbursed for the destroyed tea; the Massachusetts Government Act, which replaced the province's civilian governor with British general Thomas Gage and placed other restrictions on the colony's government; the Administration of Justice Act, which allowed royal officials charged with crimes in the colonies to be tried in Britain if it was believed they could not receive a fair trial in America; and the Quartering Act, allowing British officers to use empty buildings as barracks if colonial governments failed to provide required housing.[86]

When news of the Coercive Acts reached the American colonies in 1774, it set in motion a train of events that led to armed conflict a year later. Earlier disputes over the constitutionality of taxation were pushed to the background as the quarrel between the thirteen colonies and Britain shifted its focus to the extent of British authority over the American provinces. In the process, large numbers of colonists

---

83. Derry, "Government Policy," 58.

84. Beck, *Igniting the Revolution*, 5.

85. Bunker, *Empire on the Edge*, 188; Beck, 5; "John Hancock—Smuggling Powerhouse."

86. Derry, "Government Policy," 58.

who had taken little or no part in the protests against the Tea Act and its predecessors joined the struggle to preserve what they believed were their constitutional liberties against a perceived tyrannical government in London. This movement, which soon rendered royal officials almost powerless, began in New England in the summer of 1774 and soon spread to other colonies, where the inhabitants feared that the British government might well impose the same restrictions on them as had been placed on the people of Massachusetts. This unity was strengthened by the convening of the First Continental Congress in September 1774 and its adoption of the Continental Association the following month, which empowered local committees to enforce its resolves, and colonial unity was further cemented by the outbreak of fighting at Lexington and Concord, Massachusetts, in April 1775.[87]

Protests against the Tea Act led directly to passage of the Coercive Acts and transformed the dispute between Britain and the thirteen colonies from a debate over the respective authority of Parliament and the colonial legislatures into a struggle against British tyranny. This was not the result of oppressive taxation; the Tea Act had not increased the tax on tea. Economic historian Robert Paul Thomas's calculations revealed that the entire cost imposed on the colonists by the Navigation Acts, including the Sugar Act and Townshend duties, from 1763 to 1772 was a pittance. Based on the estimated total customs revenue raised in America during that period, Thomas found that payments to the British treasury amounted to 54 cents per $100 of annual income for each colonist, a tax rate of 0.54 percent.[88] Earl Gower indicated as much when he declared in the House of Lords that "a paltry tax upon tea, a particular insult, a single act of violence or sedition, was not the true ground of the present dispute. It was not this tax or that Act, nor a redress of a particular grievance; the great question in issue is, the supremacy of this country, and the subordinate dependence of America."[89] Thomas Jefferson would have agreed that the issue was not burdensome taxation, nor the Tea Act alone. In his 1774 pamphlet, *A Summary View of the Rights of British America*, he asserted that "single acts of tyranny may be ascribed to the accidental opinion of a day; but a series of oppressions, begun at a distinguished period, and pursued unalterably through every change of ministers, too plainly prove a deliberate and systematical plan of reducing us to slavery."[90] The issue in his view was constitutional and political, not economic.

87. T. H. Breen, *American Insurgents, American Patriots: The Revolution of the People* (New York: Hill and Wang, 2010), 16–18, 40, 46, 48, 76–78, 121, 132–33, 167, 185; Mary Beth Norton, *1774: The Long Year of Revolution* (New York: Alfred A. Knopf, 2020), xviii, 199–201.

88. Robert Paul Thomas, "A Quantitative Approach to the Study of the Effects of British Imperial Policy upon Colonial Welfare: Some Preliminary Findings," *Journal of Economic History* 25, no. 4 (December 1965): 615–38.

89. Dickinson, "Britain's Imperial Sovereignty," 83.

90. Thomas Jefferson, *A Summary View of the Rights of British America*, in Wood, *American Revolution*, 2:96.

The Role of King George III

Throughout the dispute between Britain and the colonies, the Americans blamed their troubles on the king's ministers and Parliament, viewing George III as a just ruler who would end unconstitutional taxation when he learned what his ministers had been doing. Dickinson, in the third of his *Farmer's* letters, reassured the colonists that "the constitutional modes of obtaining relief, are those which I wish to see pursued" to rectify the injustice of the Townshend duties. He urged Americans to rely on petitions because "we have an excellent prince, in whose good dispositions towards us we may confide." The British people were similarly "sensible and humane." The king and the British public "may be deceived," Dickinson noted. "They may, by artful men, be provoked to anger against us. I cannot believe they will be cruel or unjust."[91] Boston clergyman Andrew Eliot declared that "if the King can do no wrong, his ministers may; and when they do wrong, they ought to be h[an]g[e]d." Such sentiments were repeated across the colonies. The residents of Farmington, Connecticut, drew up a resolution in 1774, which stated, "that the present ministry, being instigated by the devil and led by their wicked and corrupt hearts, have a design to take away our liberties and properties, and to enslave us forever." An anonymous Philadelphian expressed similar views, insisting that "a corrupt and prostituted ministry are pointing their destructive machines against the sacred liberties of the Americans."[92]

The original opinion of Americans that exempted the king from blame for their woes was accurate. George III did not formulate policy; his responsibility was to uphold the sovereignty of Parliament over the empire. This was consistent with the views of British politicians, who "had no desire to affirm the prerogatives of the crown," nor did the king wish to do so. "In the colonial context," George III believed it was his duty to maintain "parliament's rights throughout all territories owing allegiance to the British crown."[93]

One of the first criticisms of the king appeared in Jefferson's *Summary View*, in which he urged George III "to resume the exercise of his negative power, and to prevent the passage of laws by any one legislature of the empire, which might bear injuriously on the rights and interests of another." Jefferson was suggesting that the king should have vetoed the Stamp Act and other revenue measures approved by Parliament.[94] Then, taking his argument further, Jefferson contended that "kings are the servants, not the proprietors of the people" and requested that the king listen to the colonists' complaints and secure their liberties.[95] A year later, in July 1775, the Second Continental Congress made a similar appeal to George III. In the hope of

---

91. Dickinson, *Letters from a Farmer*, Letter III, in Wood, *American Revolution*, 1:425.

92. Bailyn, *Ideological Origins*, 125–26.

93. Derry, "Government Policy," 45.

94. Jefferson, *Summary View*, 2:101.

95. Jefferson, 2:106–7.

avoiding all-out war, the delegates composed the "Olive Branch Petition," expressing their loyalty to the king and asking him to find a solution to their dispute with the parent country. King George, perhaps feeling less than charitable after Americans had battled his troops at Lexington, Concord, and Bunker Hill, declined to reply.[96]

Unlike the members of Congress, Thomas Paine did not harbor hopes of the king's benevolence, as he made clear in the attacks on monarchy and George III that filled his 1776 pamphlet, *Common Sense*. Paine described the institution of monarchy as "exceedingly ridiculous" and the idea that "the king is wiser" than the legislature as "an absurdity."[97] He attacked monarchy on religious grounds, contending that "it was the most prosperous invention the Devil ever set on foot" while denying that there was any scriptural sanction for the institution, saying rather that it was sinful in its nature.[98] Paine then shifted his attack to secular grounds, denouncing hereditary succession as ineffective and an injustice to everyone who did not belong to a royal family, as they were denied a voice in government while being forced to submit to the authority "of a rogue or a fool."[99] Tracing the origins of monarchy, Paine speculated that the first king was probably "nothing better than the principal ruffian of some restless gang, whose savage manners" or talent for deceit "obtained him the title of chief among plunderers."[100] Paine insisted that George III was no better, a "wretch," the "Royal Brute of Britain" who slept peacefully while his troops slaughtered his alleged children in America.[101]

The Declaration of Independence completed the casting of the king as a villainous tyrant responsible for all the Americans' grievances. For Jefferson, the Declaration's principal author, and the members of the Second Continental Congress, doing so was less a choice than a necessity. In arguing that their colonial legislatures were the equal of Parliament, at least regarding domestic affairs, the Americans had devised a "conception of the Empire as a set of separate political communities bound together under the King," to whom they had repeatedly pledged their loyalty.[102] Once Congress decided to break fully with Britain, the delegates could only prove the justice of their action "if the charges against the King were convincing and of sufficient gravity to warrant the dissolution of his authority over the American people. They

---

96. Robert Middlekauff, *The Glorious Cause: The American Revolution, 1763–1789* (New York: Oxford University Press, 1982), 313.

97. Thomas Paine, *Common Sense*, in Wood, *American Revolution*, 2:656.

98. Paine, *Common Sense*, 2:659.

99. Paine, 2:662.

100. Paine, 2:663.

101. Paine, 2:680.

102. Pauline Maier, *American Scripture: Making the Declaration of Independence* (New York: Alfred A. Knopf, 1997), 105.

were therefore essential to the Declaration's central purpose," historian Pauline Maier explained.[103] Hence George III became the chief villain in the Revolutionary drama.

Conclusion

There is no doubt that British efforts to tax the American colonies led to the American Revolution. Yet, the evidence is clear that for most colonists, the key issue was not that the taxes were burdensome—on the contrary, Americans conceded that the taxes were small—but that they appeared to threaten cherished rights of self-government and the foundations of the liberty the colonists prized. These convictions notwithstanding, British officials never intended to oppress the colonies. The king's ministers and most members of Parliament misunderstood the Americans' position and its implications for maintaining British authority in the colonies and therefore implemented policies that sparked unexpected, often violent, opposition. Attempts to placate the colonists only appeared to produce new American demands. At the same time, most colonists were equally ill-informed of the situation in Great Britain and the London government's need to establish effective control over a newly expanded, far-flung, and diverse empire, which required new financial outlays added to a burgeoning national debt. Asking the Americans to make a financial contribution did not constitute a conspiracy to deprive the colonists of their liberty, regardless of the alarms that writers on the fringe of British politics had raised over previous decades.[104]

Whether steeped in the political ideas described by Bailyn or concerned that taxation without representation endangered their liberty, Americans believed that they were taking an essentially conservative position as defenders of traditional English rights. In the process, they unwittingly moved ever closer to becoming revolutionaries. The arguments they advanced to support their position were a complex amalgam of political theory, interpretations of Britain's unwritten constitution, and lessons from history. They also occasionally contradicted themselves, first stating their acceptance of customs duties while declaring their opposition to the "internal" stamp tax, only to reverse themselves in the case of the Townshend duties and blaming the king's ministers and Parliament for the "oppressive" revenue acts while insisting on their loyalty to George III, then shifting position to make George III the culprit for their troubles. Just as the king became the face of British oppression, so, too, were the complex political issues surrounding taxation often reduced to the simplistic explanation that high taxes caused the Revolution. Such a reason is convenient to state and easy to understand but overlooks many essential facts and details, resulting in a distorted view of America's founders and their true motives.

---

103. Maier, *American Scripture*, 117.
104. Dickinson, "Britain's Imperial Sovereignty," 67–68.

2. THE MYTH OF BRITISH MILITARY INCOMPETENCE

Don N. Hagist

A soldier's existence was an alternative to filching in the streets, rotting in prison, or starving or freezing to death for want of food and clothing.[1]
—*James Kirby Martin and Mark Edward Lender, historians, 2015*

The British army's practice of shooting undirected volleys and advancing in line had to contend with the novelty of American sharpshooters.[2]
—*Therese-Marie Meyer, historian, 2018*

The British military system, wherein commissions were bought and aristocrats given preference, denied many men of ability roles they should have played.[3]
—*David McCullough, historian, 2005*

It is tempting to assume that a lost war was lost because one army was outfought by the other on the battlefield, regardless of strategy, logistics, national commitment, or other considerations. Perhaps it is for this reason that so many books on the American Revolution, both popular and scholarly, include a few pages pointing out inherent deficiencies in the organization, training, and battlefield performance of the British army, repeating unfounded claims of poor officers leading poor soldiers in poor tactics. This has led to a traditional view of American Patriots deftly defeating stoic British soldiers trapped in the mores of traditional European warfare.

Perceptions of the British army's operational effectiveness in the American Revolution have been largely shaped by the outcomes of the war's first two battles, Lexington and Concord in April 1775 and Bunker Hill two months later. Neither of these actions was typical of the fighting that raged for the next seven years, and neither accurately characterizes the skill and professionalism of the British army in this conflict. In assessing the background, training, and skill of officers and soldiers, a few sources, some from the time of the American Revolution and some from later years, are taken

---

1. James Kirby Martin and Mark Edward Lender, *A Respectable Army: The Military Origins of the Republic, 1763–1789*, 3rd ed. (Chichester, UK: John Wiley & Sons, 2015), 12.

2. Therese-Marie Meyer, "Stuck a Bayonet into the Grave," in *Beyond 1776: Globalizing the Cultures of the American Revolution*, ed. Maria O'Malley and Denys Van Renen (Charlottesville: University of Virginia Press, 2018), 192.

3. David McCullough, *1776* (New York: Simon & Schuster, 2005), 78.

to be generalities when in fact, they reflect specific circumstances and small segments of the overall military population. Looking at the entire eight-year war, as well as the entire population of officers and soldiers—including the fact those populations changed as the war progressed—reveals a much more professional and capable British force that was rarely beaten in battle.

Peacekeepers Thrust into War

When war broke out in America, there were about a dozen British infantry regiments in North America, ten of which were concentrated in Boston, Massachusetts. This city had been the seat of unrest in the colonies for several years. A series of events beginning with the Boston Tea Party in 1773—itself the culmination of years of protests throughout the colonies against parliamentary policies—led to open rebellion when Massachusetts colonists set up their own government in defiance of British law. A military buildup in Boston, intended to quell rising tensions, had the opposite effect. Although war was not the desired outcome of an expedition to seize military stores in Concord on April 19, 1775, the British troops were not caught wholly unprepared. They had been training since the previous summer.

For several months before April, the army had been training for the possibility of hostilities, but the 700-man force that left Boston for the twenty-mile march to Concord on April 18 was a composite organization composed of selected elite units from each of ten regiments that had never worked together before. This seems like an odd choice, but the mission was not to do battle but to locate and seize military stores, and these soldiers were the most capable of the long, fast march required to achieve surprise. The early morning march to Concord was largely uneventful—a skirmish in the town of Lexington resulted in American militia fleeing British musketry and bayonets—but a more intense clash with a large formation of militia at one of the bridges outside of Concord led to a return march that was disastrous. Discipline broke down, and the beleaguered soldiers were saved from annihilation only by a brigade that marched out of Boston to relieve them.

The popular image is of British troops naively marching in formation along the road while American snipers picked them off one by one from behind rocks and trees. This image, while not entirely inaccurate, ignores important facets of the action. Fighting began in earnest only after the British soldiers had been awake for over thirty hours and had marched for more than twenty miles. The force was composed of individual companies that had never operated together before—the grenadier company and light infantry company from each of ten regiments, specially trained in fast-paced skirmishing and marksmanship but unaccustomed to operating independently from their regiments—setting the stage for collapsing discipline when casualties occurred among officers and in the ranks. They were severely outnumbered. The road, although exposed, afforded the quickest way back to Boston. Using tactics developed during the French and Indian War in America just over a decade before and recently refined and formalized throughout the British army, flanking parties effectively swept opposition away from adjacent stone walls and woods, only to have opponents reappear elsewhere. British soldiers rushed upon their antagonists with bayonets, driving them away, but could do this only so many times before exhaustion set in.

American reports of the battle emphasized that British soldiers plundered and burned houses during their retreat but failed to mention that American militiamen fired from the windows of those houses and left their opponents little choice but to go inside to find the perpetrators. The British expedition managed to reach the safety of Boston after sustaining nearly 300 killed, wounded, and missing from a total of about 1,500 engaged.

The British troops depicted here advancing in formal lines across open ground are a staple of Revolutionary lore. While British soldiers did attack in rigid formations at Bunker Hill outside Boston on June 17, 1775, they quickly adapted to conditions in America and employed a variety of tactics against the colonists. *Battle of Bunker Hill*, painting by Howard Pyle, c. 1897. Delaware Art Museum, Wilmington.

Two months later, the arrival of a few more regiments from Great Britain provided enough force to seize Bunker Hill, a peninsular eminence north of Boston, separated from the city by about a mile of water. Learning of the impending operation, American forces built a redoubt on Breed's Hill, the slope of the peninsula facing Boston. The British assault that secured the hill but incurred tremendous casualties has been used, like the retreat to Concord, to characterize British troops as unable to adapt to warfare in the colonies. A closer analysis of the battle shows an initial plan that was sound, undone by unanticipated circumstances.

The American redoubt was on a summit, with a fortified fence extending to one side down the hill to the shore; on the other side was the town of Charlestown. The British plan was straightforward: advance slowly toward the redoubt and fence to occupy the defenders while a fast-moving column went around the end of the fence on the shoreline, outflanking the American position. It was about 3:00 p.m. before enough troops had been ferried from Boston to the peninsula to begin the assault. When sniper fire came from buildings in Charlestown, red-hot British cannon fire was used to set the town in flames, a militarily expedient move that gave the appearance of wanton destruction. Unbeknownst to the flanking column, American troops had built a barrier on the shoreline and stopped the British column cold. At the same time, the line advancing toward the fence ran into an assortment of impediments— fences, brick-kilns, and other obstructions—that made it impossible to maintain orderly ranks or rapidly charge the defensive position. As a final insult, soldiers in the flanking column that had retreated were now in the rear, firing toward American positions from a great distance but inflicting friendly-fire casualties on the soldiers advancing on the fence.

The British army carried the day, driving their foes off the peninsula, but at the cost of 1,000 casualties, about half of the attacking force—many would recover to fight again—but such losses were not sustainable. Mistakes were certainly made. Those mistakes, however, were never again made in the years and campaigns that followed. The war's two initial actions went badly for the British but were not typical of the battles that followed.

Adapting to War in America

"Britain, influenced by Frederick the Great and its own experience in the Seven Years' War, produced a regiment tailored to formal European battle," wrote an author comparing British wartime tactics to those of the Continental Army; "it deployed its battalion companies in three ranks to achieve the density needed for a bayonet charge. The Continentals turned instead to their colonial tradition of aimed fire and to the lessons of the French and Indian War for inspiration. They adopted a formation using only two ranks, with a frontage more than twice the size of that of a British battalion."[4] Peacetime training for British regiments did indeed call for three-rank formations, that is, three rows of men, each about a foot behind the man in front of him. But when the army went on the offensive in 1776, and for the remainder of the war, it used a different fundamental formation and maneuvers tailored to American terrain.

The British army that fought in America was composed primarily of infantry, and the basic organizational element of the infantry was the regiment. In the early 1770s,

---

4. Robert K. Wright Jr., *The Continental Army* (Washington, DC: U.S. Army Center of Military History, 1983), 49.

infantry regiments at full strength consisted of 35 officers, 50 noncommissioned officers, 12 drummers and fifers, and 360 private soldiers. After a year of war, the number of private soldiers was increased by 50 percent, and two years later increased again for a total of 60 noncommissioned officers and 700 private soldiers in most regiments.[5] These were divided roughly equally into ten companies.

Two companies, the grenadiers and the light infantry, were specialized, composed only of robust, reliable men with at least a year of military experience. These companies conducted skirmishing, flanking, and other actions requiring a little more fitness and independent thought than service in the other eight companies. In preparation for the 1776 campaign that drove American forces out of New York City, General Sir William Howe, a veteran of the Seven Years' War (1756–1763), reorganized the army to use fast-moving, open-order tactics that he himself had developed during the preceding years. The compact, three-deep, shoulder-to-shoulder formation was abandoned in favor of two-deep lines with the men at eighteen-inch intervals.[6] These open formations allowed each regiment a dramatically more extensive front, a front that could be maintained while moving through uneven country punctuated by woods, enclosures, and other obstacles. Howe detached the light infantry and grenadier companies from their regiments and formed them into composite battalions of light infantry and grenadiers, each with seven to thirteen companies, that remained together—with variations

GEN. SIR WILLIAM HOWE

General Sir William Howe, who commanded British forces in America from 1776 to 1778, was an expert in light infantry tactics and avoided frontal assaults on American positions, instead making use of flanking maneuvers to defeat the Americans at Brooklyn, New York, on August 27, 1776, and at Brandywine, Pennsylvania, on September 11, 1777. *Gen. Sir William Howe, British Commander in Chief*, reproduction of an engraving by C. Corbutt, 1777. Emmet Collection, New York Public Library.

5. Establishments, 1775, 1776, 1778, and 1780, War Office Papers (WO) 379/1, The National Archives, Kew, United Kingdom (TNA). Descriptions of company strength often include two fictitious "warrant men" added to companies as an allowance for expenses, yielding incorrect strengths of thirty-eight or fifty-six private men. Edward E. Curtis, *The Organization of the British Army in the American Revolution* (New Haven, CT: Yale University Press, 1926), 23.

6. General Orders, August 1, 1776, WO 36/5, TNA.

as regiments came and went from the theater—for the duration of the war. These battalions typically formed the vanguard of the army on campaign; two or three times a year, when their numbers were depleted, regiments transferred suitable men into these elite companies and took back those who were no longer fit for such active campaigning.

By the time the army took the offensive in earnest in August 1776, it was fully capable of meeting the large but relatively untrained and hodge-podge American army. At the Battle of Brooklyn on August 27, a 10,000-man force distracted American troops while an equal-sized force marched a dozen miles through the night to outflank American positions. It was a complete rout, and the momentum was maintained for months as British forces drove their adversaries out of Manhattan, Westchester County, and New Jersey. General Howe's orders directed:

> The Officers will take all proper Opportunities and especially at the beginning of the Campaign to inculcate in the mens mind, a reliance upon the Bayonet. Men of half their bodily Strength and even Cowards may be their match in firing, but the onset of bayonets in the Hands of the Valiant is irresistable. The Enemy Convinced of this truth, place their whole dependence in Entrenchments and rifle pieces. It will be our Glory and preservation to Storm where possible.[7]

The rationale was simple: if well-trained soldiers rushed in good order with bayonets, they would quickly cover the one hundred or so yards that was the effective range of typical firearms that were slow to reload; relatively raw American soldiers would not stand, even with the cover of walls or fences, to face bayonets in the hands of professional soldiers. The keys to winning battles against Americans were speed and maneuverability.

Even when their opponents relied on the cover of woods, which abounded in America, British troops were quick to adapt. By February 1777, a light infantry officer proudly proclaimed after a firefight: "The fire was prodigiously heavy at one time but per favour of some pretty large trees, which by a good deal of practise we have learnt to make a proper use of, my Company suffered very little."[8] On April 20 of that year, two years and one day after hostilities broke out, Captain William Dansey of the 33rd Regiment demonstrated not only that his light infantry company was skilled in using woods for cover but also that deception could be more effective than gunfire or bayonets in close-quarters combat:

7. General Orders, June 20, 1777. Orderly book, Major Acland's Grenadier Battalion, New-York Historical Society, New York City.

8. James Murray, *Letters from America, 1773 to 1780*, ed. Eric Robson (New York: Barnes & Noble, 1950), 40.

We have learn'd from the Rebels to cover our Bodies if theres a Tree or a Rail near us. I faced two hundred of the Rebels with my Company only in a Wood, for two minuits, myself not twenty Yards from some of them and received all their fire . . . I was so near as to call to them "by G-d my Lads we have you now" in hopes they wou'd be bullied to surrender but that wou'd not do they answer'd me with a heavy fire, however when I got my men to the Trees round about me and the other Company coming up to my Support, I bullied them another way, seeing them snug behind the Trees and showing no disposition to run, and too many of them to charge as we were rather too thin I cried as loud as I cou'd hollow that they might be sure to hear me "my G-d Soldiers they run, have at them my brave Boys" which had the desired effect, one thought the other run and they all set off as if the D—l drove them.[9]

German regiments brought to America to supplement the British army, collectively called Hessians, even though they came from several German states, had difficulty adapting to the fast-paced manner of fighting that the British adopted. In Canada, ten British regiments drove an American invading force from Quebec all the way to Lake Champlain in 1776, using open order, rapid movements, and massed light infantry and grenadiers. A German officer described the "special way of waging war which departs utterly from our system." Referring to the two-rank, open-order formations necessary for movement in the American wilderness, he wrote: "Our infantry can only operate two deep, and a man must have eighteen inches space either side to be able to march in line through woods and brush."[10] Entering the next campaign in 1777, Lieutenant General John Burgoyne established "a Constant rule in or near Woods to place Advance Centries where they may have a Tree or some other defence to prevent their being taken off by single Marksmen." His soldiers heeded his orders well. Advancing on Fort Ticonderoga at the beginning of July, "the Enemy that prided themselves in the Woods, were taught to know that even there the British Bayonet will ever make it's Way."[11]

On July 7, at the Battle of Hubbardton, British grenadiers and light infantry caught up with a much larger force fleeing southward after abandoning Fort Ticonderoga. The light infantry charged up a steep, wooded slope and met a strong American line as they crested the hill. A vicious, close firefight ensued, and the outnumbered light infantry

---

9. William Dansey, *Captured Rebel Flag: The Letters of Captain William Dansey, 33rd Regiment of Foot, 1776–1777*, ed. Paul Dansey (Godmanchester, Huntington, UK: Ken Trotman Press, 2010), 27.

10. Ray W. Pettengill, trans., *Letters from America 1776–1779, Being Letters of Brunswick, Hessian, and Waldeck Officers with the British Armies during the Revolution* (Boston, MA: Houghton Mifflin, 1924), 70.

11. Ronald F. Kingsley, "Letters to Lord Polwarth from Sir Francis-Carr Clerke, Aide-de-Camp to General John Burgoyne," *New York History* 79 (October 1998): 429.

were nonetheless able to push their opponents back. A field enclosed by log fences provided a strong position into which the Americans fled and regrouped, but the British grenadiers managed a long march, scaled another wooded slope, and appeared on the American flank. According to a British officer, the battle "did our troops the greater honour, as the enemy were vastly superior in numbers, and it was perform'd in a thick wood, in the very style that the Americans think themselves superior to regular troops."[12] Because they were greatly outnumbered, the British grenadiers and light infantry were almost repulsed at Hubbardton. At a critical moment, the day was decided by the arrival of troops armed with rifles. These weapons, with greater range and accuracy but a much slower rate of fire than military muskets, are widely seen as wonder weapons that American marksmen used to defeat the musket-armed British. But the rifles at Hubbardton were in the hands of German Jäger—hunters—a corps of skilled marksmen that routinely worked in conjunction with light infantry for scouting, skirmishing, and as an advanced guard. Rifles were also used by selected men in British light infantry companies. Only in rare cases did rifles make significant contributions to the course of battles, but throughout the war, they were used by British forces every bit as effectively as by Americans.

This was the way of war for the British soldiers throughout the American Revolution. In campaign after campaign, they made rapid advances, often fording deep streams and scaling steep hills, marching through the night to meet opponents who outnumbered them and pressed home dramatic victories. Their principal weakness was numbers: not enough men to occupy the vast territories in the colonies, too few troops to hold the ground they had gained and also launch new campaigns. Logistical difficulties and shifting strategy hampered campaign planning.

Recruiting Professional Soldiers

Adaptation and determination were possible only because of the training experience of the officers and soldiers. Both have been portrayed as little more than caricatures in countless histories, failing to look at the actual people who made up the army and their long and varied careers. Indeed, few participants in the American Revolution have been reviled, belittled, and mischaracterized as much as the soldiers in the British army. Despite the army itself being called the best in the world, somehow, writers for more than a century have presented it as composed of "the sweepings of jail, ginmills and poorhouses, oafs from the farm beguiled into 'taking the King's shillings.'"[13] This wildly inaccurate impression stems largely from a few sources, some from the time

---

12. Thomas Hughes, *A Journal by Thos: Hughes* (Cambridge, MA: Harvard University Press, 1947), 10.

13. Walter Millis, *Arms and Men: A Study of American Military History* (New Brunswick, NJ: Rutgers University Press, 1981), 17.

of the American Revolution and some from later years, taken to be generalities when in fact, they reflected specific circumstances and small segments of the overall soldier population.

Like many misconceptions, the perception that typical British soldiers were society's debris appears to come from taking information that was true of a small part of the army and assuming it to be true of the majority. It is true that in 1813 the Duke of Wellington famously wrote, "We have in the service the scum of the earth as common soldiers," and he was not the first to express such sentiments; during the American Revolution, a British officer complained to the Secretary at War, "they are the very Scum of the Earth, and do their utmost to desert, the moment they are Cloathed."[14] But both comments were made in very specific contexts: Wellington was complaining of his soldiers plundering French towns, and the other officer was describing recruits in Ireland who absconded after receiving the benefits of enlistment. There were, undeniably, low characters in the army. During the war in America, it was possible for men convicted of crimes to enlist in the army as an alternative to jail, and for a two-year period, it was legal to press men into the army. But the vast majority of British soldiers during this era enlisted voluntarily, and none of those who recorded their reasons for doing so suggested that it was a last resort; enlistment afforded some significant benefits not available in other careers.

British soldiers who served in America were recruited during three distinct time periods, during which the demand for manpower, the terms of enlistment, and the incentives offered differed. When the war began, virtually all of the British soldiers in America—about 10,000 by the end of 1775—were already in the army; they had not been recruited because of the war but had chosen to enlist during a time of peace (except, of course, those veterans of the French and Indian War who were still serving). Every peacetime recruit was a volunteer; unlike the navy, the army could not legally press, conscript, or otherwise coerce men into the service in the 1760s and early 1770s. The law required every recruit to attest before a magistrate, within four days of enlisting, that he had joined voluntarily, an important safeguard against coercion.[15]

Recruiting posters and advertisements frequently sought "gentleman volunteers," casting a military life as superior to that of a tradesman or laborer.[16] A recruiting advertisement for the 33rd Regiment of Foot sought "any able-bodied Young man . . .

---

14. Commander-in-Chief in Munster to Lord Barrington, in *Letters of Edward Gibbon*, ed. J. F. Norton (London: Cassell & Co., 1956), 2:89.

15. *Rules and articles for the better government of His Majesty's horse and foot guards, and all other forces in Great Britain and Ireland, dominions beyond the seas, and foreign parts, from the 24th of March, 1777* (London, 1777), Section III Article I; other annual editions from this era are substantially similar.

16. Recruiting poster, 45th Regiment of Foot circa 1779, Colonial Williamsburg; *Norfolk Chronicle*, March 30, 1776; *Belfast Newsletter*, March 3, 1780.

who is fixed with ambition, has a roving disposition, and whose spirit soars above the dull sameness of staying at home."[17] "Home" referred not to the prospective recruit's household but to his parish or town and, by implication, his workplace. While some historians have concluded that the army was predominantly an alternative to unemployment, the writings of soldiers, few though they are, give a different picture.[18] Almost every man who recorded his reason for enlisting was employed at the time but had some motive for leaving. Far from "outcasts of British humanity,"[19] most were working men looking for change. Men like Richard Taylor of the 63rd Regiment and Thomas Cranfield of the 39th joined to escape bad apprenticeships.[20] Valentine Duckett sought out a recruiting party because "my step-mother and I could not agree," John Robertshaw ran away from home after being "illtreated by his stepmother" and to escape working for his father, and James Andrew enlisted to be free "from the clamour of a wife."[21] Equally frequent was the allure of the army compared to the life of a laborer or tradesman: William Burke "had a wish to become a soldier"; Joshua Pell met a soldier and "had a secret inclination that I should like to go with that man"; and W. Griffith, seeing the opportunity to enlist, "could not resist it, though I could give no particular reason."[22] There are too few writings to compile statistics, but those men who wrote down their rationales for enlisting were not unemployed but instead

---

17. *British Chronicle or Pugh's Hereford Journal*, August 31, 1775.

18. For the conclusion that unemployment was a key motivation see Sylvia Frey, *The British Soldier in North America* (Austin: University of Texas Press, 1981), 9–10. The literacy rate among British soldiers cannot be determined with accuracy; just over half of discharged soldiers were able to sign their own names on their discharge forms. See Don N. Hagist, *Noble Volunteers: The British Soldiers Who Fought the American Revolution* (Yardley, PA: Westholme, 2020), 35–36, 152–53. To date, this author has found thirty-five writings of men who served in the army in the 1770s and early 1780s who gave their reason for enlisting.

19. Franklin B. Wickwire and Mary Wickwire, *Cornwallis and the War of Independence* (Chapel Hill: University of North Carolina Press, 1980), 52.

20. Edmund Bott, *A Collection of Decisions of the Court of King's Bench upon the Poor's Laws, down to the Present Time*, 2nd ed. (London: W. Strachan and M. Woodfall, 1773), 394 (Taylor); Thomas Cranfield, *The Useful Christian; a Memoir of Thomas Cranfield, for about Fifty Years a Devoted Sunday-School Teacher* (Philadelphia: American Sunday-School Union, Philadelphia, no date), 11 (Cranfield).

21. The Dying Speech of Valentine Duckett, BDSDS 1774, American Antiquarian Society, Worcester, MA (Duckett); Oressa M. Teagarden, *John Robert Shaw: An Autobiography of Thirty Years, 1777–1807* (Athens: Ohio University Press, 1992), 11 (Robertshaw); R. C. and J. M. Anderson, *Quicksilver: A Hundred Years of Coaching 1750–1850* (Newton Abbot, Devon, England: David & Charles Ltd., 1973), 174–77 (Andrew).

22. William Burke, *Memoir of William Burke: A Soldier of the Revolution* (Hartford, CT: Case, Tiffany and Co., 1837), 8 (Burke); A Narrative of the Life of Serjeant William Pell, E06–003, Grenadier Guards Archives (Pell); "Memoirs and Spiritual Experience of the late Mr. W. Griffith, Senior (Written by Himself)," *The Spiritual Magazine, and Zion's Casket*, E. Palmer and Son, London, 1848, 152.

found the army more attractive than some other aspect of their circumstances. Tales abound of men tricked into service, but primary sources do not bear out such stories for the era of the American Revolution.

The base pay of a private soldier, eight pence a day, has been used to represent the army as a miserable form of employment, worsened by deductions from wages for food, clothing, and an assortment of incidentals.[23] Eight pence per day was indeed barely competitive with rates for unskilled labor, but it had practical aspects: civilians had to pay for food and clothing out of their wages just as soldiers did; soldiers bore no cost of their own lodging, something civilian workers paid for; soldiers' pay was guaranteed while laborers and tradesmen were subject to economic changes; and soldiers had many opportunities to earn significantly more than their base wage. There was also the allure of an enlistment bounty, over a month's pay in peacetime and more in wartime, and the prospect of a pension after either long service or incurring a disability.[24] In December 1775, the War Office announced two additional incentives: a man could serve only until the end of the war, or at least three years, whichever was longer; men who had served their three years could take a land grant of one hundred acres in America when the war ended.[25] For laborers with no prospect of owning land in Britain, this was a significant temptation—as well as a way to encourage settlement in colonial lands.

Almost all British soldiers who served in the American Revolution enlisted under the terms described above: voluntarily, with an enlistment bounty and the possibility of a pension. Wartime enlistees had the additional incentives of a fixed term of service and the option of a land grant (whereas peacetime recruits generally served for life). These benefits, at least to some extent, offset the difficult lifestyle of a soldier and give some insight into why British soldiers were so effective on the battlefield—soldiers had something to lose if they fled from their duty and were also subject to severe punishments, including the death penalty, for desertion.

---

23. The base pay and various deductions are described in John Williamson, *A Treatise on Military Finance* (London: T. Egerton, 1782).

24. The bounty offered before 1775 was typically one guinea (a coin valued at 21 shillings or £1 1 shilling). A template set of recruiting instructions directed that "no more than £1 11s 6d. shall be given to each recruit as bounty-money" and also directed that a receipt be made "for the bounty-money agreed on," suggesting flexibility in the amount offered. In 1778, the government established a bounty of £3, and in 1779 to £3 3s. Thomas Simes, *The Military Medley* (London: 1768), 34; Curtis, *Organization of the British Army*, 55, 57; Don N. Hagist, *British Soldiers, American War: Voices of the American Revolution* (Yardley, PA: Westholme Publishing, 2012), 186–89.

25. *London Gazette*, December 16, 1775.

Convicts, Press Gangs, and Lashes?

Men convicted of petty larceny or misdemeanors could be offered military service as an alternative to prison. Like recruiting in general, enlistment was voluntary—enlistment was a choice, not a requirement, and regimental officers accepted only those they thought would make good soldiers. Surveys of available records indicate that only a few hundred such men entered the army between 1775 and 1781, during which period some 50,000 British soldiers served in America. There are no records of the number of convicts who served in regiments in America, but it certainly was small.[26] The careers of a handful can be traced and show that the army was a good alternative; the 46th Regiment of Foot took six men confined "for petty offenses," of whom four went on to serve in America, two eventually becoming noncommissioned officers.[27]

In response to France's 1778 declaration of war, the army raised new infantry regiments, requiring rapid recruiting of thousands of men. In May of 1778, a new law allowed pressing men into the army for the first time since the previous war. The Recruiting Act initially allowed men to be pressed only in "the City of London, The City and Liberties of Westminster, and . . . parts of the County of Middlesex" as well as in Scotland. Only men who were "able-bodied and idle" and those who were "disorderly" and "could not, upon Examination, prove themselves to exercise and industriously follow some lawful Trade or Employment" or other means of support could be pressed. There were other limitations based on trade, age, and physical condition. In February 1779, a new press act superseded the 1778 act. It expanded the age range and some of the other limits and applied to all of Great Britain but was suspended throughout England and Wales from the end of May through the end of November; the London area excepted to ensure that it would not interfere with farming.[28] In May 1780, the press act was repealed, in no small part due to the corrupt practices it invited—the few surviving accounts of men tricked into enlistment date from the two years the press act was in effect. Impressment remained illegal for the remainder of the war. The number of pressed men sent to America was negligible, amounting to fewer than 100 of the over 1,300 replacements sent in 1779 and only 71 of the roughly 2,700 men in three new regiments sent to America that year.[29]

Military discipline applied to all soldiers regardless of background. "The lash was used to punish offences whether trivial or heinous. Nor was it applied either lightly or

---

26. Stephen R. Conway, "The Recruitment of Criminals into the British Army, 1775–81," *Historical Research*, LVIII (May 1985): 46–58.

27. John Ridout to the Secretary at War, August 10, 1776, WO 1/993; muster rolls, 46th Regiment of Foot, WO 12/5797.

28. Curtis, *Organization of the British Army*, 59–60.

29. WO 34/150 folio 129, TNA (recruits); WO 4/966, 402–7, TNA (regiments).

sparingly," wrote a historian in 1926.[30] Like most since then, this writer characterized martial discipline only in terms of malefactors without considering it in full context. Regiments maintained records of trials and punishments, and although only a few such records survive, they reveal that harsh discipline was applied only to that portion of the soldiers whose behavior warranted it. Punishment books for four regiments in Ireland from 1773 through 1777 record every trial held during that period, the sentence handed down by the military court, and whether the sentence was carried out in full, in part, or the offender was pardoned. Comparing these records to muster rolls reveals the portion of men tried and of those, how many received lashes. During this four-year period approximately 3,500 sergeants, corporals, drummers, and private soldiers spent time in these regiments, a high number because substantial numbers were drafted from them into regiments serving in America and were replaced by new recruits. In 972 trials, 723 individual soldiers were tried; many defendants were repeat offenders, some individuals being tried as many as eight times in four years. There were some not guilty verdicts, some pardons, some sentences of non-corporal punishment, and some remittances of punishment, resulting in a total of 355 men being lashed, about 10 percent of the total who served, some of them lashed multiple times.[31] A punishment book for the 44th Regiment, serving in the New York garrison and then in Canada from 1778 through 1785, shows similar numbers: 203 men tried in 400 trials, again many of them several times, out of 1,524 men altogether; 125, or 8 percent of the total, were lashed for crimes.[32] These records reveal that punishment was neither arbitrary nor a soldier's certain fate; instead, as in any community, a small portion of the population committed the majority of crimes and received most of the punishment. Every regiment had its "notorious scoundrel" and "incorrigible thief," but they were few.[33]

"Punishments were never meant only to affect Criminals, but also as Examples to the rest of Mankind," wrote Lieutenant John Barker of the 4th Regiment of Foot in Boston in 1774.[34] Lashings were administered in a somewhat ritual manner, witnessed by the rest of the regiment, as a warning to them. Brutal though it was, lashing was seldom fatal. Among the witnesses to any punishment was the regiment's surgeon, the medical officer charged with caring for soldiers' health, observing that lashes were applied so as not to endanger vital organs, and halting punishments that risked

---

30. Curtis, *Organization of the British Army*, 28.

31. Punishment Books, 3rd, 36th, 67th and 68th Regiments of Foot, HL/PO/JO/10/7/544, House of Lords Record Office, London.

32. Punishment Book, 44th Regiment of Foot, MG23, K6(2), Public Archives of Canada.

33. John Peebles, *John Peebles' American War: The Diary of a Scottish Grenadier, 1776–1782* (Mechanicsburg, PA: Stackpole Books, 1998), 456–57 (scoundrel); John Nairne to Richard Lernoult, September 3, 1782, John and Thomas Nairne fonds, MG 23, GIII23, vol. 3, 234–35 (thief).

34. John Barker, *The British in Boston: The Diary of Lt. John Barker*, ed. Elizabeth Ellery Dana (Cambridge, MA: Harvard University Press, 1924), 14.

endangering the life of the victim.[35] This ensured that most lashings were, as intended, corporal punishment, not capital.

Well-Trained Career Soldiers

When the war broke out, Britain's army was composed entirely of career soldiers. Although nearly half of the troops had served less than five years, inspections of twenty-three infantry regiments in 1774 recorded about 28 percent of soldiers with five to ten years of service in the army, and 23 percent with more than ten years, up to as much as thirty-five years.[36] The wartime need for soldiers meant a lot of recruiting, but the War Office, recognizing the need for experience as well as numbers, directed regiments remaining in Great Britain to transfer ("draft," in the parlance of the day) substantial numbers of experienced soldiers into regiments deployed to America. The result was that, in 1775 and 1776, about half of the new soldiers added to regiments deployed in America were transfers—drafts—so that the deployed regiments, after their size was increased, included less than 20 percent new recruits.[37]

The British army, far from being the rigid, tradition-bound institution of popular belief, utilized different types of troops to carry out battlefield operations. These soldiers from General William Howe's army in 1778 include a light infantryman (no. 1), grenadier (no. 5), line infantrymen of various units (nos. 2, 4, 6, 7), and a cavalry trooper (light dragoon, no. 3). *Types of British Soldiery of General Howe's Army in Philadelphia, 1777–78*, engraving by Frank H. Taylor, 1905, in Frank H. Taylor, *Valley Forge, a Chronicle of American Heroism* (Philadelphia: J. W. Nagle, 1912).

Training was as important as motivation and years of service, and here, too, folklore pervades the literature. "British soldiers were taught not to aim, but merely to point the piece towards the target," wrote one historian,[38] while a more recent author

---

35. Robert Hamilton, *Duties of a Regimental Surgeon Considered* (London: J. Johnson, J. Murray, T. Longman, and J. Shave, 1787), 2:25–87.

36. Inspection Returns, WO 27/32, TNA.

37. See, for example, muster rolls, 22nd Regiment of Foot, WO 12/3872, and 23rd Regiment of Foot, WO 12/3960, TNA. Proportions varied in each regiment but followed these general trends.

38. Robert Leckie, *The World Turned Upside Down: The Story of the American Revolution* (New York: Putnam, 1972), 45.

went so far as to say, "Not only was there no attempt made to aim, British regulars were taught to look the other way, so as not to have the musket flash blind them."[39] One need only look at the army's training manual to see that this is incorrect. There was no command called "aim," but this is a semantic detail; the command for aiming was called "Present," and described holding the musket with the butt on the right shoulder, "the right Cheek to be close to the Butt, and the left Eye shut, and look along the Barrel with the right Eye from the Breech Pin to the Muzzel."[40] As to the common assertion that muskets were inaccurate due to "a lack of sights,"[41] military texts describing the parts of the musket called the fitting at the muzzle, used to attach a bayonet, the "sight,"[42] and grooves filed into the breech aligned with this sight[43]— crude by modern standards, but allowing aimed fire.

In peacetime, soldiers fired live ammunition only a few times each year,[44] but that changed for soldiers in America before hostilities broke out. In the four months before April 1775, British soldiers in Boston practiced firing at targets with live ammunition on average twice a month, enough to achieve moderate proficiency.[45] Other preparations for warfare included regular marches of five or ten miles into the countryside laden with knapsacks and weapons "to give the men a little exercise."[46] Wartime enlistees spent anywhere from a few weeks to over two years training in Great Britain before embarking to join their regiments in America. This recruiting and training process yielded men who arrived in America already versed in military fundamentals, ready to learn the specific practices required for warfare in America.[47]

---

39. Mike Wright, *What They Didn't Teach You about the American Revolution* (New York: Presidio Press, 2009), unpaginated e-book.

40. *The Manual Exercise, As Ordered by His Majesty, in 1764*. The copy used here was printed by Hugh Gaine, New York, 1775. Although this document was very widely reprinted, the text of the manual exercise portion does not vary with the exception of typographical changes.

41. Rick Atkinson, *The British Are Coming: The War for America, 1775–1777* (New York: Henry Holt, 2019), 62.

42. See, for example, William Windham, *A Plan of Discipline Composed for the Use of the Militia of County of Norfolk* (London: J. Shuckburgh, 1759), Plate 1.

43. See, for example, George C. Neumann, *Battle Weapons of the American Revolution* (Texarkana, TX: Scurlock Publishing, 1998), 55, 63, 67, 74, 167, 172.

44. J. A. Houlding, *Fit for Service: The Training of the British Army, 1715–1795* (Oxford, UK: Clarendon Press, 1981), 144–45.

45. Regimental Orders for December 1, 1774 (10 rounds per man), January 16 (8), February 7 (8) and 21 (8), March 14 (10), 23 (10) and 31 (15), April 15 (15), 1775. Orderly Book, 18th Regiment of Foot, National Army Museum, London.

46. Barker, *The British in Boston*, 11, 18, 23, 25, 27–28; Frederick Mackenzie, *The Diary of Frederick Mackenzie* (Cambridge, MA: Harvard University Press, 1930), 13, 15.

47. Hagist, *British Soldiers, American War*, 9–13.

Professional Officers

Leading these men were regimental officers who were, for the most part, career professionals with a vested interest in doing well by their men and the army as a whole. In general, each infantry company was led by a captain, a lieutenant, and an ensign. A few regiments raised during the war had larger companies and added another lieutenant. The grenadier and light infantry companies were composed only of experienced men; since ensigns were the most junior officers and, therefore, the least experienced, none served in these companies; instead, they had a captain and two lieutenants. Besides the company officers, there was an adjutant, a quartermaster, a surgeon, a surgeon's mate, and a chaplain.[48]

A nuance that is challenging to understand is that three of the company captains had dual ranks—the regimental colonel, lieutenant colonel, and major were also company commanders.[49] Further complicating the structure was that these three senior officers also held additional ranks or positions. Most regimental colonels were also general officers with commands that kept them away from their regiments, leaving the lieutenant colonel with the day-to-day command of the regiment during times of peace or when posted away from a war zone.[50] During the American Revolution, the wartime-only rank of brigadier general was put into use, and several lieutenant colonels were appointed as brigadiers.[51] This left the regiment under the care of the major, although the regiment might be in a brigade commanded by their own lieutenant-colonel frocked as a brigadier. And sometimes the major, too, took a wartime post, commanding a battalion—a regiment-sized formation of companies detached from their regiments— or a staff position. Captains, too, were occasionally away filling specialized wartime roles—aide-de-camp, town major, or deputy adjutant general.[52]

On the other end of the seniority scale were ensigns, newly commissioned officers learning their profession on the job. Called cornets in the cavalry and second lieutenants in the artillery and three infantry regiments that had historical connections to the artillery,[53] ensigns usually received their commission in their late teens and advanced into higher ranks within two or three years.[54] With only eight ensigncies available in each infantry regiment, one in each of the eight line companies, some aspiring men

---

48. Houlding, *Fit for Service*, 419.

49. Muster rolls, WO 12, TNA.

50. Muster rolls, WO 12, TNA; Army Lists, WO 65, TNA.

51. See, for example, orders for June 6, 1775, WO 36/1, 102, TNA.

52. See, for example, appointments of regimental officers to the command of grenadier and light infantry battalions, brigade major, town major, and other posts, general orders, June 19, 22, 24, 1775; *General Sir William Howe's Orderly Book*, ed. B. F. Stevens (Port Washington, NY: Kennikat Press, 1980), 5–16.

53. Army Lists, WO 65, TNA.

54. Houlding, *Fit for Service*, 109.

waiting for a vacant ensigncy served in the ranks, or in any role where they might be useful, for a few months or even years until a commission became available.[55] Other men, however, received commissions in Great Britain for regiments that were on service in America and might require several months to over a year before joining the regiment in the field.[56] And for reasons not stated—probably the challenges of managing administrative matters while fighting a war—some ensigncies remained vacant for extended periods.[57]

All of this put pressure on the officers actually present with the regiment. In late 1780, for example, eight companies of the 22nd Regiment of Foot had only fifteen of their twenty-four company officers present to manage day-to-day operations; six were serving in other roles, and three positions for ensigns were still awaiting men to fill them.[58]

About two-thirds of regimental commissions were obtained by purchase, a system often poorly understood and, therefore, much maligned. Purchase implies that anyone with enough money could obtain a commission regardless of qualifications, but this was not the case. Each commission required approval by both the colonel of the regiment and the king himself. Both of these individuals had a strong interest in ensuring that only qualified aspirants were approved, and although connections and influence were a factor in obtaining such approval, this served to ensure qualification rather than circumvent it. A young gentleman hoping for a military career needed recommendations by men of good standing, and those recommendations came only from those willing to stake their reputation on the young man's performance. Did he have a basic education in literature, languages, mathematics, and other disciplines typical of young gentlemen? Was he physically and mentally capable of meeting the demands of campaigning? Did he have the bearing of a gentleman, essential for commanding respect from soldiers? Had he shown a genuine passion for the military profession?[59]

The purchase itself, a substantial sum of money—the cost of an ensigncy was equal to about six years' pay at that rank—was a form of insurance toward the young officer's performance.[60] Someone with sufficient wealth—a family member or wealthy sponsor—put up the money that was then held by the government for the duration of the officer's career. Advancement in rank was also by purchase but required the

55. Hagist, *British Soldiers, American War*, 237–47.

56. Muster rolls of several regiments in America, 1775–1783, WO 12, TNA.

57. Muster rolls of several regiments in America, 1775–1783, WO 12, TNA.

58. State of Troops under the Command of His Excellency General Sir Henry Clinton, November 1, 1780, CO 5/100, 311, TNA. Present were the major, five captains, six lieutenants, and three ensigns. Five ensigns were not present, or the position was not filled at all.

59. Mark Frederick Odintz, "The British Officer Corps, 1754–1783" (PhD diss., University of Michigan, 1988), 285–306.

60. Curtis, *Organization of the British Army*, 160; Houlding, *Fit for Service*, 102.

same approval as the initial commission. With great competition for advancement, only men who had proven their abilities were allowed to purchase into the next rank. When an officer finally retired, he sold his final commission and regained the purchase money as his retirement fund.[61] The importance of this financial stake was that it could be lost; a court martial that found an officer guilty of poor performance—cowardice or another failure to do duty—could sentence the officer to be cashiered, that is, removed from the army with the forfeiture of his purchase money, a financial sacrifice that could leave him destitute. Thus, the system that appeared to allow any well-to-do person to obtain any rank desired instead largely guaranteed that only men of suitable qualifications obtained commissions and provided a strong incentive for them to work hard and well in their profession.[62]

Commissions could also be preferred, that is, granted based on merit alone rather than purchased, which was more common in wartime when demand for officers was high due to both attrition and the multitude of staff positions required for wartime operations. Preferment also required recommendation, either by demonstrated performance or testimony of a sponsor, and approval by the colonel and the king. This opened opportunities to men with merit but not means. In the 1770s and 1780s, about a third of commissions were granted by preferment, resulting in a corps of regimental officers, those leading men into battle and managing everyday operations, composed of career officers with surprisingly diverse backgrounds. Some were from true aristocracy. The majority were sons of landed gentry, educated in literature, classical languages, and mathematics, well-versed in sports, hunting, riding, and traveling, and accustomed to being leaders in their communities. A significant proportion were children of career military men, mostly sons of officers but including some sons of long-service noncommissioned officers, literally born and bred to their profession. A few rose through the ranks, receiving commissions not as teenagers but after long careers, mostly as sergeants, intimate with the administration and internal workings of corps on campaign.[63]

Enough has been written about the generals who commanded the armies in America—Thomas Gage, Sir William Howe, John Burgoyne, Sir Henry Clinton, and Charles, Lord Cornwallis—that there is no need to discuss their strengths and foibles here.[64] They, too, were career officers, and all had served in regimental posts early in their careers. Like most senior officers, their career paths were closely tied to their political connections, an advantage for men whose roles as commanders-in-chief required significant political as well as military acumen, especially in an era when

---

61. Houlding, *Fit for Service*, 101–2.

62. Houlding, 102.

63. Odintz, "British Officer Corps, 1754–1783," 178–84.

64. For a detailed treatment of higher British leadership, see Andrew Jackson O'Shaughnessy, *The Men Who Lost America: British Leadership, the American Revolution, and the Fate of the Empire* (New Haven, CT: Yale University Press, 2013).

communication with the government required many weeks of turnaround time. These were men every bit as invested in their careers as the officers and soldiers they led. Their failure to extinguish a popular rebellion far from home by military force reflects a common thread in military history rather than inadequate individual performance on any of their parts.

Campaigning in America

A popular painting by Howard Pyle depicts British grenadiers stoically marching in three close-order ranks up the slopes of Bunker Hill, laden with heavy knapsacks. Nothing like this ever happened in America, not even at Bunker Hill. As seen above, even though the engagements at Lexington, Concord, and Bunker Hill were costly, the British army quickly adapted warfare in America and used tactics designed for rapid movement. Most of the time, soldiers and officers alike carried minimal baggage. Soldiers typically had only their weapons, blankets, and a few days' worth of provisions, leaving tents and knapsacks on wagons that caught up with the army every few days.[65] "I have neither bed or baggage; my clothes are all on my back and I am often obliged to wrap my cloak and blanket round me while I get my rags mended," wrote a grenadier officer at the end of a four-month campaign in December 1776; two months later a light infantry officer wrote from New Jersey that "Two Shirts and other Necessaries just as a Soldier are enough for any Officer under the rank of General."[66]

"No tents, built wigwams," recorded an officer after landing on Manhattan Island in September 1776, referring to the makeshift shelters built almost everywhere the army stopped for the night.[67] A British military dictionary defined wigwam simply as "a hut used in America";[68] an officer recalled of campaigning in Virginia in early 1781: "Our encampments were always chosen on the banks of a stream, and were extremely picturesque, as we had no tents, and were obliged to construct wigwams of fresh boughs to keep off the rays of the sun during the day. At night, the blazing fires which we made of fence-rails illuminated the surrounding scenery, which, in this part of America, is of the most magnificent description."[69] Sometimes there was no shelter at all. An officer wrote in September 1776, near the city of New York, that "It is now

---

65. Typical marching orders can be found in August 19, 1776, WO 36/5, TNA.

66. Dansey, *Captured Rebel Flag*, 21.

67. William Bamford, *A Redcoat in America: The Diaries of Lieutenant William Bamford, 1757–1765 and 1776* (Warwick, UK: Helion & Company, 2019), 214.

68. Charles James, *A New and Enlarged Military Dictionary* (London: T. Egerton, 1805), s.v. "Wigwam."

69. Samuel Graham, *Memoir of General Graham*, ed. Colonel James J. Graham (Edinburgh: R. & R. Clark, 1862), 269.

a fortnight we have lain on the Ground wrapt in our Blankets," and after the Battle of White Plains a month later, "it rained excessive hard the whole night so that we who lay in the open air had most of our ammunition spoil'd & ourselves drip[p]ing wet notwithstanding which the men were in high spirits eager for the attack."[70]

"Light Infantry accustomed to fight from tree to tree, or charge even in woods; and Grenadiers who after the first fire lose no time in loading again, but rush on, trusting entirely to that most decisive of weapons the bayonet; will ever be superior to any troops the Rebels can ever bring against them. Such are the British, and such the method of fighting which has been attended with constant success," boasted a British officer in a letter home from Philadelphia in March 1778.[71] In the context of the battlefield, he was right. Anomalous actions like the retreat from Concord and Bunker Hill in 1775 are often used to characterize British officers and soldiers as unable to cope with conditions in America, overlooking the predominant outcome of battles during an eight-year war. Long Island, White Plains, Fort Washington, Brandywine, Paoli, Germantown, Camden, Guilford Courthouse, and countless lesser-known actions were British victories, often accomplished after long marches and against superior numbers. Capitulations at Saratoga and Yorktown occurred only after outnumbered, undersupplied armies were trapped in defensive positions.

The British loss of the American colonies was not due to the failure of an incompetent army outfoxed by a clever enemy. It was the culmination of strategic rather than tactical failures, the inability of government and military officials to understand the basis and magnitude of the rebellion, and the futility of attempting to suppress it by force alone—problems encountered in countless conflicts before and since the American Revolution. When seen in this light, it is clearer why the war lasted eight years. A good army sent to put down a rebellion in a foreign land can succeed on the battlefield, time and again, but fail to end the rebellion.

---

70. Marianne Gilchrist, "Captain Hon. William Leslie (1751–76): His Life, Letters and Commemoration," *Military Miscellany II* (Stroud, Gloucestershire: Sutton Publishing, for the Army Records Society, 2005), 153–54, 160; some words abbreviated in the original have been spelled out for clarity.

71. William Hale, *Some British Soldiers in America*, ed. W. H. Wilkin (London: H. Rees, 1914), 245.

3. Citizen-Soldiers or Regulars? The Revolutionary Militia Reconsidered

Mark Edward Lender

> By the rude bridge that arched the flood,
> Their flag to April's breeze unfurled,
> Here once the embattled farmers stood,
> And fired the shot heard round the world.[1]
> —*From Ralph Waldo Emerson, "Concord Hymn" (1837)*

> The militia has been so insufferably bad, that we find it impossible to support the war by their means, and therefore a powerful army of regular troops must be obtained, or all will be lost.[2]
> —*Richard Henry Lee, September 1776*

The War for American Independence bequeathed two iconic symbols of the Patriot military effort. There was the "Embattled Farmer." He was the independent yeoman of Concord Bridge fame, enshrined in Daniel Chester French's sculpture and memorialized in Emerson's poem—the man who embodied the American militia tradition of the citizenry in arms. Then there was the "ragged Continental." Often drawn from the margins of society, he was the American regular soldier who endured the long years of war, suffered the privations of the Valley Forge and Morristown winters, and served ill-paid, poorly supplied, and under-appreciated by the cause he enlisted to defend. There is more than a kernel of truth to both of these images, for the "embattled farmers" and the "ragged Continentals" were both essential to the struggle for independence.

Yet after the conflict, and even during it, these now iconic images were often an uneasy pair. Americans were conflicted over the best means of waging the war: Should they rely mostly on militia or on regulars? And which forces deserved the lion's share of credit for the ultimate Patriot victory? Opinions differed sharply. George Washington was adamant in his preference for regulars. "To place any dependence on Militia," he warned Congress in the autumn of 1776, "is, assuredly resting upon a broken staff.

---

1. Ralph Waldo Emerson, "Concord Hymn," in *Yale Book of American Verse*, ed. Thomas R. Lounsbury (New Haven, CT: Yale University Press, 1912), 85.

2. Richard Henry Lee to Patrick Henry, September 15, 1776, in *Letters of Delegates to Congress, 1774–1789*, ed. Paul H. Smith and Ronald M. Gephart, 26 vols. (Washington, DC: Library of Congress, 1976–2000), 5:175.

Men just dragged from the tender scenes of domestick life—unaccustomed to the din of Arms—totally unacquainted with every kind of Military skill, which being followed by a want of Confidence in themselves," would "fly from their own Shadows" when confronted by "regularly traind" and disciplined professionals.[3] On the other hand, Dr. Benjamin Rush, an ardent Revolutionary and Signer from Pennsylvania, was every bit as sure that the militia was the key to victory. He spoke for others of a similar mind when he wrote John Adams: "The militia began, and I sincerely hope the militia will end the present war."[4]

The respective contributions of the militia and the Continental regulars have endlessly fascinated historians of the Revolutionary era, and some of their judgments have been barbed. In fact, one side of the argument has gone so far as to create something of a popular myth: that the militia, so dear to patriotic imagery—and verse in Emerson's case—was all but ineffectual in the field and that the Revolution would have failed but for the efforts of the Continental Line. This was the import of Richard Henry Lee's letter to Patrick Henry. And if one writer was responsible for the modern persistence of this myth, it was certainly Colonel Emory Upton. Upton was no lightweight. He was a celebrated Union Civil War commander and a prominent military thinker. His posthumous and influential work, *The Military Policy of the United States* (1903), was one of the first serious studies to disparage the American militia tradition. It was a blistering attack. "In the Revolution," he insisted, "the Continentals or Regulars often displayed a valor deserving of victory, but which was snatched away by the conduct of undisciplined [militia] troops." He made his case with a lengthy analysis of the War for Independence, concluding that any military policy that relied on short-term militia was folly. "Regular troops engaged for the war"—the policy Washington had urged—"are the only safe reliance of a government, and are in every point of view the best and most economical," he wrote.[5]

Most modern historians have elected not to argue directly with Colonel Upton. They have conceded that, with certain prominent exceptions, militiamen were not the equal of regulars in prolonged campaigning or stand-up fighting. But in a tacit answer to the colonel, the modern consensus is: So what? Colonial and state governments, as any number of historians have correctly observed, never intended the militia for traditional battle. In his influential *Arms and Men* (1956), Walter Millis pointed out that "if less than ideal combat troops," the militia controlled the local scene and stymied

---

3. George Washington to John Hancock, September 25, 1776, in *The Papers of George Washington Digital Edition*, Revolutionary War Series, ed. Theodore J. Crackel et al. (Charlottesville: University of Virginia Press, Rotunda, 2007), 6:396.

4. Benjamin Rush to John Adams, October 1, 1777, in *Letters of Benjamin Rush*, 2 vols., ed. Lyman H. Butterfield (Princeton, NJ: Princeton University Press, 1951), 1:157.

5. Emory Upton, *The Military Policy of the United States* (Washington, DC: Government Printing Office, 1912), viii, xi, 2–67, 67.

"Britain's only practicable weapon, that of counter-revolution."[6] Some twenty years later, John Shy drove this point home. "Once established," Shy explained, "the militia became the infrastructure of revolutionary government." The militia was a political weapon. Through "indoctrination or intimidation"—and Shy might have mentioned outright violence—the militia was the critical factor in suppressing Loyalism and maintaining Patriot authority.[7] Like Millis and Shy, Don Higginbotham, in his comprehensive *The War of American Independence* (1971), also emphasized the political significance of the militia, and this perspective is now near orthodoxy.[8]

However, in a more recent survey of the subject, James Kirby Martin and Mark Edward Lender (*A Respectable Army*, 2015) have offered a somewhat different interpretation. While fully appreciating the militia's political and military contributions, they have stressed that the Continentals formed the essential core of Patriot military resistance. They allowed the best means of confronting the British and their allied German professionals and gave the Patriot war effort necessary long-term staying power. The American regulars also accorded the Revolution international credibility the militia could not provide. Martin and Lender also noted another continuing thread in the literature. There is a general consensus that, however imperfect in practice, militia service reflected an ideological ideal of "a universal military obligation," at least among free property owners. A citizen was expected to defend his stake in society, an expectation that again anchored the militia to a given locality or region.[9] In addition, most modern authors have also agreed that the Revolutionary generation inherited a colonial expectation that heavy fighting and long-term service was *not* the business of the middle-class yeomen of the militia. Society assigned the really

---

6. Walter Millis, *Arms and Men* (New York: New American Library, 1956), 34–35.

7. John Shy, "Mobilizing Armed Force in the American Revolution," in *The American Revolution: A Heritage of Change*, ed. John Parker and Carol Urness (Minneapolis, MN: Associates of the James Ford Bell Library, 1975), 105. In an earlier (1963) essay, Shy found that most historians "regarded [the militia] as both politically healthy and militarily inefficient, but in any case relatively uncomplicated." Shy differed from this view in finding colonial—and one can conclude much the same for state—militias rather more complex. Legal and administrative arrangements, organizational structures, and operational readiness (including levels of training and logistical support) varied from colony to colony according to circumstances. Yet whatever the regional differences, colonial militias were consistently local in orientation and never were intended as a main combat force. See Shy's "A New Look at the Colonial Militia," *William and Mary Quarterly* 20, no. 2 (1963): 175–85.

8. Don Higginbotham, *The War of American Independence: Military Attitudes, Policies, and Practice, 1763–1789* (New York: The Macmillan Company, 1971), 11–13; Don Higginbotham, "The American Militia: A Traditional Institution with Revolutionary Responsibilities," in *Reconsiderations on the Revolutionary War: Selected Essays*, ed. Don Higginbotham (Westport, CT: Greenwood Press, 1978), 83–103.

9. James Kirby Martin and Mark Edward Lender, *"A Respectable Army": The Military Origins of the Republic, 1763–1789*, 3rd ed. (Malden, MA: Wiley Blackwell, 2015), 17–18. For a similar view, see Lawrence D. Cress, *Citizens in Arms: The Army and Militia in American Society to the War of 1812* (Chapel Hill: University of North Carolina Press, 1982), 5–8.

tough soldiering to those in marginal socio-economic circumstances—that is, to the poor and others with little stake in society.[10] In other words, it was a job for the often socially down-and-out regulars of the Continental Line.[11]

So which was it? Should we credit the militia or the Continentals with the lion's share of the Revolutionary victory? And why did the partisans of each hold the sentiments they did? We will revisit these questions with a specific interest in clarifying the militia's contributions to the Patriot war effort and deal especially with the militia's performance in relation to the service of the Continental regulars. We will also ask if historians have scanted a truly interesting query: When it came to assigning credit to the regulars or the militia, was it ever *really* an "either-or" question? And if it wasn't—and this chapter will argue that it wasn't—we can go a long way toward dispelling the myth (and Colonel Upton's insistence) that the Revolutionary militia was not worth its pay.

The Militia: Expectations and Preparations

As Americans moved from protest to rebellion in early 1775, realistic Patriots accepted that fighting was a distinct possibility. Almost no one, however, envisioned the prospect of confronting the British with a regular American army. Rather, preparations focused on militia, ideally the citizenry in arms, which colonists preferred for both traditional and ideological reasons. For more than a century before the Revolution, without British troops on hand, colonial militias had defended the frontiers against

---

10. On the matter of leaving the serious campaigning to the poor and marginalized, see Martin and Lender, *A Respectable Army*, 16; James Titus, *The Old Dominion at War: Society, Politics, and Warfare in Late Colonial Virginia* (Columbia: University of South Carolina Press, 1991), 40–45, 59–61, 78–99; Harold E. Selesky, *War and Society in Colonial Connecticut* (New Haven, CT: Yale University Press, 1900), 144–94; Michael A. McDonnell, *The Politics of War: Race, Class, and Conflict in Revolutionary Virginia* (Chapel Hill: University of North Carolina Press, 2007), 39, 298–99, 385–88, 452–61.

11. None of this is to suggest, however, that historians have written off the militia as serious combatants. A number of excellent campaign histories and biographies of militia leaders have amply demonstrated that the American irregulars saw plenty of action in engagements large and small. These works have contributed further to our understanding of the political and social significance of the militia while reminding us forcefully of the militia's role in military operations. For example, see Rod Andrew Jr., *The Life and Times of General Andrew Pickens: Revolutionary War Hero, American Founder* (Chapel Hill: University of North Carolina Press, 2017); Lawrence E. Babits, *A Devil of a Whipping: The Battle of Cowpens* (Chapel Hill: University of North Carolina Press, 1998); Ben Z. Rose, *John Stark: Maverick General* (Waverley, MA: Tree Line Press, 1996); Mark V. Kwasny, *Washington's Partisan War, 1775–1783* (Kent, OH: Kent State University Press, 1996); and the older, but still useful, Robert Bass, *Gamecock: The Life and Campaigns of General Thomas Sumter* (New York: Holt, Rinehart, and Winston, 1961).

Indians and the French.[12] Generally, the militia comprised all white males (usually including indentured servants) between the ages of sixteen and fifty. The exception was Quaker-dominated Pennsylvania, which refused to establish a militia. In the rest of the North, militia companies were based on townships; junior officers were elected, while colonial governments appointed senior commanders. In the South, counties provided companies and, in larger counties, regiments (two or more companies). In addition to frontier defense, southern militias also regularly patrolled localities against potential slave rebellions or escape attempts. Militias throughout the colonies served locally and usually for short terms, but in all colonies, the militia also served as a recruiting pool for units raised for longer enlistments and for missions farther afield. Militia operations seldom worked smoothly, but Americans were used to the system, and while hardly proof against surprises or major attacks, the militia did provide a modicum of local defense during the colonial era.[13]

The militia also fit nicely into the ideological preferences of the day. A key tenet of "republicanism" was that regular standing armies were the tools of tyrants. Recruited from the margins of society, professional soldiers, republicans insisted, had no attachments to the liberties or rights of the citizenry—as we have noted, they had no "stake" in society—and too often, they simply followed the dictates of the kings or autocrats who paid them. This was a lesson from history, as the examples of Julius Caesar and Oliver Cromwell supposedly demonstrated. The militia, however, was different. Comprised in theory of the liberty-loving citizenry—men with every stake in society—the militia was a safeguard against tyranny. Motivated by a love of their rights, in the republican view, militiamen were more than a match for professionals.[14] If it came to a showdown with the mother country, colonials would put their faith in their citizen-soldiers. If this sentiment turned out to be naive (and it certainly did), it was nevertheless genuine.

In fact, the rebels resorted to militia action well before independence. In almost every colony, Patriot leaders used the militia to consolidate their political and social control. They weeded out officers suspected of Loyalist sympathies, put rebel officers in charge, and then tasked the militia with enforcing rebel authority. This involved

---

12. For militia on the frontiers, see for examples, Mark Edward Lender, "The Western Theater: The Theater of Fear," in *Theaters of the American Revolution: Northern, Middle, Southern, Western, Naval*, ed. James Kirby Martin and David L. Preston (Yardley, PA: Westholme, 2017), 141, 144; Andrew, *Andrew Pickens*, 15, 23, 28; Glenn F. Williams, *Dunmore's War: The Conflict of America's Colonial Era* (Yardley, PA: Westholme, 2017), 121–31.

13. E.g., Shy, "A New Look at the Colonial Militia," 175–85; Williams, *Dunmore's War*, 81–111, 123–31; Harold E. Selesky, ed., *Encyclopedia of the American Revolution*, 2nd ed., 2 vols. (Detroit: Thomson Gale, 2006), 2:722–25; John Shy, *Toward Lexington: The Role of the British Army in the Coming of the American Revolution* (Princeton, NJ: Princeton University Press, 1965), 3–19.

14. The republican ideological loathing of standing armies and preference for militia is explained in Bernard Bailyn, *The Ideological Origins of the American Revolution* (Cambridge, MA: Harvard University Press, 1967), 62–63, 84.

local law enforcement, policing boycotts of trade with the British, discouraging use of British goods, and cowing Loyalists through threats of or actual physical violence, forcing them to swear loyalty oaths to the Patriot cause, disarming them in some instances, boycotting their businesses, and ostracizing them socially. Long before Lexington and Concord, the militia had swept through the Carolina and Georgia backcountries and swiftly secured rebel control of the region (or thought they had; the Loyalists would bide their time). In New England, militias enforced political authority at all levels, silencing terrified Loyalists and sending many fleeing to British-occupied Boston. Even in heavily Quaker Pennsylvania, which initially had no formal militia, volunteer militia units formed to assist the Patriot cause.[15] Much of this activity wasn't pretty—to fight for democracy is *not* necessarily to practice it—but the militia gave muscle to the new Revolutionary governments.

Indeed, the militia's ability to enforce Patriot authority at the local level proved critical to the Revolution's ultimate success. With Loyalists thoroughly off-balance, the militia drastically lessened the chances of any successful counter-revolution. When the war started in earnest in April 1775, Patriot authorities could work from a generally secure political base and a home front loyal to the cause (or at least not actively opposed)—an enormous advantage. And militia activity also afforded rebel governments a fairly effective intelligence base; militiamen were the eyes and ears of the Revolution locally and could move to preempt or warn of most domestic threats. The Continental Army was never large enough to provide this crucial local coverage. And even when Continentals occupied an area in force, they were often unfamiliar with local conditions and personalities; they relied on the resident militia to inform them of regional security concerns. In fact, throughout the war, the maintenance of local political and social control would prove the militia's most important mission.[16]

This political-social mission, however, as well as the real possibility of militia involvement in more formal military operations, necessitated considerable administrative and organizational effort. By early 1775, all the colonies had taken steps to put their militias on a war footing. Military leadership was a problem. The colonies had no traditional officer corps, and while there were some veterans of the French and Indian War (1754–1763), there were too few of them to staff expanding militia organizations. Rebel authorities, therefore, followed the traditional colonial precedents of drawing their officers from among local notables. Most units elected their junior officers, usually (but not always) from among socially prominent families, while commissions above company grades went to government appointees. This process commissioned any number of bungling amateurs, but across the colonies, militia leaders of considerable talent emerged as well. We will return to some of them later.

---

15. This is detailed at length in T. H. Breen, *American Insurgents, American Patriots: The Revolution of the People* (New York: Hill and Wang, 2010).

16. Millis, *Arms and Men*, 34–35; Selesky, *Encyclopedia*, 2:722–25.

In general, the new militia organizations mirrored colonial arrangements, with adjustments for population growth. Most plans called for more companies and regiments; some states eventually even provided for divisions. Laws also called for improved militia support services to provide adequate equipment, munitions, and training. Where formal legislation lagged, many Patriots joined volunteer militia companies funded by private donations. As Patriot authorities were caught up in such Revolutionary fervor, however, most of the volunteer outfits were absorbed into the formal militia. Some of these legislated organizations were ambitious. Virginia laws called for the enrollment of all free white men between the ages of sixteen and fifty in the regular militia, with a potential enrollment of 50,000 men. From these ranks would come 1,020 men to serve in a long-service force, which Virginia could send on missions virtually anywhere within the state. There also would be an organization of some 8,000 "minutemen" who would receive special training and be ready to turn out at a moment's notice.[17] North Carolina, Maryland, and Delaware also provided for minutemen. In theory at least, such preparations promised to mobilize an enormous number of militia troops, and ideally, as New Jersey's governor William Livingston told the state assembly, militia laws should "oblige" "every Man capable of bearing Arms to . . . turn out."[18]

New England was generally successful in maintaining its militia forces. Towns were responsible for ensuring enough men turned out, and authorities often provided arms for men unable to afford their own. Governments also did their best to purchase arms, munitions, artillery, and matériel. The British recognized the danger such efforts represented; indeed, it was just such a collection of military stores that prompted General Thomas Gage to dispatch the ill-fated mission to Concord in April 1775. Royal authorities were less aware, however, of militia abilities to respond quickly to threats. Massachusetts, New Hampshire, and Connecticut militia regiments had des-ignated minutemen—in the case of Massachusetts, a third of the regular militia— ready to spring into action on short notice. And the system could be effective. The seemingly spontaneous militia response to the British at Lexington and Concord was no fluke; it was the result of carefully prepared contingency plans. And in the actual fighting on April 19, officers retained a reasonable level of command and control.[19]

Soon enough, the war would reveal many faults with militia organizations across the colonies. The Virginia experience was telling: to the fury of many citizens, the new militia law ended the traditional practice of allowing militiamen to elect their own junior officers. Poorer Virginians also resented militia exemptions for major slave

17. McDonnell, *Politics of War*, 92–94.

18. William Livingston to the Assembly, February 3, 1777, in *The Papers of William Livingston*, 5 vols., ed. Carl E. Prince and Dennis P. Ryan (Trenton: New Jersey Historical Commission, 1979–1988), 1:209.

19. David Hackett Fischer, *Paul Revere's Ride* (New York: Oxford University Press, 1994), 84, 90–91, 149–64, 249, 250–54.

owners, and middle-class farmers objected to call-ups that disrupted agricultural routines. In fact, no state was ever able to compel full compliance with militia service, and over time, militia laws changed to eliminate some of the more unworkable or expensive regulations. Maryland and North Carolina got rid of separate minutemen; they cost too much and were administratively cumbersome.[20] Some states were more successful than others in mobilizing their militia (we have noted the New England experience), but debates, sometimes quite acrimonious, over who should serve and under what circumstances persisted until the end of the war. William Livingston, one of the two longest-serving wartime governors and a former militia brigadier general, lamented that New Jersey's militia laws allowed men to pay fines or hire substitutes in lieu of personal service. The practice had introduced "the invidious Distinction between Rich & Poor, which is always attended with disagreeable Circumstances."[21] Even so—and this is the key point—militiamen were usually numerous enough, North and South, to control the home fronts for Patriot authorities, or at least to prevent the enemy from controlling them. And none of this negates the fact that early in the war, Patriots took militia planning seriously—and that, if necessary, they fully intended to fight the war with citizen-soldiers.

Arming the Militia

In theory, the militia offered the colonies (later the states) not only a large pool of manpower but also a fiscally economical military. Militiamen were expected to arm themselves. In Virginia, Thomas Jefferson noted that the law required every man to acquire "arms usual in the regular service."[22] Requirements in the rest of the states were fairly similar, and in the earliest days of the independence struggle, Patriots, indeed, relied on private arms. The forces that cowed and disarmed suspected Loyalists in the Carolinas and confronted the redcoats on Lexington Green carried personally owned weapons. Patriot authorities supplied powder, shot, and basic equipment, although some laws also mandated that militiamen own cartridge pouches and at least a minimal supply of ammunition. When the British commander-in-chief, Lieutenant General Thomas Gage, reported he was facing the "whole Country . . . assembled in Arms," he meant a population armed with weapons with which they were thoroughly familiar.[23]

---

20. Selesky, *Encyclopedia*, 2:685, 851–52, 1212–14.

21. William Livingston to Israel Putnam, in Prince and Ryan, *Livingston Papers*, 1:222.

22. Thomas Jefferson, *Notes on the State of Virginia*, intro. Thomas Perkins Abernathy (1784; repr. New York: Harper & Row, 1964), 86–87.

23. Thomas Gage to the Earl of Dartmouth, April 22, 1775, Teaching American History, https://teachingamericanhistory.org/documents (accessed Nov. 9, 2019).

The smooth-bore flintlock musket was the usual weapon. They were of various types: including Dutch, French, and other European muskets acquired in trade; a scattering of locally manufactured pieces (there were few colonial gunsmiths); and various models of the popular British "Brown Bess," many of which were left over from the French and Indian War. Most muzzle-loaders fired a lead ball of approximately .75 caliber (a ball of approximately three-quarters of an inch in diameter and weighing about an ounce), which was the Brown Bess standard. As the war dragged on, Patriot authorities did encourage local weapons manufacturing, and local "committees of safety" and similar organizations commissioned muskets from a growing (but still limited) number of gunsmiths. An experienced soldier could get off three shots per minute (and *very* occasionally more), although this rate of fire was probably beyond the competence of most militia, at least until they acquired considerable experience. The smooth-bore musket, however, if relatively easy to use, had some serious disadvantages. It was terribly inaccurate and virtually useless at ranges over a hundred yards, often considerably less.[24] The smooth-bore could mount a bayonet, the weapon essential for close-quarter combat. However, early in the war, most militiamen lacked bayonets—and the few who had bayonets were seldom trained in their use. The experience of Bunker Hill grimly demonstrated how helpless militia could be in the face of a determined British bayonet assault.

A limited number of the militia carried rifles, especially on the frontiers. In fact, Jefferson noted that militia in the South, west of the Blue Ridge, "are generally armed with rifles."[25] These were privately owned and usually the product of Pennsylvania gunsmiths, often of German origin. Later, smiths operated on the Virginia (including Kentucky) frontier. Like the smooth-bore musket, the long rifle was a flintlock muzzle-loader. But unlike the musket, the rifle had a longer barrel (thus "long rifle") as well as spiral grooves—rifling—inside the barrel that gave the lead ball a twist that stabilized its flight. These attributes greatly improved range and accuracy, and competent riflemen usually could hit a man-sized target at 200 yards. In hunting and war (on the frontiers, hunting was a critical source of food, and Indian warfare was a frequent reality), this was an immense advantage over the smooth-bore musket. The rifle had disadvantages, however. It did not mount a bayonet and took a long time to load. A rifleman had to hammer the lead ball down the barrel to engage the rifling. Thus, the rifle was of limited value in traditional linear combat that saw lines of infantry blazing away at relatively close range and then closing with the bayonet. But the rifle was deadly in skirmishing and longer-range fighting. The British, who made

---

24. Firearms of the Revolutionary period are detailed in Harold L. Peterson, *The Book of the Continental Soldier* (Harrisburg, PA: Stackpole Books, 1968), 23–58.
25. Jefferson, *Notes on the State of Virginia*, 87.

only limited use of rifles (although Hessian jaegers—light infantry—used the weapon effectively), hated the American riflemen.[26]

Militia carried a variety of other weapons as well. Officers sometimes owned and carried swords; many men carried tomahawks (an item sometimes required by law) or knives for hand-to-hand fighting. Pistols appeared in militia ranks as well, usually among the officers. Mounted militia units carried sabers and pistols, although missions generally focused on scouting duties. Militia horsemen were neither numerous enough nor sufficiently trained to engage in heavy combat. Over time, the militia would acquire a variety of other firearms and edged weapons, often from Continental stores or captured from the British.[27] But through the end of the war, the standard smooth-bore flintlock remained the militia's mainstay.

Over the course of the war, Patriot authorities gradually assumed responsibility for arming the militia. That is, personal weapons gave way to state-issued arms and supplies. There were exceptions: in the Carolinas and Georgia, as well as on the frontiers, where rebel governments held little sway or Continental quartermasters were either absent or unable to offer material support to local forces, militia often had to depend on their own resources and captured arms until the end of the war. The other states, however, wanted to standardize weaponry, which made for more efficient supply operations. Militia expectations changed as more men expected governments to arm them, and occasionally entire militia units reported for duty unarmed and asking for government weapons. As the war lengthened, authorities also organized and supplied militia artillery and horse units (with horsemen often riding their own mounts) along with depots and logistical personnel. All states established financial, legal, and administrative structures to support militia operations. These efforts were time-consuming and increasingly expensive, and militia affairs generally occupied a prominent place on the agendas of all of the Revolutionary state governments.

Combat: The Test of Reality

The first year of open war seemed to confirm rebel faith in militia. The Lexington and Concord affair was a classic confirmation of republican expectations; the swarming minutemen along the long road back to Boston came within an ace of overwhelming the retreating redcoats. Gathering militia then besieged the British army in Boston; even the pyrrhic royal victory at Breed's (Bunker) Hill seemed to prove that the militia could stand the ferocious test of battle. By the end of June, Patriot irregulars had taken Fort Ticonderoga and several other small British outposts in New York and

---

26. Jefferson, *Notes on the State of Virginia*, 38–44. For a thoughtful evaluation of the long rifle in the War for Independence, see Neil L. York, "Pennsylvania Rifle: Revolutionary Weapon in a Conventional War?" *Pennsylvania Magazine of History and Biography* 103, no. 3 (July 1979): 302–24.

27. Peterson, *Book of the Continental Soldier*, 44–53, 83–112.

across the border in Quebec province. Various New England and New York militia parties were tangling with British foraging parties and trading shots with British ships from shore and from small boats. By December, American volunteer forces drawn largely from militias had thrown the British on the defensive in Canada. In the South, the militia from Georgia to Virginia moved aggressively against British landing parties and occasional Loyalist bands. In larger actions in early December 1775, Virginia militia defeated a force of Loyalists and British sailors at Great Bridge, causing the final collapse of royal authority in the colony; in February 1776, North Carolina

Challenging the widespread belief that the American militias were largely responsible for success in the Revolution, others have argued that the war was won by the Continental Army, whose soldiers enlisted for long terms of service and were trained to fight in the manner of European troops. Untitled illustration of Continental Army soldiers, watercolor by Charles M. Lefferts, c. 1910–1920. Anne S. K. Brown Collection, Brown University.

militia shattered a Loyalist rising at Moore's Creek Bridge, securing that colony for the Revolution for some four years. When the British evacuated Boston in March 1776, Patriots were in control of all thirteen of the rebellious colonies, and the military credit undisputedly belonged largely to the spirited conduct of the militia.

Success of this magnitude, however, seldom inspires sober second thoughts. In their elation at the course of events, few Patriots considered that these early militia achievements owed much to favorable circumstances and just plain good luck. In fact, in all of these early conflicts, militia forces had engaged with odds heavily in their favor, aided by poor judgment on the part of their opponents. The rebels enjoyed numerical superiority against the exposed and unsupported British column that retreated from Concord. At Bunker Hill and Moore's Creek Bridge, they fought from behind excellent defensive works against redcoats advancing bravely (and foolishly) over open ground or against Loyalists with broadswords rushing pell-mell over a narrow and partially dismantled bridge into concentrated musketry and artillery fire. In upper New York, they surprised small and isolated British garrisons at Ticonderoga, St. John's, and elsewhere. At no time did they face a major British formation in the open field; at no time did they undertake operations requiring the maneuver of large units in battle. The war was far from over, and it remained to be seen if the army of citizen-soldiers could sustain its winning momentum.

In fact, it could not. In July 1776, the heavily reinforced British landed on Staten Island, and in August, they attacked on Long Island in overwhelming strength. By late November, they had driven Washington's army out of New York City and off Manhattan Island, inflicting painful defeats along the way. And by early December, the redcoats and their Hessian allies had forced the rebels across New Jersey, over the Delaware River, and into the relative safety of Pennsylvania. In the process, the royal advance had laid bare the deficiencies of militia as a main field force. They had crumbled in the face of the enemy, often dispersing in confusion and terror. Militias were poorly trained and ill-prepared to face well-trained professionals in open combat. If militiamen were usually brave enough, they lost confidence in the face of regulars who delivered massed volley fire, maneuvered in compact formations under experienced officers, and enjoyed excellent supply services and equipment, including bayonets, which they knew how to use with deadly effect. Moreover, militiamen served only for short terms, usually only for several months or less, and many went home as their enlistments expired, no matter the needs of the army. Units had simply melted away during the retreat across New Jersey.[28] This behavior, of course, did little to foster cohesion in Patriot ranks. In Pennsylvania, Washington was in despair and utterly furious at what he saw as militia incompetence and inconstancy. He already

---

28. Arthur S. Lefkowitz, *The Long Retreat: The Calamitous Defense of New Jersey, 1776* (Metuchen, NJ: The Upland Press, 1998), 35–126.

had warned Congress of the dangers of depending on militias, and now he was certain that the cause was hopeless without a major change in the Patriot military.[29]

The commander-in-chief saw salvation only in the creation of a regular Continental Army; he wanted to fight European professionals with American professionals. His goal was an army of well-disciplined, long-term soldiers—with enlistments of a minimum of three years—trained in uniform drill and tactical movements. The general knew there would be little chance of recruiting many volunteers from the landowning yeomanry who comprised the bulk of the militia; as in Europe, most of a regular army would come from the lower ranks of colonial society—but so be it. Washington also knew republican purists would oppose the idea, and they did. Ideological qualms about regular armies were quite real. Pennsylvania radical Benjamin Rush, to note a prominent example, wanted to fight on with militia and had no use for a military he feared would consist of the dregs of society. He declared to Samuel Adams that he would "despair of our cause if our country contained 60,000 men abandoned enough to enlist for 3 years or during the [duration of the] war."[30] But the situation was desperate, and most of Congress conceded the general's argument. In late 1776, it voted to give Washington his "respectable army" of 88 battalions, with battalions allotted to the states by population.[31] Most Americans would now look to the Continental Army, not the militia, to do the heavy fighting.

We should note that Washington already had the core of his regular force. During the siege of Boston, many of the assembled militia, many of them from the ranks of the minutemen, had signed on for another eight months, and the states had raised additional regiments of one-year men.[32] They were far from the army Washington wanted, but they were a start. In early 1777, many of these veterans enlisted in the new regiments the states sent to the reorganizing Continental Line. Often the new recruits had no prior militia experience, but many did. And here was a continuing trend: as in the colonial era, the militia would be a recruiting pool for the regular army throughout the war. The Fourth New Jersey Regiment, for example, drew its recruits almost entirely from the militia. The same was true of Colonel John Glover's 14th Continental Regiment of 1775–1776, raised almost entirely from the Marblehead, Massachusetts militia of fishermen and seamen.[33] Indeed, from time to time over the course of the struggle, various states resorted to conscription to fill their Continental

---

29. George Washington to John Hancock, Crackel, *Papers of Washington*, 6:396.

30. Benjamin Rush to Samuel Adams, October 1, 1777, in Butterfield, *Letters of Benjamin Rush*, 1:156–57.

31. September 16, 1776, in *Journals of the Continental Congress, 1774–1789*, 34 vols., ed. Worthington C. Ford et al. (Washington, DC: U.S. Government Printing Office, 1904–1937), 5:762–63.

32. Selesky, *Encyclopedia*, 2:727–28; Robert K. Wright Jr., *The Continental Army* (Washington, DC: Center of Military History, U.S. Army, 1983), 51–52, 54–55.

33. "Sketch of Colonel Ephraim Martin, of the New Jersey Continental Line," *Pennsylvania Magazine of History and Biography* 34 (1910): 480–82; Fred Anderson Berg, *Encyclopedia of Continental*

regiments, and the draftees came from the organized militia units. In 1778 and 1780, New Jersey drafted hundreds of frequently reluctant militiamen for nine or six months of Continental duty. A drafted militiaman could hire a substitute rather than serve in person, but either way, the regular army got a man. In the South, Virginia drafted militia for its Continental regiments as well, often in the face of vociferous complaints from the affected militia.[34] Whether they served happily or not, however, draftees and volunteers from militia ranks across the rebellious states blurred the distinction between the militia and regular forces—manpower often overlapped.

Creation of the regular Continental Army hardly meant the end of the militia's war. It did, however, reorient militia responsibilities, returning the militia to its initial focus on the local scene. As it had even before independence, the militia assured Patriot authorities of social and political control at the local level. Regular militia patrols kept a vigilant eye on political loyalties and not infrequently clashed with British foraging parties and Loyalist raiders. In Virginia, as in the rest of the South, Patriot authorities saw the militia as "the first line of defense" against slave revolts.[35] Militiamen operating near Continental forces gathered intelligence for the regulars and provided security for rebel governments. They served as guides for Continental units on the march, kept watch on British positions, and warned of enemy movements. From late 1776 on, the latter role was especially important in sections of New Jersey and New York state in close proximity to the main British army in and around New York City. Pennsylvania and New Jersey militia did the same after the British occupied Philadelphia in 1777. In South Carolina, the militia would serve a similar function in British-occupied regions of the state after the fall of Charleston in 1780. On the western frontiers from New York to Georgia, militia—formal units and ad hoc parties—were constantly on the alert against Indian raids or were planning raids of their own. The militia, in other words, remained busy.

But how busy? In fact, we can actually offer a rough measure that suggests the War for Independence was, in some respects, largely a militia war. Historian Howard H. Peckham's meticulous compilation of Revolutionary engagements and casualties makes this point abundantly clear. Peckham counted 1,546 land and naval actions between 1775 and 1783; of the 1,331 land actions, only 60 were primarily engagements between the regular armies. The rest were fights (not necessarily small) between Patriots and Loyalists or Native Americans (sometimes both), with regulars playing only peripheral roles, if any at all. Moreover, Peckham's count was conservative. This is the implication of David Munn's more detailed compilation

Army Units: Battalions, Regiments, and Independent Corps (Harrisburg, PA: Stackpole Books, 1972), 34, 82.

34. Mark Edward Lender, "The Conscripted Line: The Draft in Revolutionary New Jersey," *New Jersey History* 103 (1985): 23–46; on the draft in Virginia, see McDonnell, *Politics of War*, 274–75, 384.

35. Lender, "Conscripted Line," 93.

While many Americans attribute victory in the Revolutionary War to the actions of the militia, these colonial citizen-soldiers seldom defeated regular troops in battle. A rare occasion when the militia did succeed against regular troops (in this case, German professionals fighting for the British), occurred at the Battle of Bennington on August 16, 1777. *Battle of Bennington*, engraving from a painting by Alonzo Chappel, 1874. National Archives, College Park, MD.

of New Jersey battles and skirmishes. Munn verified over 600 military and naval engagements in New Jersey or off its immediate coast. Of these, only fourteen pitted the regular armies against one another.[36] The clear implication of the Peckham and Munn studies is that most combat was local and took place without major British or Continental forces on the scene. These were the actions that brought the war home to the vast majority of North Americans of all political persuasions, ethnicities, and social circumstances.

The price for such a level of military activity could be high. There is no statistical breakdown of casualties between the Continentals and the militia. But one suspects that the militia shared the burden in killed, wounded, captured, and missing in action and deaths from disease. Battles with Loyalists, Indians, and the occasional redcoat

---

36. Howard H. Peckham, ed., *The Toll of Independence: Engagements and Battle Casualties of the American Revolution* (Chicago: University of Chicago Press, 1974), 130, passim; David C. Munn, ed., *Battles and Skirmishes of the American Revolution in New Jersey* (Trenton, NJ: Bureau of Geology and Topography, Dept. of Environmental Protection, 1976), passim.

at Oriskany, New York (1777), Wyoming, Pennsylvania (1778), Minisink, New York (1779), and in the Mohawk, Schoharie, and Cherry Valleys of New York (1780) exacted murderous tolls. At Oriskany alone, on August 6, 1777, some 800 militiamen blundered into an ambush by about 500 Indians, Loyalists, and British regulars. The Patriots fought to a bloody draw but lost 385 dead, 50 wounded, and 30 captured in one of the costliest American engagements of the war.[37] In August 1782, frontiersman Daniel Boone barely escaped from an Indian-Loyalist ambush at Blue Licks in present-day Kentucky, then Fayette County, Virginia; the disaster cost the militia over 80 killed (including Boone's son, Israel) and wounded, almost half of the Patriot force engaged.[38] Such grim events were repeated, usually on a smaller scale, North and South, throughout the conflict. The militia did not have an easy war.

None of this is to suggest that militia could not show to advantage in major engagements. In many instances, they did quite well. The New Jersey militia, recovering from the shock of invasion in late 1776, rose en masse (a rising that had begun even before Washington's counterattack at Trenton) and drove the British from all but a narrow strip of the state. During the Saratoga campaign in 1777, the militia under New Hampshire's John Stark destroyed two German columns at the Battle of Bennington (called after the nearby town of Bennington, in present-day Vermont, but actually fought in Walloomsac, New York). The engagement cost Lieutenant General John Burgoyne's army some 900 men. As Burgoyne continued to move south, New York and New England militias moved into his rear and sealed the northern communications routes, even attacking and destroying supplies the British had left at Fort Ticonderoga. No further supplies or reinforcements reached Burgoyne, and the militia effectively choked off any chance the British had of retreating to Ticonderoga. These militia actions, even if not involving major battles, contributed significantly to forcing Burgoyne's eventual surrender—and thus to one of the most important victories in American (maybe even world) military history.

These victories were impressive, and like the militia successes of 1775 and early 1776, they shared certain similarities. The militia engaged largely on their own terms. In New Jersey, at Bennington, and during the Saratoga campaign, they hit isolated or unsupported enemy units that had advanced into the countryside—too far away from larger British formations that could come to their aid. In all of these cases, the militia had the choice of fighting or pulling back if a redcoat or other enemy force looked too strong or if an attack appeared too costly. This pattern was consistent after 1777, and one wonders at the British learning curve. Too many senior royal commanders

---

37. Peckham, *Toll of Independence*, 38; Gavin K. Watt, *Rebellion in the Mohawk Valley: The St. Leger Expedition of 1777* (Toronto: Dundurn Press, 2002), 316–20; Joseph T. Glatthaar and James Kirby Martin, *Forgotten Allies: The Oneida Indians and the American Revolution* (New York: Hill and Wang, 2006), 163–68.

38. Michael C. C. Adams, "An Appraisal of the Blue Licks Battle," *Filson Club Quarterly* 75, no. 2 (2001): 181–203.

consistently underestimated the dangers militia posed to units venturing unsupported into the countryside.

The South

The pattern was much the same in the South, although in crucial ways, matters there constituted a special case. Northern militia units generally (but not always) fought within an organized political context that provided logistical support, more or less regular pay, and predictable rotating tours of duty. After 1780 this was not true in most of the Carolinas and Georgia, where Patriot governments had either collapsed or were unable to exert effective control in major parts of their states and localities. British troops had already restored the royal government in Georgia in 1779. Then, in a major Patriot disaster, in May 1780, the southern branch of the Continental Army was all but lost when Charleston surrendered to British commander-in-chief Lieutenant General Sir Henry Clinton. Continental remnants were largely destroyed in subsequent actions at Waxhaws and Camden. With the Continentals reduced to a minuscule and barely functional rump in North Carolina and with rebel political institutions teetering (the government of South Carolina, such as it was, was in exile in North Carolina), it appeared that the royal "Southern Strategy"—an effort to tap a supposed reservoir of Loyalist support and win the South back for the empire—was working.

Many well-regarded modern historians have considered British estimates of Loyalist strength and hope for Loyalist support naive or wrong-headed. But in fact, the British invasion of the South, especially the captures of Savannah and Charleston, sparked a considerable Tory resurgence. Many Georgians and South Carolinians deeply resented their treatment at the hands of Patriots in 1775 and 1776, and they grasped the chance for payback. Jim Piecuch has argued that royal plans to take advantage of Tory numbers and perhaps tap the strength of the enslaved and Indian populations in the South for the royal cause were not necessarily unrealistic. They failed in the face of a number of impediments, including the inability to effectively coordinate the often-diverse interests of Loyalists, Indians, and slaves. Indeed, Lieutenant General Charles, Lord Cornwallis showed little interest in doing so, fixating instead on tactical concerns.[39] There were also too few redcoats, Hessians, and provincial regulars to protect the king's friends. And this last critical factor owed much to the southern Patriot militias.

---

39. This is the thrust of Jim Piecuch's *Three Peoples, One King: Loyalists, Indians, and Slaves in the Revolutionary South, 1775–1782* (Columbia: University of South Carolina Press, 2008). See also Piecuch's "The Southern Theater: Britain's Last Chance for Victory," in *Theaters of the American Revolution: Northern, Middle, Southern, Western, Naval,* ed. James Kirby Martin and David L. Preston (Yardley, PA: Westholme, 2017), 136.

The American political collapse in the South did not entail a military collapse. However, at least until the Continental Army was revived in 1781, the war in the South would be a militia war, often waged on an ad hoc partisan basis. The effort would lack central direction; there would be nothing approaching a unified command. The states had established formal militia organizations early in the war, and after 1780 southerners struggled to maintain what formal units they could—which often proved impossible amid the political and social chaos that engulfed the region. Thus, most militiamen were volunteers fighting in pick-up units, usually self-supplied and mounted, often without pay and formal terms of enlistment. They subsisted off the countryside, frequently plundering Tories for food, horses, and whatever booty they could find in lieu of pay. Until limited Continental supplies became available in 1781, they frequently replenished ammunition and other matériel from captured enemy stores.

The militia war produced some leaders of genuine talent. The three main commanders were Andrew Pickens, the "Wizard Owl," the bane of Loyalists in western South Carolina and Georgia; Thomas Sumter, the "Carolina Gamecock," who proved a magnetic militia recruiter and whose raids drove the British to distraction; and Francis Marion, the "Swamp Fox," who kept the lowcountry outside of Charleston in turmoil. Sumter and Marion had been Continental officers earlier in the war. These men caused the British no end of grief. Cornwallis hated Marion. "Colonel Marion had so wrought the minds of the people," he later recalled, "partly by the terror of his threats and cruelty of his punishments, and partly by the promise of plunder, that there was scarcely an inhabitant between the Santee and the Pee Dee [lowcountry rivers north of Charleston] that was not in arms against us."[40] There was a host of other partisan leaders as well, sometimes working with one of the "big three" and sometimes independently. But together, beginning in May 1780 (after the fall of Charleston) and continuing to the end of the struggle, these partisans waged a campaign that kept the Revolution alive in the deep South.

It was a brutal campaign. In fact, it was a civil war pitting Patriots against Loyalists—Americans against Americans—with all of the passion, cruelty, and bloodlust such conflicts unleash. Responding to British calls to rally to the king, many southern Loyalists had organized in militia units and enlisted in provincial regular battalions, often cooperating with British units. They became the targets of rebel partisans in bloody contests to control the countryside. When a main British force left a region uncovered, Patriot militia moved in with vengeful reprisals against anyone who had welcomed the king's soldiers. Both sides claimed victories and suffered defeats, and there were instances when neither side cared particularly about taking prisoners. Most of this fighting was a guerrilla struggle. The militia staged hit-and-run attacks, quickly pulling out of harm's way in the face of large enemy units or when a fight was going

---

40. Cornwallis quoted in Franklin Wickwire and Mary Wickwire, *Cornwallis and the War of Independence* (London: John Dickens & Co, 1971), 190–91.

badly. As in the North, the southerners made it dangerous for the British to penetrate the countryside in anything but real force, and royal troops had to be constantly on guard against bushwhackers and snipers, if not more serious ambushes. Small British parties moved only at risk. Even when not suffering casualties, the constant tension was enervating, and morale among the royal troops suffered accordingly. For the British, the South had become a quagmire.

If most of the fighting was on a small scale, there were larger engagements. On August 19, 1780, militia under Isaac Shelby, Elijah Clarke, and James Williams caught some 500 tory provincials and militiamen at Musgrove's Mill, near present-day Spartanburg, South Carolina. At a cost of 4 killed and 12 wounded, the rebels killed over 60 of the Loyalists and captured another 70.[41] In October, Patriot militia struck one of the most devastating blows of the war. On October 7, a combined force of some 900 "Overmountain men"—settlers from western Virginia and Tennessee who lived over the Blue Ridge—and Virginia and North and South Carolina militia surrounded and defeated over 1,100 Loyalist militia and veteran provincial regulars under Major Patrick Ferguson at King's Mountain, South Carolina. The fight pitted Americans against Americans—Ferguson, who was killed, was the only British soldier there—and resulted in the loss of the entire Loyalist force. Many of the attacking militiamen had used rifles to deadly effect. Cornwallis was stunned at the news. Ferguson's command had been the left wing of his army, and it was clear that the shattering defeat would dampen any efforts to rally Carolina Loyalists to the king.[42] Learning of King's Mountain, Henry Clinton later remarked that the defeat "unhappily proved the first link in a chain of evils that followed each other in regular succession until they at last ended in the total loss of America."[43]

The "chain of evils" proved a long one, but Clinton was right about where it led. Sumter had not joined the rebel march to King's Mountain, but he was not long out of action. The following month his militia mauled the command of the feared British dragoon Lieutenant Colonel Banastre Tarleton in a violent clash at Blackstock's Farm (near the town of Union, South Carolina). Some of the South Carolinians were riflemen who emptied British saddles before the riders could close with them. Sumter was hit badly in the fray, but Blackstock's Farm was Tarleton's first defeat, and American

41. John Buchanan, *The Road to Guilford Courthouse: The American Revolution in the Carolinas* (New York: John Wiley & Sons, 1997), 176–79.

42. For a full study of the battle, see J. David Dameron, *King's Mountain: The Defeat of the Loyalists, October 7, 1780* (Cambridge, MA: Da Capo Press, 2003); Buchanan, *Road to Guilford Courthouse*, 223, 225–41.

43. Henry Clinton, *The American Rebellion: Sir Henry Clinton's Narrative of His Campaigns, 1775–1782, with an Appendix of Original Documents*, ed. William B. Willcox (New Haven, CT: Yale University Press, 1954), 226.

morale soared. (In reporting to Cornwallis, however, Tarleton implausibly claimed a victory at Blackstock's. The militia knew better.)[44]

Beyond these dramatic actions, the protracted nature of the conflict was discouraging for the Crown. No one could land a knockout blow, but for the Southern Strategy to work, the British and their Loyalist allies needed to do just that. Without a pacified countryside, a critical mass of civilians with Loyalist sympathies could never be secure enough to declare openly for the Crown. Nor could they establish civil institutions beyond the effective control of British troops, and the British never had enough men to provide the necessary coverage. By simply keeping in the field, Patriot militias were defeating the British strategic design.

Compound Warfare

That is not to say, however, that the rebels were winning the southern war. They were not. The British adapted to militia threats, and Cornwallis ordered his troops to move only in numbers large enough to protect themselves. His dragoons could move swiftly against militia concentrations or unwary rebel parties, and they did. In August 1780, for instance, Tarleton caught a careless Sumter by surprise at Fishing Creek, South Carolina. Sumter got away, but Tarleton took 300 prisoners and all of Sumter's supplies.[45] The militias were never strong enough to confront a main British field army, and redcoats were able to prevent Patriots from re-establishing effective civil institutions in many areas. Moreover, with the Crown firmly in control of the largest cities in the deep South—the ports of Charleston; Savannah, Georgia; and Wilmington, North Carolina—as well as some key towns in the interior, they could throttle much of the southern economy. Planter prosperity depended on exports, and there was some question as to how long many southerners could tolerate what amounted to economic isolation at British hands. Time was not necessarily on the rebel side. They needed the means to defeat Cornwallis and his senior subordinates, and the militia alone could not provide it.

What Patriots needed was an effective force of American regulars to support and cooperate with the militia campaign and confront the British regulars. The war in the North had already demonstrated how the arrangement could work. In modern terminology, this is "compound warfare": "The simultaneous use of a regular or main force and an irregular or guerilla force against an enemy." In compound warfare, a combatant "increases his military leverage by applying both conventional and

---

44. Buchanan, *Road to Guilford Courthouse*, 251–60.

45. John Pancake, *This Destructive War: The British Campaign in the Carolinas, 1780–1782* (Tuscaloosa: University of Alabama Press, 1985), 107.

unconventional force at the same time."[46]

Despite his early misgivings about the militia, Washington learned to work effectively with the citizen-soldiers. They provided a crucial intelligence function for the Continentals, screened the regular army's movements, and participated in joint patrolling and foraging operations. Later in the conflict, a core of northern militia became quite war-wise and worked closely with the Continentals in major operations. In 1777, as noted earlier, militia played a prominent role against Burgoyne during the Saratoga campaign, and militia units served next to the Patriot regulars in some of the major fighting. In 1778, some 2,000 New Jersey and Pennsylvania militiamen harassed Henry Clinton's army as it trekked through New Jersey during the Monmouth campaign, linking their operations with Continental formations. At Connecticut Farms and Springfield in 1780, militiamen rallied to offer effective resistance to yet another British push into New

Despite the arguments made on behalf of the militia and the Continental Army, in fact, neither can claim the bulk of the credit for American victory. Fighting together in what has been termed "compound warfare," the combined efforts of the Continentals and militia and the proper use of their different capabilities managed to defeat the British, as ably demonstrated by Brigadier General Daniel Morgan at the Battle of Cowpens on January 17, 1781. *Daniel Morgan*, painting by Alonzo Chappel, 1861. National Archives, College Park, MD.

Jersey, serving alongside regular troops and under the overall command of Continental officers.[47] In the long run, the regular-militia combination proved impossible for the British to counter effectively in the middle colonies.

46. Thomas M. Huber, "Compound Warfare: A Conceptual Framework," in *Compound Warfare: That Fatal Knot*, ed. Thomas M. Huber (Fort Leavenworth, KS: U.S. Army Command and General Staff College Press, 2002), 1.

47. For compound warfare in the War for Independence, see Jerry D. Morelock, "Washington as Strategist: Compound Warfare in the American Revolution, 1775–1783," in Huber, *Compound Warfare*, 79. For the Monmouth and Springfield campaigns, see Mark Edward Lender and Garry Wheeler Stone, *Fatal Sunday: George Washington, the Monmouth Campaign, and the Politics of Battle* (Norman: University of Oklahoma Press, 2017); and Edward G. Lengel, *The Battles of Connecticut Farms and Springfield, 1780* (Yardley, PA: Westholme, 2020). Although he does not use the term compound warfare, in *Washington's Partisan War*, Kwasny describes a similar militia-regular interaction.

Farther north, a small Continental force based in Albany, with an occasional presence westward in the Mohawk Valley, did its best to support militia operations confronting Loyalist and Indian raids (sometimes with redcoat help) out of Canada. Many of these attacks were destructive and kept the northern New York frontier in turmoil; in places like Ballston and Stone Arabia, both in mid-October 1780, and a year later at Warrensborough, militia forces and civilians suffered serious losses trying to deal with them. But the militia hit back, often under Continental colonel Marinus Willett, and by later 1781, they proved increasingly effective.[48] Indeed, the militia gave pause to one of the most aggressive British officers. This was Lieutenant General Frederick Haldimand, governor of Quebec province, who had orchestrated an active raiding campaign, both to hurt the rebels and to keep them from launching an offensive into Canada. Late in the war, however, he gave up on the strategy. Continental forces were not really the problem, but the Americans, he informed Henry Clinton, had produced a war-wise "multitude of militia men in arms" that had become a potent threat. British forces venturing into the New York interior risked being overwhelmed.[49]

The king's forces did no better in the South. In October 1780, Washington tasked Major General Nathanael Greene with reconstituting the Continental Army in the southern theater. Greene, a Rhode Islander and former Quaker who had been appointed a general in 1775 despite a lack of military experience, but whose abilities were quickly recognized by Washington, was, by common consent among modern historians, one of Washington's most talented subordinates, if not *the* most talented. He had served brilliantly as the army's quartermaster general and had a full appreciation of logistics management. Long before 1780, Greene had learned to appreciate the defensive capabilities of militia fighting on their home ground. Still, like Washington, Greene was a firm believer in regular soldiers as the key to victory. He had made no secret of his aversion to dependence on rebel militia, and he once told his brother Jacob that congressional hopes for the militia were "the most absurd and ridiculous imaginable. . . . A military force established upon such principles defeats itself."[50] But as the war dragged on, Greene had proved adept at commanding in mixed

---

48. For the fighting in northern New York and the increasing effectiveness of the militia, see Peckham, *Toll of Independence*, 92; Christopher Ward, *The War of the Revolution*, 2 vols. (New York: Macmillan, 1952), 2:651–52; Richard A. Preston, "Ross, John," *Dictionary of Canadian Biography*, vol. 4, *1771–1800* (Toronto: University of Toronto/Université Laval, 1979), www.biographi.ca/en/bio/ross_john_1762_89_4E.html (accessed Nov. 11, 2019).

49. Frederick Haldimand to Henry Clinton, April 28, 1782, *Collections of the Vermont Historical Society* (Montpelier, VT: J. & M. Polard, printer, 1871), 2:266.

50. Nathanael Greene to George Washington, October 18, 1778, in *The Papers of General Nathanael Greene*, 13 vols., ed. Richard K. Showman and Dennis M. Conrad (Chapel Hill: University of North Carolina Press, 1976–2005), 3:3, 5; Greene to George Washington, January 5, 1779, in Showman and Conrad, *Papers of Nathanael Greene*, 3:145; Greene to Jacob Greene, September 20, 1776, in Showman and Conrad, *Papers of Nathanael Greene*, 1:103–4.

regular-militia actions, notably at Springfield, New Jersey, in June 1780.[51] In the South, he would emerge as the Revolution's master of compound warfare.

In December 1780, Greene arrived in Charlotte, North Carolina, to assume command of what remained of the southern army. He did not like what he saw. He found no more than a thousand poorly provisioned and supplied Continentals under arms, and he was skeptical of the southern militia. The demoralized rebel forces were "without Discipline and so addicted to plundering, that the utmost Exertions of the Officers cannot restrain the Soldiers."[52] Greene, however, made the best of things. Luckily the few Continentals were hardened veterans and responded to his efforts to restore discipline. And the major general was a quick study. He knew his regulars were insufficient to confront Cornwallis on anything near equal terms. Thus he swallowed his reservations about the militia and quickly communicated with the key partisan leaders. He grasped that only coordinated Continental-militia operations—compound warfare—stood a chance of reclaiming the South in the face of Cornwallis's advantages of superior numbers of regulars, better equipment and artillery, and experienced supply services. Greene found ready allies in Marion and Pickens, although Sumter, aloof and jealous of his command prerogatives, proved a difficult partner.[53]

We should note, however, that Greene's decision to reach out to the militia commanders was more than a matter of necessity (which it certainly was). It was also a leap of faith—because the new theater commander's qualms about the militia were well-founded. Some five months earlier, on August 16, 1780, militia troops had performed disastrously at the Battle of Camden. Much of the fault lay with the American commander, Major General Horatio Gates. Gates was a true believer in the citizen-soldiers, and the more ardent congressional republicans adored him for it. At Saratoga, Gates had done well in a largely defensive battle in which the militia had harassed Burgoyne's army, cut off his communications, and interdicted his supplies. The Continentals, however, had done most of the serious fighting. But at Camden, Gates committed the militia to the front line of a traditional stand-up fight in the open field. Worse, he aligned most of his militia against the cream of Lord Cornwallis's army, and the irregulars broke and ran in the face of disciplined British fire and bayonets. Only one regiment of North Carolina militia, fighting next to the Continentals, performed

---

51. "III. To George Washington from Major General Nathanael Greene, 23 June 1780," *Founders Online,* National Archives, https://founders.archives.gov. [Original source: *The Papers of George Washington,* Revolutionary War Series, vol. 26, *13 May–4 July 1780,* ed. Benjamin L. Huggins and Adrina Garbooshian-Huggins (Charlottesville: University of Virginia Press, 2018), 522–23.]; Terry Golway, *Washington's General: Nathanael Greene and the Triumph of the American Revolution* (New York: Henry Holt, 2005), 223–24; Lengel, *Connecticut Farms and Springfield,* passim.

52. Greene to Robert Howe, December 29, 1780, Showman and Conrad, *Papers of Nathanael Greene,* 7:17.

53. On Greene's assumption of command and his initial efforts to revive the southern theater, see Golway, *Washington's General,* 236–39.

well. Camden was a shattering rebel defeat.[54] And in a snarky note to his New York friend and politico James Duane, Alexander Hamilton observed of Gates that "His passion for Militia, I fancy will be a little cured, and he will cease to think them the best bulwark of American liberty."[55] For that matter, Camden did nothing to bolster *anyone's* faith in the militia (or in Horatio Gates). Only time would tell if Greene's hopes for militia cooperation with his regulars would prove a winning combination.

Whatever his doubts about his army, Greene began his campaign in dramatic fashion. Defying conventional military wisdom not to divide an inferior force in the face of a larger enemy, Greene did just that. He marched most of his command to the southeast to fence directly with Cornwallis while detaching a force to the southwest under Brigadier General Daniel Morgan. Morgan was to threaten British outposts in western South Carolina. Confronted with Greene's startling move, Cornwallis sent Banastre Tarleton's British Legion—crack Loyalist troops—with supporting infantry to catch Morgan while he dealt with Greene. It was a prelude to one of the classic engagements of the war and an equally classic example of compound warfare in action.

On January 17, 1781, Morgan, knowing Tarleton was closing in and having prepared his defensive ground carefully, stood to fight at Hannah's Cowpens in western South Carolina. Morgan deployed his regulars, including Continental dragoons, behind two advanced lines of militia. By design, the militia fired only a couple of volleys, which staggered the charging British, before pulling back and reorganizing behind the Continental main line, which then shattered Tarleton's disorganized command. Among the re-engaged men pouring fire into the reeling enemy were South Carolinians under Pickens and Virginia militiamen, some of whom had seen prior Continental service—another example of manpower shared between the regulars and irregulars. Tarleton was utterly routed, and the Battle of Cowpens stands as one of the war's tactical masterpieces.[56]

Cornwallis was furious. He turned his main force on Morgan, hoping to recover the approximately 600 prisoners lost at Cowpens, but the rebels got away. Cornwallis then chased Greene all the way across North Carolina, with Greene escaping over the Dan River into Virginia on February 14 (this was the so-called "race to the Dan"). During Greene's long retreat, North Carolina militia skirmished several times with the pursuing British, slowing them down at river fords and helping Greene's main body to stay ahead of the frustrated Cornwallis. The race had exhausted the British,

---

54. For a full account of Gates's defeat at Camden, including his flawed deployment of the militia, see Paul David Nelson, *Horatio Gates: A Biography* (Baton Rouge: Louisiana State University Press, 1976), 232–37.

55. Alexander Hamilton to James Duane, September 6, 1780, *The Papers of Alexander Hamilton*, ed. Harold C. Syrett (New York: Columbia University Press, 1961), 2:420.

56. For the definitive account of Cowpens, see Babits, *A Devil of a Whipping*, esp. 61–136.

who remained in North Carolina to rest and regroup, only to have a reinforced and resupplied Greene cross back into Carolina looking for a fight.[57]

As the rival army commanders looked for opportunities to strike, smaller actions continued. Sumter was especially active. On February 19 and 20, Sumter, attacking alone (he really was stubbornly averse to cooperating with Greene), unsuccessfully besieged the British post of Fort Granby. Three days later, he captured a British supply train near Belleville, inflicting some fourteen casualties on the escorting troops. On February 28, the Gamecock lost several men in a botched attack on Fort Watson.[58] Yet, even such disappointing (from the Patriot perspective) engagements kept the British off balance, and there were some stunning successes. On February 23, in cooperation with Henry Lee's Continental Legion, Pickens's militia surprised 400 Tory militiamen under Colonel John Pyle near the Haw River. The savage Patriot assault killed 96, wounded many others, and scattered the survivors in the so-called "Pyle's Massacre." Two weeks later, Marion, the "Swamp Fox," was in action as well; on March 6, he came off second-best with a force of redcoats and Loyalist regulars in a tough action at Wiboo (sometimes Wyboo) Swamp in Clarendon County. Wiboo Swamp was a tactical setback, but it frustrated a British move into the interior and cost them casualties they could ill afford.[59] This list could go on, but the picture was clear enough: with Greene in the fight, supplying and coordinating with the militia, the Revolution was very much alive in the South.

Working with the militia, Greene's operations hinged on his Continentals posing a constant threat to British units and their key positions while avoiding battle unless on favorable terms. He never engaged without substantial militia adjuncts to his regulars. And, as the "race to the Dan" had shown, he refused to be caught. But he did fight. Over the rest of 1781, Greene, or his senior Continental commanders, fought major actions or engaged in sieges at Guilford Courthouse, Hobkirk's Hill, Ninety Six, Augusta, and Eutaw Springs. He never won a clear-cut victory, but even in defeat or in tactical draws, he bled the royal forces, inflicting casualties the Crown could ill afford while keeping his own forces intact. After losing at Hobkirk's Hill near Camden, South Carolina, on April 25, he was philosophical. "*We fight,*" he famously wrote to the French minister in America, Anne-Cesar de la Luzerne, "*get beat rise and fight again.*"[60] These battles, and many smaller ones—Clinton's "chain of evils"—progressively wore down the King's forces and led to their steady retreat to Charleston

---

57. Stanley D. M. Carpenter, *Southern Gambit: Cornwallis and the British March to Yorktown* (Norman: University of Oklahoma Press, 2019), 175–88.

58. John Buchanan, *The Road to Charleston: Nathanael Greene and the American Revolution* (Charlottesville: University of Virginia Press, 2019), 73–74.

59. Andrew, *Andrew Pickens*, 119–21; John W. Gordon, *South Carolina and the American Revolution: A Battlefield History* (Columbia: University of South Carolina Press, 2003), 142.

60. Greene to Chevalier Anne-Cesar de la Luzerne, April 28, 1781, in Showman and Conrad, *Papers of Nathanael Greene*, 8:168.

and its immediate environs. With the exceptions of Charleston, Savannah, and Wilmington, by the time Washington and the French had trapped Cornwallis at Yorktown, Greene had reclaimed the Carolinas and Georgia.

Greene, that is, and the militia. All of his major battles had seen heavy commitments by the southern militia. At the siege of Augusta, Georgia, in May 1781, Pickens and Elijah Clarke teamed with Continental lieutenant colonel Henry ("Light Horse Harry") Lee's Legion. The surrender of the British garrison in June broke the Crown's hold on backcountry Georgia. Marion and Pickens also played significant roles at Eutaw Springs in September. The last major combat in the Carolinas, Eutaw Springs was a brutal tactical draw that cost the British heavily, compelling them to withdraw.[61] The Swamp Fox, Pickens, and other militia leaders had rallied the numbers Greene needed to fight in the open field, and the militia's constant raids, harassing attacks, screening work, and intelligence gathering made the Continental Army a greater threat to the British than it otherwise could have been. Indeed, after the war, Sumter uncharitably claimed the victory was the militia's alone. That was nonsense. It was a joint victory, a model of compound warfare.

A Parallel War: Militia on the Frontier

While the war raged—or sputtered, as it often did in the North and South—there was another theater in which it was impossible to underestimate the role of militia forces. The Continental Army barely set foot in the West, the vast area of Trans-Appalachia beyond the Blue Ridge. There, the scattered white settlers largely looked to themselves for protection against the various American Indian tribes who, quite rightly, dreaded a Patriot victory they knew would open a tsunami of white settlers. Most of the tribes allied with the British; they accepted (indeed, demanded) royal aid and cooperated with the regulars and Loyalists on operations large and small. But they had no particular love for the Crown; they fought not only to protect their lands but also their very ways of life. The result was some of the most savage fighting of the war, and it usually had little to do with action to the east of the Blue Ridge.[62]

In the South, fighting with the Indians began before the colonists exchanged a shot with the redcoats. In 1776, militia from Georgia, the Carolinas, and Virginia took the war to the Cherokees, forcing most of them to move west. Pickens and other future Revolutionary commanders were involved in these operations.[63] In the Virginia-Pennsylvania backcountry, the Shawnees and smaller tribes bore the brunt

---

61. The best account of Eutaw Springs, including the militia's role, is Robert M. Dunkerly and Irene B. Boland, *Eutaw Springs: The Final Battle of the American Revolution's Southern Campaign* (Columbia: University of South Carolina Press, 2017).

62. For the war in the West, see Lender, "Western Theater," 139–78.

63. Andrew, *Andrew Pickens*, 15–18.

of rebel assaults. Stunned at first, the Indians fought back effectively, and the frontiers were aflame for the rest of the war and beyond—Yorktown meant little beyond the Blue Ridge. While Congress did formally organize a Western Department, Continental units had little luck moving west of Fort Pitt (Pittsburgh). Thus, for Americans living below the Ohio River in Kentucky and present-day Tennessee, defense became a local affair. Scattered white settlements usually constructed blockhouses or other fortifications manned with almost anyone able to handle a weapon. Depending upon the locale, westerners attempted to organize formal militias, but more often, they relied on ad hoc parties gathered for particular operations. The Overmountain men who helped defeat Ferguson were a prominent example. Other hastily recruited volunteers, often men with militia experience, would participate in much of the frontier fighting.[64]

Eastern governments occasionally did try to lend a hand to western settlers. In 1778, Virginia sent an expedition under Colonel George Rogers Clark to attack the tribes in the Ohio River Valley. Clark's men were state troops, not Continentals, and were constituted outside of the regular militia. The expedition took some pressure off the region, but the Indians were anything but out of the fight.[65] The following year, after desperate pleas from the New York and Pennsylvania frontiers, Washington finally acted. He sent Major General John Sullivan and a full third of the Continental Army against the Iroquois in New York state. Sullivan fought and won a sizeable battle at Newtown (close to present-day Elmira) and burned his way through Iroquois country. The impact on the Iroquois was devastating, and the frontiers enjoyed a season of relative peace. But the Iroquois were back with a vengeance in 1780, often in league with Loyalist raiders, and once again, the burdens of local defense fell on the militia.[66] So it would be in New York until the end of the war.

The Militia in the Balance

For all of their successes—and these successes were quite real—the militia never overcame some of the shortcomings that had attracted the criticisms of Washington and other advocates of regular troops. Training and proficiency in field maneuvers never approached the levels expected of the Continental regulars. Short tours of duty compromised unit cohesion, and many militiamen objected—to the point of refusing—to serve far from home, much less to following the Continentals out of state. Militias also were expensive to maintain. Members of organized militias were paid

---

64. Lender, "Western Theater," 139–78.

65. Lender, "Western Theater," 157–61.

66. Glenn F. Williams, *The Year of the Hangman: George Washington's Campaign Against the Iroquois* (Yardley, PA: Westholme, 2005), 293–96.

and equipped, and over the course of the war, militia expenses became a significant part of the Revolutionary debt that Alexander Hamilton dealt with years later.

There also were objections to repeated call-ups. New York and New Jersey militia—their states subject to frequent raids—complained that the burdens of frequent duty interrupted important civilian pursuits. They were right. In an economy that was over 90 percent agricultural, numerous militia call-ups were bound to have an impact on planting, harvests, and the normal routines of maintaining crops and livestock. In New Jersey, Governor William Livingston lamented that so many militiamen tried to evade service that the burdens of the war fell largely on "the willing." The Virginia experience is the most illustrative. While the state had seen some fighting earlier in the war, it became a major theater for the first time in 1781. Benedict Arnold (then a British officer) invaded Virginia in January 1781, followed by the subsequent incursion of Lord Cornwallis. Major general the Marquis de Lafayette, reinforced by Anthony Wayne, could muster fewer than 3,000 Continentals in opposition. During the months-long campaign, calls on state militia came with a frequent and often frantic regularity. By the late summer, plenty of Virginia militia troops were in the field, although many others simply had had enough; they refused to turn out, and there were even instances of Virginians rioting in protest. In the end Virginia authorities, like their counterparts in the other states, were unable to effectively compel the service of many of their citizen-soldiers.[67] Americans, even committed Patriots, *did* get war-weary.

Another persistent problem was the speed of turn-outs, even among willing militiamen. The regular army, embodied on a full-time basis, could react relatively quickly to emergencies and could prepare more readily for offensive operations. The militia could do neither. In the face of major enemy initiatives, it could take considerable time to pull together militia forces. True, even relatively small militia forces could skirmish with and harass a large opposing force, buying time for Continentals to come up. But as we have seen, it was generally the case that with the militia, discretion proved the better part of valor; in the absence of a Continental response, the irregulars wisely would back off to fight another day. There also were instances when the Continentals pulled out of a fight because hoped-for militia support did not arrive. Fortunately for the Revolution, there were critical times—before Trenton, at Saratoga, during the Monmouth campaign, and at Cowpens and Eutaw Springs— when the militia had the time to rally and make all the difference. But no Continental commander ever took sufficient militia support for granted.

One thing is clear, however: experience mattered in militia performance. North and South, the militia of 1781 was not the militia of 1775 and 1776. Constant call-ups, the availability of better arms and equipment, frequent skirmishing and patrolling, cooperation with Continental units, the policing of Tories and enforcing the

---

67. McDonnell, *Politics of War*, e.g., 340–41, 370–72, 374–78, 387–88, 398–434; Selesky, *Encyclopedia*, 2:1215.

authority of rebel local and state governments, and the occasional pitched battle had produced a war-wise and even battle-hardened militia. For all of its shortcomings, it was a force vastly more effective than the citizen-soldiers of the war's early years. In addition, over time, the states (at least in the North) gradually improved the administrative and legal structures governing militia affairs. There were fairly regular efforts to perfect company and regimental organizations and even to assure competent leadership at higher command levels. Without garnering the fame of Sumter, Pickens, or Marion, northern militias produced some first-class talents in the likes of Brigadier General John Cadwalader of Pennsylvania and Major General Philemon Dickinson of New Jersey.[68]

Laws to compel militiamen to turn out had some effect, especially later in the conflict. This was true despite frequent popular resistance (we have noted the Virginia experience). In New Jersey, for instance, the scene of more combat than any other state, authorities at one time or another were able to mobilize virtually every available male of military age (not counting the substantial pacifist Quaker population, losses to Loyalism, and men officially deferred for government or other essential service).[69] Of course, mere numbers never guaranteed effectiveness in the field, but numbers certainly were important. The British could never easily replace losses in the field—Clinton, in particular, was highly casualty averse—but as long as the rebels maintained the will to fight on, the militia could make good its losses. The old military aphorism is germane here: at some point, quantity assumes a quality all its own.

Conclusion: The Question Answered

So, where does all of this leave our original question? Who won the war, the militia or the Continental regulars? And what about the popular myth of the problematic militia? Clearly, the questions are moot—and the myth is "busted." Both militia and regular forces played critical parts in the military drama. The Continentals gave the Revolution the means to confront the British main armies, or at least threaten them, which alone circumscribed royal military and political initiatives. The militia could (and did) keep the British off balance, but in most cases, militia alone could not prevent major enemy forces from moving at will. Significantly, the Continental Army gave the rebel cause international standing, something the militia alone could never do. The Continental Army, however, was never large enough to offer protection to civilian populations and Patriot political establishments over vast swaths of the rebellious colonies. North and South (and especially South), the militia served this

---

68. Ashley Hanson, "John Cadwalader," Mount Vernon, https://www.mountvernon.org (accessed February 24, 2023); "Dickinson, Philemon," *Biographical Dictionary of the United States Congress*, http://bioguide.congress.gov (accessed Nov. 11, 2019).

69. Selesky, *Encyclopedia*, 2:806.

purpose—enforcing the rule of local authorities, supporting regional law enforcement, and suppressing and intimidating Loyalists. To the militia belongs the credit for the fact that Tories were nowhere able to mount an effective counter-revolution. In the West, the Continental presence was negligible; local militia forces bore the brunt of frontier combat.

That both militia and regulars were essential to the Patriot victory was nowhere more evident than in the record of combat. The Continentals, while usually bearing the main burdens of heavy combat, did provide a core around which the militia could rally in major engagements. This was the case at Saratoga, Monmouth, and Cowpens. On the other hand, the regulars depended routinely on the militia for local intelligence, screening and skirmishing operations, guarding supply trains, and similar duties. The militia also could act independently; we have noted their victories at Bennington and King's Mountain. And even their bloody stand-off at Oriskany accrued to the Patriots' benefit in 1777. The militia was particularly valuable, however, in the small-scale guerrilla operations that made Pickens, Sumter, and Marion famous (or infamous, depending on one's perspective). And the militia was most effective when teamed with the regulars in the compound warfare that combined the strengths of both armed forces. Neither force could have won the War for Independence alone; they did it together.

The militia, however, did take a final bow. On November 25, 1783, when the last British troops evacuated New York City, Continental artillery chief Henry Knox led a small contingent of American regulars into town, taking formal possession. There were few Continentals left for Knox to lead. The war was over and Congress, all but insolvent, sent most of the regulars home with promissory notes—there was no money actually to pay them—and with a rather ungracious (indeed, callous) reference to the republican aversion to maintaining standing armies in time of peace. Hours later, with the few regulars dispatched to various posts, they were absent as escorts when Washington entered the city in triumph. Instead, the general and a high-level political entourage made do with an escort of un-uniformed mounted Westchester County militia.[70] Benjamin Rush, that arch-ideological partisan of militia, in effect got his wish: The militia had indeed begun the war—and it had finished it.

---

70. Mark Plus, *Henry Knox: Visionary General of the American Revolution* (New York: Palgrave Macmillan, 2008), 185; Edward G. Lengel, *General George Washington: A Military Life* (New York: Random House, 2005), 351; Thomas Fleming, *The Perils of Peace: America's Struggle for Survival After Yorktown* (New York: Smithsonian Books, 2007), 312.

4. British Atrocities

Jim Piecuch

> Sacred to the memory of the Patriots who on this
> spot fell a sacrifice to British barbarity.[1]
> —*Monument on the site of the September 20, 1777, Battle of Paoli, Pennsylvania*

> Tarleton . . . was in the midst of them, when commenced a scene of indiscriminate
> carnage never surpassed by the ruthless atrocities of the most barbarous savages.[2]
> —*Dr. Robert Brownfield on the May 29, 1780, Battle of the Waxhaws*

> There was 8 died of a day while I was there. They were carried on shore in heaps
> and hove out the boat on the wharf.[3]
> —*Christopher Vail's account of occurrences on the British prison ship* Jersey

From the beginning of the War for Independence, the Revolutionaries accused British soldiers of committing atrocities against American troops and sometimes civilians. The first such charges were leveled immediately after the first day of fighting on April 19, 1775; Connecticut governor Jonathan Trumbull was among the colonists who claimed "that such outrages have been committed as would disgrace even barbarians" during the British retreat from Concord.[4] The chorus of condemnation grew as American leaders and newspapers almost continually alleged that British troops slaughtered rebels while they slept, when they attempted to surrender, or after taking them prisoner. The Crown's Loyalist and Indian allies were said to have acted with even greater brutality, ignoring pleas for mercy as they murdered innocent women and children along with helpless soldiers. Nearly every battle brought fresh accusations, and several were specifically denoted "massacres" to illustrate the savagery of the

---

1. Kieran J. O'Keefe, "Monuments to the American Revolution," *Journal of the American Revolution*, September 17, 2019, https://allthingsliberty.com/2019/09/monuments-to-the-american-revolution/ (accessed Jan. 3, 2020).

2. "Recollection of Dr. Robert Brownfield," in *A Sketch of the Life of Brig. Gen. Francis Marion and a History of His Brigade from Its Rise in June 1780 until Disbanded in December, 1782*, by William Dobein James (Charleston, SC: Gould and Riley, 1821), Appendix, 3–4.

3. Edwin G. Burrows, *Forgotten Patriots: The Untold Story of American Prisoners during the Revolutionary War* (New York: Basic Books, 2008), 178.

4. Jonathan Trumbull to General Thomas Gage, April 28, 1775, in *Reporting the Revolutionary War: Before It Was History, It Was News*, ed. Todd Andrlik (Naperville, IL: Sourcebooks, 2012), 127.

British and their supporters. These allegations helped motivate the Revolutionaries to continue fighting despite numerous demoralizing defeats.

The accounts of British brutality were reinforced in public memory after the war in the early histories and in monuments erected to commemorate important events of the Revolution. Kieran J. O'Keefe noted in his study of Revolutionary War monuments that those built in the late eighteenth and early nineteenth centuries "often emphasized the perceived barbarity of the British." This theme declined in the twentieth century, however, as the Anglo-American alliance in the world wars contributed to a more favorable view of the British among the public.[5]

Historians continue to debate whether British and Loyalist soldiers and allied Indians deliberately slaughtered American troops. Although many of the more recent studies offer a balanced view of this controversy, many writers continue to repeat the atrocity stories that originated during the war and were perpetuated in the early histories. The fact that the majority of British officers and enlisted men despised the treasonous colonists is undisputed. Matthew H. Spring, in his study of the British army in the Revolution, noted that "British troops appear to have viewed the rebels with considerable hostility. This antipathy probably contributed to the grim reputation for ruthlessness that the redcoats earned in America because of the frequency with which they seem to have killed enemy combatants attempting to surrender in the heat of the action and finished off the wounded."[6] Attitudes, however, do not necessarily reflect actions. The British soldiers' reputation for cruelty may not have been deserved, especially when those who made the accusations despised the British and had much to gain by portraying their enemies as vicious murderers. Atrocity stories involving British troops, Loyalists, and especially their Indian allies were perpetuated in large part because they helped unite Americans against a ruthless common enemy.[7] A careful examination of the most notorious British atrocities during the War for Independence reveals that the allegations of massacre on the battlefield were either false or exaggerated. There is more evidence to support accusations that British soldiers often sexually assaulted American women, an issue now largely forgotten, as is another case of unjustifiable cruelty, the deaths of American prisoners of war in British custody.

The Battle of Paoli

After defeating the American army at the Battle of Brandywine, Pennsylvania, on September 11, 1777, British general Sir William Howe marched his forces toward

---

5. O'Keefe, "Monuments."

6. Matthew H. Spring, *With Zeal and Bayonets Only: The British Army on Campaign in North America, 1775–1783* (Norman: University of Oklahoma Press, 2008), 232.

7. See Robert G. Parkinson, *Thirteen Clocks: How Race United the Colonies and Made the Declaration of Independence* (Chapel Hill: University of North Carolina Press, 2021), esp. 82, 99, 123, 165.

Philadelphia. As he retreated, American commander-in-chief General George Washington sent three detachments on September 18 to harass Howe's flanks and slow the British advance. One of these forces, consisting of 1,500 men under General Anthony Wayne, marched that night and occupied a position between the town of Paoli and White Horse Tavern, only four miles from Howe's left flank. Wayne found the position promising and sent two letters to Washington the next day urging him to bring the rest of the Continental Army to attack the British. Washington declined to undertake such a risky move. Meanwhile, Howe learned the location of Wayne's troops and realized their isolation made them vulnerable. Wishing to clear his flanks before resuming his advance, Howe summoned General Sir Charles Grey to head-quarters on September 20 and ordered him to attack Wayne's force. Howe believed the defeat of Wayne would eliminate one of the threats to his flanks and frighten the other two American detachments into withdrawing.[8]

At 10:00 p.m. that night, Grey set out for Wayne's camp with a large force of infantry and a small number of cavalry troopers amounting to about 5,000 men. A second British detachment of two regiments moved to the Lancaster Road to block Wayne's expected route of retreat. To ensure that he achieved surprise, Grey ordered his soldiers to remove the flints from their muskets to prevent accidental gunfire that might warn the Americans; he intended to make his attack with bayonets. Grey also took into custody all the civilians he encountered on his march to prevent anyone from warning Wayne. The latter precaution failed as a local resident discovered the British intentions and notified Wayne of the enemy's movement. The American general ordered additional infantry and cavalry guards to patrol the approaches to his camp. However, the troops posted on Swedes Ford Road somehow failed to notice Grey's force as it marched on that route. Wayne's first warning of the impending attack came around 11:00 p.m. when some sentries saw the British and fired a few warning shots before scattering. Ten minutes later, Wayne heard more gunfire and ordered his soldiers to retreat along White Horse Road.[9]

Grey's troops quickly dispersed the sentries who had fired and then pushed forward to the line of pickets guarding Wayne's camp. The pickets had either ignored the firing or failed to realize its significance, and most were killed or wounded by British bayonets. The British charged into the American camp, where the troops had not yet responded to Wayne's retreat order. Some soldiers were trying to form a line of battle while others remained in their shelters. British troops overwhelmed the disorganized resistance and drove the Americans from their camp, while Wayne managed to save his four pieces of artillery from capture. After a short time, Grey halted the pursuit,

8. Paul David Nelson, *Sir Charles Grey, First Earl Grey: Royal Soldier, Family Patriarch* (Madison, NJ: Fairleigh Dickinson University Press, 1996), 42–43.

9. Nelson, *Sir Charles Grey*, 43–44.

united with the troops who had been guarding the Lancaster Road that Wayne had fortunately avoided, and the combined British force returned to camp.[10]

Grey had achieved surprise and won an overwhelming victory. The British had lost only 3 men killed and 7 wounded. Estimates of American casualties varied, though figures of nearly 200 killed, 150 wounded, and 71 captured have been generally accepted. The Americans also lost nine wagons loaded with supplies and a number of horses and cattle. General Howe praised his soldiers' "Steadiness in Charging with their Bayonets without firing a single Shot" and asserted such boldness was proof of "their Spirit and Discipline" as well as "their evident Superiority over the Enemy."[11] Nevertheless, the encounter was exceedingly violent. Major John Andre, a British staff officer, recorded a bloodier description of the battle. The British "rushed along the line putting to the bayonet all they came up with," he wrote, "and overtaking the main herd of the fugitives, stabbed great numbers and pressed on their rear till it was thought prudent to order them to desist."[12]

If the British took pride in their victory at Paoli, the Americans, not surprisingly, saw the battle in a different light. They seized on the lopsided casualties and carnage to describe the engagement as a massacre and portray Grey "as a monster who had encouraged his soldiers to murder poor Continental troopers in the act of surrendering. This line became a staple of rebel propaganda, accepted as undeniable truth."[13] Continental Major Samuel Hay described the action in terms similar to Andre's. "The annals of the age cannot produce such a scene of butchery," he told his superior, Colonel William Irvine. "The enemy rushed upon us with fixed bayonets and made the use of them they intended." Hay, however, blamed the debacle not on Grey or his soldiers but squarely upon the American commander, General Wayne. "So unguarded was our camp that they were amongst us before we either formed in any manner for our safety, or attempted to retreat, notwithstanding the General had full intelligence of their designs two hours before they came out."[14] The implication of Hay's letter was clear: the disastrous results of the British attack resulted from Wayne's failure to respond properly to the warning he had received.

Wayne, stung as much by the criticism as the defeat, fought to preserve his reputation and was cleared by a military court of inquiry. However, other officers continued to disparage him, including fellow Pennsylvanian Colonel Richard Humpton, who repeatedly declared that Wayne "had timely notice of the enemy's intention to attack"

---

10. Nelson, 44–45.

11. Nelson, 45.

12. John Andre, "Journal," September 20, 1778, in *The Spirit of 'Seventy-Six: The Story of the American Revolution as Told by Participants*, 2 vols., ed. Henry Steele Commager and Richard B. Morris (Indianapolis, IN: Bobbs-Merrill Co., 1958), 1:621–22.

13. Nelson, *Sir Charles Grey*, 45.

14. Samuel Hay to William Irvine, September 29, 1777, in Commager and Morris, *Spirit of 'Seventy-Six*, 1:622.

yet failed to take adequate precautions.[15] These accusations even reached Congress, where one member asserted that Wayne was guilty of "unpardonable negligence." Wayne, in turn, blamed the pickets for failing to provide warning of Grey's approach and argued that Humpton had not reacted promptly to the British attack. Wayne demanded a formal court-martial before which he could defend himself, and as he hoped, the court found his actions proper.[16]

Neither Washington nor Congress desired to publicize command failures and disputes within the Continental Army when American affairs were at a low point. Washington's defeat at Brandywine and the loss of Philadelphia two weeks later were serious blows to the Revolutionaries' morale. A second disastrous defeat resulting from a commander's poor leadership would further undermine the American cause. On the other hand, a brutal massacre perpetrated by the British could energize the rebels, encouraging them to continue the fight against a barbaric foe. Propaganda triumphed over fact.

Most historians since the latter half of the twentieth century have accurately described the Battle of Paoli as a tragic American defeat rather than a massacre. Others, such as Robert Middlekauff, have straddled the issue; he described the Americans as "carelessly asleep" while adding that British soldiers "used their bayonets with cruel efficiency" and that "many of the sleepers never left their blankets."[17] Despite efforts to dispel the myth, the massacre story survives. The History Channel's *This Day in History* feature on its website contains the entry for September 20 titled "Redcoats Kill Sleeping Americans in Paoli Massacre," inaccurately stating that British soldiers stabbed American soldiers to death as they slept, although the account correctly notes that "the Paoli Massacre became a rallying cry for the Americans against British atrocities for the rest of the Revolutionary War."[18] Likewise, a 2010 article by Max Hunsicker favored the view that the engagement was a massacre, asserting "evidence shows that this 'battle' was simply barbaric" and noting that British soldiers "had no problems attacking defenseless men with swords and bayonets."[19]

15. Hugh F. Rankin, "Anthony Wayne: Military Romanticist," in *George Washington's Generals and Opponents: Their Exploits and Leadership*, 2 vols., ed. George Athan Billias (New York: Da Capo Press, 1994), 1:267.

16. Stephen R. Taaffe, *Washington's Revolutionary War Generals* (Norman: University of Oklahoma Press, 2019), 119.

17. Robert Middlekauff, *The Glorious Cause: The American Revolution, 1763–1789* (New York: Oxford University Press, 1982), 389.

18. "This Day in History, September 20, 1777," History Channel, https://www.history.com (accessed Jan. 4, 2020).

19. Max Hunsicker, "The Paoli Massacre: A Battle Won by Bayonet," Pennsylvania Center for the Book, https://www.pabook.libraries.psu.edu (accessed Jan. 4, 2020).

The Battle of Wyoming

One of the most notorious massacre stories originated in Pennsylvania's Wyoming Valley, where on July 3, 1778, British forces inflicted a severe defeat on the Americans. An 1833 monument to the event reflected the viewpoint that had existed since the battle; the marker honored the Americans who fought against "a combined British, Tory and Indian force" that left a path of "wide-spread havoc, desolation, and ruin" in the wake of their "savage and bloody footsteps."[20] The fact that the British force consisted of Loyalist rangers and allied Indians, both groups being particularly detested by the Revolutionaries, reinforced the tales of a massacre, although, as Joseph R. Fischer noted, "little evidence exists to support the stories."[21]

On July 3, 1778, a combined force of Indians and Loyalists attacked and defeated American troops in Pennsylvania's Wyoming Valley. Americans charged their enemies with committing numerous atrocities, as depicted here. Note the Indian scalping a fallen American and the Loyalist Rangers wielding tomahawks to indicate their savagery. As with other alleged atrocities, evidence of systematic, intentional brutality is scant. *Massacre at Wyoming*, oil painting by Alonzo Chappel, 1858. Chicago Historical Society.

---

20. O'Keefe, "Monuments."

21. Joseph R. Fischer, *A Well-Executed Failure: The Sullivan Campaign Against the Iroquois, July–September 1779* (Columbia: University of South Carolina Press, 1997), 28.

Even aspects of the battle not associated with the alleged massacre have been the subject of disagreement among historians. One source states that the attacking force numbered 800 men, including Colonel John Butler's Loyalist rangers; a large contingent of allied Iroquois, mostly of the Seneca nation; and a small number of British regular troops. Another historian provided a lower figure of 450–500 rangers and Indians. There is general agreement that the Americans numbered 400 militiamen, and some accounts mention an additional 60 Continental troops. Adding to the confusion is that while John Butler commanded the British attackers, Colonel Zebulon Butler led the Americans, so it is sometimes uncertain which Butler was being discussed in the sources.[22]

The course of events is more easily clarified. John Butler's force left Canada to strike at the rich agricultural lands of the Wyoming Valley that provided food for American forces. Forewarned, the Americans took refuge in forts and blockhouses. Butler surrounded two blockhouses on July 3, demanded their surrender, and took the occupants prisoner. He then marched to the largest post, Forty Fort, where his surrender demand was refused. Butler opted not to risk a costly attack, instead deciding to burn the captured blockhouses and feign a retreat, hoping to lure the Americans out of their defenses. The Americans fell into the trap. Four hundred militiamen and 60 Continentals marched out of the fort and into an ambush, where they were quickly overwhelmed. The fleeing Americans were pursued by the Indians and rangers. Most accounts agree that 227 Americans were killed in the battle and subsequent pursuit, and only 5 were taken prisoner, apparently not including those who surrendered in the blockhouses and Forty Fort, which capitulated after the battle. One Indian and 2 Loyalists were killed and 8 wounded.[23]

Stories of a brutal and deliberate massacre immediately began to circulate. According to one account, an American militiaman fell to his knees in front of his Loyalist brother, but his pleas for mercy were ignored, and his brother shot him in the head. Another tale described a woman of mixed Indian-European ancestry who had accompanied the Senecas, coldly directing the execution of 16 captives. American newspapers quickly spread the horrible tale of settlers "scalped and butchered," Loyalists, Indians, and British troops "committing the most horrid murders on defenceless farmers, women and children," and estimating the death toll at 2,000 people.[24]

Loyalist colonel John Butler saw the matter in a different light, reporting that "not a single person has been hurt of the Inhabitants, but such as were in arms."

---

22. Fischer, *Well-Executed Failure*, 27; Barbara Alice Mann, *George Washington's War on Native Americans* (Westport, CT: Praeger Publishers, 2005), 16.

23. Fischer, *Well-Executed Failure*, 27; Mann, *Washington's War on Native Americans*, 16; Isabel Thompson Kelsay, *Joseph Brant, 1743–1807: Man of Two Worlds* (Syracuse, NY: Syracuse University Press, 1984), 219; Robert G. Parkinson, *The Common Cause: Creating Race and Nation in the American Revolution* (Chapel Hill: University of North Carolina Press, 2016), 411, 412.

24. Fischer, *Well-Executed Failure*, 27–28; Parkinson, *Common Cause*, 412–13.

Many historians have agreed. One declared that "contrary to American propaganda, the [Indians] killed no noncombatants that day." Another noted that "little evidence exists to support the [atrocity] stories" while conceding that during the pursuit of the fleeing Americans, the Indians killed "nearly every soldier who fell into their hands," adding that "this no-quarter brand of war was not unusual and was practiced by both sides" on the frontier.[25] Thus, while the consensus among historians is that no massacre occurred in the Battle of Wyoming, the lurid details of slaughter, their credibility reinforced by the actual scalping that took place, continue to be repeated. For example, a website focused on Pennsylvania's history describes the battle as "the 'surpassing horror of the American Revolution' because of the brutal and horrific acts committed by Iroquois Confederation warriors and their British and Loyalist allies."[26]

Baylor's Massacre

A year after the Battle of Paoli, General Grey was involved in another alleged massacre in New Jersey. In September 1778, the British commander-in-chief, General Sir Henry Clinton, dispatched a party of 5,000 men from the British lines around New York City to gather supplies for his army. General Charles, Lord Cornwallis led the expedition and had orders to eliminate any American forces he might encounter during the operation. On September 27, Loyalists informed Cornwallis that Lieutenant Colonel George Baylor's 3rd Regiment of Continental Light Dragoons was camped outside the town of Old Tappan in present-day Bergen County.[27]

That night Cornwallis detached Grey with several hundred infantrymen and fifty cavalry troopers to strike Baylor's force. Grey marched along the Hackensack River and approached the American camp at 3:00 a.m. on September 28. He decided to employ the same tactics he had used at Paoli and ordered his troops to attack with bayonets. The British encountered a guard of twelve men near Baylor's headquarters and overcame them before they could give any warning. Charging among and into the houses and barns where the Americans were sleeping, the British killed sixteen Americans, wounded another sixteen, and captured thirty-eight. Baylor was wounded and taken prisoner. All the American horses and equipment were seized by the British, and only about thirty-five of Baylor's troops escaped.[28]

The initial American report indicated that Baylor had not taken adequate precautions to secure his camp. General Israel Putnam informed George Washington that Baylor's regiment had been taken completely by surprise, noting that "they had only

25. Fischer, *Well-Executed Failure*, 27, 28; Mann, *Washington's War on Native Americans*, 16.

26. "Battle of Wyoming Historical Marker: Beyond the Marker," Explore PA History, http://explorepahistory.com (accessed Jan. 4, 2020).

27. Nelson, *Sir Charles Grey*, 66–67.

28. Nelson, 67–68.

one man out to Reconnoiter," who was captured before he could give the alarm.[29] Some accounts indicated, however, that a massacre did occur. Americans made the accusation, as might be expected. However, this time they received some support from British sources, including Colonel Charles Stuart, one of Grey's subordinates, who wrote, "the credit that might have been due to the Corps" for their victory "is entirely buried in the barbarity of their behaviour."[30] The massacre story became a staple of local history throughout the nineteenth century; in 1872, a New Jersey newspaper published an article based in part on earlier oral accounts relating how "Grey burst through the door on a moonless autumn night" and how "unarmed American dragoons, barely roused from sleep, had been bayoneted." These and similar stories are commonly found online.[31] Grey's biographer, Paul David Nelson, accepted the accuracy of that allegation, writing that the British turned a deaf ear to "unarmed" Americans who "asked for quarter," with the result that "a few Americans were unnecessarily slaughtered."[32] Spring rendered a harsher judgment, citing the incident as "the best example" that British soldiers' "ruthlessness was sometimes not spontaneous but was instead (allegedly) put into effect on the direct orders of officers."[33] If, as is probable, "a few" Americans were killed without justification, an atrocity was committed, albeit on a small scale. It is obvious from the number of prisoners taken that no systematic slaughter occurred.

The Cherry Valley Massacre

Four months after striking the Wyoming Valley settlements, Loyalists and Indians targeted the New York frontier town of Cherry Valley for attack. The settlement was protected by a fort and a garrison of 450 men under Colonel Ichabod Alden. A party of over 600 Loyalist rangers and Iroquois Indians under Captain Walter Butler and Mohawk leader Joseph Brant launched their assault on November 11, 1778. Despite having received warnings of their approach, Alden took no precautions. He was away from the fort when the attack began and hurried to his post upon hearing gunfire, only to be killed on the way. An effort by the rangers and Indians to storm the fort failed, and the attackers withdrew and sacked the town, destroying every building except the fort and killing or capturing many of the residents. After a second assault

29. Israel Putnam to George Washington, September 28, 1778, in *The Papers of George Washington: Revolutionary War Series*, ed. Theodore J. Crackel (Charlottesville: University of Virginia Press, 2008), 17:165.

30. Nelson, *Sir Charles Grey*, 68–69.

31. Kevin Wright, "Overkill: Revolutionary War Reminiscences of River Vale," Bergen County Historical Society, http://www.bergencountyhistory.org (accessed Jan. 4, 2020; article since removed from site).

32. Nelson, *Sir Charles Grey*, 69.

33. Spring, *Zeal and Bayonets*, 233.

on the fort failed on November 12, the raiding party left, having killed an estimated 16 soldiers and 32 civilians and taken 14 soldiers and 40 civilians prisoner. Butler released the captives when his force departed.[34] He gave them a letter to deliver to the American commander in the region, General Philip Schuyler, stating that he did everything possible "'to restrain the Indians . . . but they were to[o] much enraged by the destruction' of Oquaga."[35]

There is solid evidence that some Americans were murdered during the two-day raid. Walter Butler wrote that he "could not prevent some of them [women and children] falling unhappy Victims to the Fury of the Savages" and later claimed that the Iroquois were angered at having been falsely accused of murdering noncombatants at Wyoming. Brant intervened to prevent several killings. Some reports indicated that the Loyalist rangers also killed civilians. Several historians, however, have noted Butler's statement and argued that the Indians' execution of civilians was in retaliation for earlier American attacks against the Iroquois towns of Unadilla, Tioga, and Oquaga, where many Indian noncombatants were alleged to have been murdered by the Revolutionaries. The inaction of the American commanders was also criticized. Butler wrote that the fort's garrison "remained Spectators of our Depredations," and one historian charged that those officers were "neglectful to the point of mindlessness."[36]

Clearly, noncombatants were killed by Indians and probably by Loyalist rangers. Some of the victims were possibly Loyalists; Brant, for example, was a friend of Robert Wells and his family, all of whom were killed in the attack. Accounts quickly circulated in the press denouncing the British and their allies for "inhuman barbarities," including a story attributed to an officer who claimed to have watched as men were scalped and infants and women were murdered and mutilated.[37] Captain Benjamin Warren, who was in the fort, praised the "spirit and alertness" with which the soldiers repulsed the first attack, noting that twelve soldiers, in addition to Colonel Alden, were killed in the fighting and nearly twenty captured. On November 13, Warren reported that "we sent out parties after the enemy withdrew" to gather the dead and assist the wounded. "Such a shocking sight my eyes never beheld before of savage and brutal barbarity," he wrote, stating that a woman and four children lay dead together, "mangled, scalpt," and dismembered, while another family had twelve members killed, four of them burned in their house.[38]

---

34. Mann, *Washington's War on Native Americans*, 23–24; Kelsay, *Joseph Brant*, 230, 232; Parkinson, *Common Cause*, 421.

35. Parkinson, *Common Cause*, 421–22.

36. Mann, *Washington's War on Native Americans*, 24–25; Kelsay, *Joseph Brant*, 230, 232; Parkinson, *Common Cause*, 421, 422.

37. Parkinson, *Common Cause*, 421, 423.

38. "Diary of Captain Benjamin Warren," New River Notes, https://www.newrivernotes.com (accessed Jan. 4, 2020).

Undoubtedly a massacre took place at Cherry Valley, even if the Indians' violence toward noncombatants was, in the opinion of the Iroquois, legitimate retaliation for American atrocities committed against their people. Such brutality may have been commonly practiced by both sides in frontier warfare, as Joseph R. Fischer observed, yet that does not absolve either Americans or their opponents from moral responsibility for resorting to excessive violence.[39]

"Bloody" Tarleton at the Waxhaws

The most infamous and consequential of the alleged British atrocities occurred on May 29, 1780, at the Waxhaws in South Carolina. The brief battle, involving less than 700 soldiers, ended in an overwhelming British victory that was almost immediately labeled a massacre by Americans. Lieutenant Colonel Banastre Tarleton emerged with a reputation as a murderous

British Lieutenant Colonel Banastre Tarleton, commander of the British Legion, was a highly effective officer who won several victories over American forces. He was accused of ordering the massacre of Americans who tried to surrender at the Battle of Waxhaws on May 29, 1780, earning the nicknames "Bloody Tarleton" and "Butcher." However, there is little evidence to support claims that Tarleton deliberately perpetrated such atrocities. *Sir Banastre Tarleton*, oil painting by Joshua Reynolds, 1782. National Gallery, London.

villain, and Revolutionaries eager to avenge the slaughter of their fellows responded with merciless attacks on their enemies, provoking a cycle of retaliatory violence that made the war in the South particularly vicious.

---

39. Fischer, *Well-Executed Failure*, 27.

In late March 1780, Colonel Abraham Buford led a newly recruited regiment of 350 Virginia Continental troops to reinforce the Americans defending Charleston. By the time this force approached Charleston in early May, the British had isolated the city's garrison, and Buford withdrew northward, halting at Camden on May 26. The next day, British lieutenant general Charles, Earl Cornwallis, learned of Buford's position and ordered his cavalry commander, Tarleton, to defeat the Continentals or drive them from South Carolina. Tarleton set out with 230 cavalry and infantry of his British Legion and 40 troopers from the 17th Light Dragoons. Buford left Camden that same day.[40]

On May 29, near the end of a forced march that would cover 105 miles in fifty-four hours, Tarleton learned that the Americans were only a short distance ahead and sent an officer to demand Buford's surrender, offering the same terms given to the defenders of Charleston, who had capitulated on May 12. Buford refused the demand without halting his column. The Americans covered another two miles before Tarleton reached their position and overwhelmed a small rear guard. The Continental infantry formed a line of battle across and east of the road they were using; Buford ordered his wagons, artillery, cavalry, and militia to continue their retreat. Tarleton deployed his infantry on his flanks with his cavalry in the center while he took position on the left of his line. At 3:30 in the afternoon, the British charged and almost instantly overran the American defenders. About the time the British attack began, Buford sent an officer with a white flag to surrender, but the officer returned with the message that the offer had been refused.[41]

According to American accounts, what followed was a bloody slaughter of the Continental troops, who were sabered and bayoneted as they threw down their weapons and begged for quarter. The casualties seem to support this version of events: Tarleton reported that 113 Americans were killed, 150 wounded, and 53 captured, against British losses of 5 killed and 12 wounded.[42] Buford's report, written on June 2, stated that many of his men were killed and injured "after they had lain down their arms."[43] Similar stories spread rapidly among the Virginia and North Carolina troops who were nearby and met the Americans fleeing from the battle, and soon circulated throughout the Carolinas.[44]

News of the alleged massacre galvanized Americans, many of whom had lost hope in the Revolutionary cause and were ready to accept British rule after the disaster at

---

40. Jim Piecuch, *The Blood Be Upon Your Head: Tarleton and the Myth of Buford's Massacre* (Lugoff, SC: Southern Campaigns of the American Revolution Press, 2010), 11, 14–15, 16.

41. Piecuch, *Blood Be Upon Your Head*, 18–19, 21–22, 23.

42. Banastre Tarleton, *A History of the Campaigns of 1780 and 1781, in the Southern Provinces of North America* (London: T. Cadell, 1787), 84.

43. Abraham Buford to Virginia Assembly, June 2, 1780, Thomas Addis Emmet Collection, New York Public Library.

44. Piecuch, *Blood Be Upon Your Head*, 26, 37.

Charleston. South Carolinian Joseph Gaston typified this reaction. He wrote that he and his friends had been considering taking the oath of allegiance to Britain when they learned of "the shocking massacre of Colonel Bradford's [Buford's] men, by Tarleton," whereupon they all swore to continue to fight and never surrender.[45] The massacre story thus served as valuable propaganda to revitalize American resistance in the South. As one historian observed, "Tarleton's cutting down of unarmed men was a ready-made atrocity story" for the American press.[46] The story of Americans driven to resist the savage British has retained its power after more than 200 years; in the film, *The Patriot*, the peaceful South Carolinian Benjamin Martin, portrayed by Mel Gibson, takes up arms after witnessing atrocities committed by British colonel William Tavington, a character based on Banastre Tarleton.[47]

The story of the massacre, reinforced by early historians of the Revolution, grew in credibility until it became accepted fact. Dr. David Ramsay, writing in 1785, described how "the British legion was directed to charge men who had laid down their arms. In consequence of this order, the unresisting Americans praying for quarters, were chopped in pieces."[48] Loyalist Charles Stedman wrote a decade later that at the Waxhaws, "the virtue of humanity was totally forgot," though he was not present at the battle and elsewhere in his history expressed contempt for Tarleton.[49]

Further confirmation of the horrid atrocity came from two individuals who claimed to have been eyewitnesses. Forty years after the battle, Dr. Robert Brownfield's account was published as an appendix to a biography of Francis Marion, and Major Henry Bowyer's story, which had been written much earlier, appeared in an 1888 volume.[50] These detailed confirmations of British barbarity became the foundation for subsequent historians' recounting of the battle. John Richard Alden, Russell F. Weigley, John Buchanan, and Tarleton biographer Robert D. Bass all denounced Tarleton for his murderous behavior.[51] Only a few historians differed in opinion. Sir John Fortescue, in his history of the British army published in 1911, praised Tarleton's victory, declaring

---

45. Joseph Gaston, "A Reminiscence of the War of the Revolution, in South Carolina," *Historical Magazine, Third Series*, vol. 2, no. 2 (August 1873), 90.

46. Parkinson, *Common Cause*, 499.

47. *The Patriot*, directed by Roland Emmerich (Columbia Pictures, 2000).

48. David Ramsay, *The History of the Revolution of South-Carolina, from a British Province to an Independent State*, 2 vols. (Trenton, NJ: Isaac Collins, 1785), 2:109–10.

49. Charles Stedman, *The History of the Origin, Progress, and Termination of the American War*, 2 vols. (London: privately published, 1794), 2:193, 325.

50. Brownfield, "Recollection," Appendix, 2–5; Frederick Johnston, "Sketch of Colonel Henry Bowyer," in *Memorials of Old Virginia Clerks*, by Frederick Johnston (Lynchburg, VA: J. P. Bell, 1888), 92–93.

51. John Richard Alden, *The South in the American Revolution* (Baton Rouge: Louisiana State University Press, 1976), 242; John Buchanan, *The Road to Guilford Courthouse: The American Revolution in the Carolinas* (New York: John Wiley & Sons, 1997), 84; Russell F. Weigley, *The Partisan War: The South Carolina Campaigns of 1780–1782* (Columbia: University of South Carolina Press, 1970), 7;

that it "brilliantly closed an extraordinary march."[52] Don Higginbotham more cautiously wrote that descriptions of the battle "are hopelessly confused" and conceded that Tarleton "may not have been a butcher" but "was ruthless."[53] John S. Pancake was also cautious in his judgment, stating that the engagement at the Waxhaws gave Tarleton "a notoriety that he may not have altogether deserved" and noting that the British commander's actions in sending for surgeons from the towns of Camden and Charlotte to treat wounded Americans were "hardly consistent" with accounts of a deliberate massacre.[54]

A close examination of surviving documents, many of which were not easily accessible to earlier historians, reveals a combination of facts and inconsistencies that sheds doubt on the accuracy of the massacre story. Buford's assertion that a massacre occurred cannot be considered reliable because one of his soldiers reported that the American commander "Broke from them" and fled the field soon after his line was broken. He was in no position to witness the aftermath.[55] But one part of his letter was evidently accurate. Buford wrote that when his men "gave way" before the British charge, he "sent a flag to the commanding officer to offer a surrender which was refused in a very rude manner."[56] Clearly, Buford sent out a single offer of surrender, and the bearer of the white flag returned to report that it had been rejected.

This point conflicts with the two accounts most heavily relied upon to portray the battle as a massacre. Brownfield, whose version of the engagement was published in 1821, wrote that Ensign John Cruit was the bearer of the flag and that when he advanced, he "was instantly cut down"; however, Cruit survived the battle.[57] If Cruit had been wounded without making contact with British officers, he could not have returned to Buford to report a "rude" refusal. Henry Bowyer, an officer on Buford's staff, told an equally incredible story. He insisted that Buford had ordered him to carry the flag and that he had protested, as he might be hit by musket fire. Buford insisted, and Bowyer rode forward with a handkerchief on the point of his sword. He

Robert D. Bass, *The Green Dragoon: The Lives of Banastre Tarleton and Mary Robinson* (New York: Henry Holt & Co., 1957), 80–83.

52. Sir John Fortescue, *The War of Independence: The British Army in North America, 1775–1783* (repr., London: Greenhill Books, 2001), 169.

53. Don Higginbotham, *The War of American Independence: Military Attitudes, Policies, and Practice, 1763–1789* (Boston, MA: Northeastern University Press, 1981), 361.

54. John S. Pancake, *This Destructive War: The British Campaign in the Carolinas, 1780–1782* (Tuscaloosa: University of Alabama Press, 1985), 71.

55. Charles Harmon (Harman), Pension Application W7645, February 8, 1834, National Archives, Washington, DC.

56. Buford to Virginia Assembly, June 2, 1780.

57. Brownfield, "Recollection," Appendix, 2–5.

was attacked by British troops, and his horse was wounded though he escaped unhurt "to a place of security"; he made no mention of returning to Buford.[58]

Given Buford's statement, the soldier who carried the white flag could not have been either Cruit or Bowyer. Bowyer's account also contains other inaccuracies. For example, he identified British major Archibald McArthur as a participant, although neither McArthur nor his regiment was present. Nor does Bowyer's description of the danger of traversing the field while exposed to dangerous musket fire match other accounts. Major Charles Cochrane, commanding the Legion infantry on the British right, reported that he ordered his men to rely on their bayonets, and they advanced without firing.[59] Furthermore, the American troops had time to fire only one volley during the British charge; any firing afterward was sporadic, yet Bowyer's account implies that both sides engaged in sustained firing, something certainly not true of the saber-wielding British cavalry.

The inaccuracies in the Brownfield and Bowyer accounts render them unreliable for historians in presenting an accurate depiction of events and thus call into question the massacre tale in its entirety. The only eyewitness evidence is Tarleton's own account, in which he noted that while leading the charge on the British left, his horse was killed, and he was pinned beneath it. Thinking that their commander had been slain, some of his men grew angry and responded with "a vindictive asperity not easily restrained."[60] The implication is that some of the British troops near Tarleton deliberately killed Americans in retaliation for the perceived death of their colonel. This was an atrocity, but nothing near the scale of the systematic slaughter of prisoners and wounded soldiers that has been generally described. Furthermore, Tarleton put a stop to his men's actions as soon as he was extricated from his horse.

The question of what happened to the actual American bearing the white flag cannot be answered definitively. Neither Tarleton nor his second-in-command, Cochrane, reported seeing the flag. They were on the left and right of the line, respectively, unusual positions since commanders in that era usually took posts behind the center of their position. Furthermore, both officers advanced into battle with their men, demonstrating great courage but giving up effective command of troops outside their immediate vicinity. We can surmise that Buford would have expected Tarleton to be at the center and rear of the British position and that he would have directed the flag bearer there. The soldier would then have encountered either Captain Erasmus Corbett or Captain David Kinloch, as both were in that vicinity, but neither had the authority to accept a surrender. That would explain Buford's statement that the flag bearer returned with a refusal of the surrender offer.

---

58. Johnston, "Sketch of Bowyer," 92–93.

59. Report of Capt. Charles Cochrane, enclosed in Lord George Germain to Jeffery Amherst, November 30, 1780, Jeffery Amherst Papers, UK War Office Series 34/128/37, David Library of the American Revolution, Washington Crossing, PA, microfilm.

60. Tarleton, *History of the Campaigns*, 31.

Finally, as with the alleged massacres previously discussed, the question of American command competence must be addressed. American brigadier general William Moultrie, who had been captured at Charleston and had access to the prisoners taken at the Waxhaws, never described the battle as a massacre in his postwar memoirs. Instead, he compared it to similar European engagements where cavalry attacked and defeated infantry forces and inflicted disproportionate casualties. He also pointed out "capital mistakes" made by Buford. First, Moultrie noted that Buford ordered his troops to hold their fire until the attacking British were within ten yards, too close to allow them to reload and fire a second volley before the cavalry broke their line. Moultrie also suggested that Buford should have formed his soldiers into a hollow square with the supply wagons for protection and the artillery inside the position. Had he done so, Moultrie asserted, "the enemy could have made no impression upon him: nay, Tarleton would never have attacked him."[61] Matthew Spring came to the same conclusion.[62] Instead, Buford ordered his wagons and artillery to continue retreating, depriving his men of defensive barricades and the supporting fire of two artillery pieces. Nor did Buford order his men to fix bayonets to their muskets, a measure that would have deterred both horses and the troopers on them from making a close approach.

Buford's mistakes, in conjunction with the mortal injury to Tarleton's horse that caused some of his soldiers to retaliate in the erroneous belief that their commander had been killed, resulted in some Americans being killed unnecessarily. However, the number was undoubtedly a small percentage of the total casualties suffered by Buford's command. The systematic murder of helpless men so often described in accounts of the battle never actually occurred. But the execution of British and Loyalist troops by Americans in retaliation for this mythical massacre was very real during the remainder of the war in the South. Revolutionaries frequently shouted "Tarleton's quarter" as they killed fleeing or captured enemies.[63]

Sexual Assaults

Accusations that British troops had sexually assaulted American women were commonplace throughout the war. A Loyalist leveled the first of these charges after the Battle of Long Island in August 1776; he asserted that General Howe's soldiers had raped women without distinguishing between rebels and Loyalists.[64] Captain John

---

61. William Moultrie, *Memoirs of the American Revolution, So Far as It Related to the States of North and South Carolina, and Georgia*, 2 vols. (New York: David Longworth, 1802), 2:205–8.

62. Spring, *Zeal and Bayonets*, 271–72.

63. Pancake, *This Destructive War*, 71.

64. Holger Hoock, *Scars of Independence: America's Violent Birth* (New York: Crown Publishing, 2017), 115.

Peebles of the 42nd Regiment confirmed that such assaults had occurred, writing of an incident involving a "poor old man and his daughter in Long Island" that "was very bad indeed."[65]

In the fall of 1776, as British forces pursued the retreating American army across New Jersey, women in that state began reporting that they had been raped by British troops. The accounts were so numerous that the Pennsylvania Council of Safety began collecting them; they were published in Philadelphia newspapers in December. Among the incidents was the rape of a young Princeton woman by two British cavalrymen who ordered her to guide them through a barn where they claimed rebel troops were hiding; once inside, the pair assaulted her. The woman's name was not revealed to protect her reputation, but other women, such as Mary Campbell and Rebekkah Christopher, testified that they had been raped repeatedly by several British soldiers; Christopher declared that her ten-year-old daughter was similarly assaulted. Another victim, thirteen-year-old Abigail Palmer, stated that she and two other girls had been held captive and for "three Days successively" were raped "by a great number of soldiers belonging to the British army." When one of the girls screamed, the soldiers ordered her to be silent, threatening to stab their bayonets into her eyes if she did not comply.[66]

Such reports were so numerous that in addition to Pennsylvania officials, the government of New Jersey and the Continental Congress also began investigating the charges. They found that the rapes were not confined to younger women and girls—one victim was almost seventy years old—and that British officers, as well as enlisted men, perpetrated sexual assaults. In one instance, a New Jersey man killed an officer he found raping his daughter, only to be wounded in turn by two other British officers who were present.[67]

General Howe dismissed complaints of rape as fabricated for propaganda purposes, claiming that he was aware of only one case in which the victim had declined to press charges against the offender. However, Captain Peebles noted on December 24, 1776, that a soldier condemned to death for rape was pardoned "at the intercession of the injured party," adding that "there have been other shocking abuses of that nature that have not come to public notice" and observed that "hard is the fate of many who suffer indiscriminately in a civil war."[68] However, the British army did prosecute and punish troops accused of rape, but not to the extent that they punished other breaches of discipline, and convictions were difficult to obtain since many American women did not risk entering the army's camp to inform officers of the assaults, nor were they likely to testify at courts-martial.[69]

---

65. David Hackett Fischer, *Washington's Crossing* (New York: Oxford University Press, 2004), 179.

66. Fischer, *Washington's Crossing*, 178, 510n.

67. Fischer, 178–79.

68. Fischer, 179.

69. Hoock, *Scars of Independence*, 171, 173.

Knowing they were unlikely to be punished, soldiers continued to rape women throughout the war. For example, when the British raided New Haven, Connecticut, in July 1779, Mercy Otis Warren of Massachusetts learned that the troops had committed numerous sexual assaults. She termed these "barbarous abuse of the hapless females" who became "sacrifices to the wanton and riotous appetites of the soldiers."[70]

American leaders used sexual assaults by British troops to foment outrage against their enemy. "Rape was an extraordinary political tool for the Patriots," one historian noted.[71] Washington supplied accounts of rape to congressional investigators while admonishing his own soldiers that "it is expected that humanity and tenderness to women and children will distinguish brave Americans, contending for liberty, from mercenary ravagers, whether British or Hessians."[72] Yet this did not stop American troops, both Continentals and militia, from committing acts of rape. However, far fewer such incidents were reported, primarily in Loyalist newspapers. There are indications that some Continental soldiers were convicted of rape and whipped for their crimes, but the records provide few details. The relatively lax attitude of British officers toward sexual assault, and the silence surrounding cases involving American troops, probably reflects eighteenth-century beliefs that rape was an inevitable, if regrettable, consequence of war.[73]

The British Prison Ships

Although most accounts of British cruelty toward American troops on the battlefield were either exaggerations or outright fabrications, there is well-documented evidence of a far more serious atrocity: British mistreatment of American prisoners of war. Over the course of the war, the British captured more than 30,000 prisoners on the battlefields of North America and at sea.[74] Most of these men were confined under harsh conditions that resulted in the deaths of more than half of the captives.

The official British policy toward prisoners was established at the beginning of the war by Lord George Germain, the secretary of state for the American Department and the royal minister responsible for directing military operations against the rebels. He declared that anyone "seized or taken in the act of high treason, committed in any of the colonies, or on the high seas" would be kept in custody without trial unless the king's cabinet altered the policy. Germain explained that "the revolted provinces not being on the foot of a foreign enemy their prisoners are not deemed prisoners of

---

70. Rosemarie Zagarri, *A Woman's Dilemma: Mercy Otis Warren and the American Revolution* (Wheeling, IL: Harlan Davidson, 1995), 146.

71. Hoock, *Scars of Independence*, 166.

72. Hoock, 168.

73. Hoock, 171, 173.

74. Burrows, *Forgotten Patriots*, 200–201.

war in England but are committed for high treason upon proof of their having borne arms against the King," thus making the captives ineligible for parole or exchange because they were not classified as prisoners of war. Historian Carl P. Borick noted that in addition to these instructions, the treatment of prisoners was affected by "the military situation, local conditions, and the attitudes of British leaders toward captured Americans."[75]

To handle the anticipated prisoners, General Howe appointed Joshua Loring, a Loyalist refugee from Boston, as commissary general of prisoners in March 1776. Howe's victories in the New York campaign the following summer and fall resulted in the capture of thousands of Americans, leaving Loring with the problem of finding secure places to hold them.[76] He and other British officials decided to separate captured officers from enlisted men, recognizing that it would be far easier to recruit the latter into British service if they were away from their officers' influence.[77]

As prisoners arrived in New York City during the fall of 1776, Loring found insufficient buildings to house them. The approximately 1,000 enlisted men in British custody were confined in a church and two sugar refineries, known as "sugar houses," with 700 crammed into the Old North Dutch Church. One prisoner in the church recalled that the window shutters were kept closed, and they were fed only green apples for ten days before finally being issued bread. Providing food for the captives was an ongoing problem for the British, even though the standard practice was to issue rations for prisoners amounting to two-thirds of the quantity provided to British soldiers. Howe's troops and the sailors in the Royal Navy required the immense quantity of thirty-two tons of food per day, far more than could be obtained locally in British-occupied areas. The shortfall had to be made up by shipments from Britain, a long journey subject to disruption by bad weather that often resulted in supply shortages. Lack of provisions for British troops resulted in further reductions in prisoners' rations, leaving captives subject to malnutrition and, therefore, more susceptible to scurvy, dysentery, typhus, and other diseases.[78]

By the end of November, the number of prisoners in New York had swelled to over 5,000, and Loring resorted to another method of housing them. Two older ships, the *Whitby* and *Grosvenor*, were anchored in the harbor and stripped of their armament, masts, and other equipment. Two hundred-fifty prisoners were put aboard the former and 500 on the latter; both were eventually berthed at Brooklyn's Wallabout Bay. The vessels were so crowded that some Americans suffocated. Those who survived were hungry, lacked the ability to bathe or procure clean clothing, and frequently

---

75. Carl P. Borick, *Relieve Us of This Burthen: American Prisoners of War in the Revolutionary South, 1780–1782* (Columbia: University of South Carolina Press, 2012), xi.

76. Burrows, *Forgotten Patriots*, 10, 11.

77. Burrows, 13.

78. Burrows, 19–20, 23–24.

became sick without access to medical care. As a result, between 2,000 and 2,500 prisoners died by the end of 1776.[79]

William Slade of Connecticut, captured when the British took Fort Washington on November 16, recorded his experiences aboard the *Grosvenor*. He was placed on the ship on December 2, and on December 14, he wrote, "Deaths prevail among us, also hunger and naked." He noted that the weather was growing colder. "Sorrow increases," he observed two days later. On December 22, he recorded: "Last night nothing but grones all night of sick and dying. . . . sickness prevails fast. Deaths multiply." Twenty men enlisted with the British the next day and left the ship. Slade added that smallpox was spreading among the prisoners. Three men from his battalion died during the night of December 26–27, and smallpox continued to spread rapidly. Fortunately for Slade, he was removed from the ship the next day and confined on shore.[80]

Actual atrocities, in the form of unnecessarily cruel treatment of captured American soldiers confined in harsh conditions aboard prison ships in the harbors of New York, Charleston, and Savannah, have received far less attention than the alleged massacres on the battlefield. The illustration incorrectly depicts a British soldier on guard duty among the prisoners; British guards rarely ventured into the crowded prisoners' quarters for fear of exposing themselves to disease. *Interior of the Old* Jersey *Prison Ship, in the Revolutionary War*, engraving by Edward Bookhout from a drawing by Felix Octavius Carr Darley, 1855. Library of Congress.

79. Burrows, 50, 52, 56, 64.

80. "William Slade's Account of a Prison Ship," in Commager and Morris, *Spirit of Seventy-Six*, 2:855–56.

In March 1777, Parliament passed a law proposed by the king's chief minister, Lord North, to regulate the treatment of captured Americans, but it brought no relief. Basic judicial rights were denied to American prisoners while making them subject to prosecution for treason. Those taken at sea were liable to be prosecuted for piracy as well. North justified the harsh law on the grounds that tough measures were required to subdue the rebellion.[81]

British victories on land and the capture of American vessels at sea continued to bring numerous prisoners to New York, resulting in the conversion of many more vessels to prison ships, including the *Jersey*, which became the most notorious. The majority were moored in Wallabout Bay. Aboard, conditions for the captives remained miserable, marked by overcrowding, poor sanitation, insufficient food, contaminated drinking water, and diseases that were a natural consequence of such situations. In contrast, officers enjoyed far better treatment. Many were placed in private homes on Long Island, where they had adequate food and were free to move about.[82]

For the enlisted captives, there was one rapid route out of the prison ships: enlistment in the British army or navy. Recruiters regularly visited the prisoners and urged them to join the royal forces. Some did, in many cases seeking an opportunity to desert later. Most, however, stood firm and refused to enter British service, especially in the early years of the war.[83]

American officials reached an agreement with the British in November 1777 that allowed the shipment of supplies to the prisoners in New York. During the following three months, large quantities of clothing and blankets were sent to alleviate the captives' distress. Meanwhile, George Washington had been attempting to negotiate a prisoner exchange. Howe agreed to have representatives of the two armies meet at Germantown, Pennsylvania, in March 1778. The Continental Congress, however, tried to impose conditions that threatened to sabotage a potential agreement, insisting that Loyalists who had served with the British be subject to harsh penalties and that the British pay in gold and silver for the cost of maintaining their prisoners held by the Americans. Washington finally convinced Congress to moderate its demands, but in mid-April, after two weeks of fruitless discussion, the British declared that General Howe had no authority to make agreements with rebels, and the talks ended.[84]

In October 1779, David Sproat, a Philadelphia Loyalist, was appointed commissary of naval prisoners. He worked in conjunction with Loring, who was widely blamed for the harsh treatment of the captives, and in American eyes, Sproat was even worse than his counterpart. During the following extremely harsh winter, despite no food shortages in New York, prisoners died in large numbers from the cold and

81. Burrows, *Forgotten Patriots*, 80.

82. Burrows, 92–93, 98.

83. Burrows, 112–13.

84. Burrows, 118, 125–27.

malnutrition. According to one account, only 250 of 600 men held on the ironically named prison ship *Good Hope* survived the winter. In March 1780, the enraged survivors managed to set the vessel on fire and destroy it. Their action, however, only caused Sproat to resort to harsher treatment.[85]

The British capture of Charleston, South Carolina, on May 12, 1780, brought 2,861 Continental enlisted men into captivity. Lieutenant General Sir Henry Clinton, commander of the British army in North America, considered these men valuable because they might be exchanged for British prisoners in American hands or enlisted into British service. As had been done in New York, officers were separated from enlisted men to facilitate recruitment. The former were quartered in empty buildings in Charleston and at nearby Haddrell's Point and Mount Pleasant; the latter were confined to barracks in the city. Also, as in New York, Continental officers received far better treatment than enlisted men.[86]

Initially, the British treated the Charleston prisoners well, issuing more generous rations than the Americans had received during the siege. Some captives enlisted in the royal forces, but others took advantage of their occasional ability to leave the barracks and escaped. Lord Cornwallis estimated that 500 Continentals had done so by the end of June 1780. The British responded by increasing the number of guards at the barracks and barring prisoners from leaving their place of confinement, warning that anyone who attempted to escape would be put aboard a prison ship. Nevertheless, the escapes continued.[87]

In mid-August, the British won another major battle at Camden that brought hundreds more prisoners to Charleston, where the commandant, Lieutenant Colonel Nisbet Balfour, struggled to find space for them. He encouraged officers to step up recruiting efforts among the captives, which produced a substantial number of enlistments but did not solve the problem. Clinton hoped to exchange the Charleston prisoners for the soldiers of General John Burgoyne's army who had been captured at Saratoga in October 1777. Both the Continental Congress and Washington refused, however. Washington admitted that such an exchange would remove large numbers of Americans from the rigors of confinement yet argued against it because he believed the British would receive the greater benefit. The exchange "would throw into the Enemy's hands a very respectable permanent augmentation to their present force," he wrote, while many of the freed Americans whose enlistments had expired would return home. With no exchange possible and the strength of the British garrison in Charleston weakened by illness brought on by the late summer heat, Balfour followed the example of British officials in New York and ordered the Americans aboard prison

---

85. Burrows, 148–49, 150–51.

86. Borick, *Relieve Us*, 3, 4–5, 46.

87. Borick, 7–8, 10–11.

ships. Since fewer than 1,300 men could be held aboard the available vessels, many prisoners remained on land in the barracks.[88]

Conditions aboard the prison ships in Charleston harbor were no better than in New York. Jammed together in narrow holds with poor sanitation, the men quickly fell victim to smallpox, dysentery, and other illnesses. Heat and humidity were worse than in New York, and the swampy coastal areas of South Carolina were home to mosquitoes that spread malaria and yellow fever, diseases not seen in the North. Benjamin Burch, a Maryland soldier who contracted yellow fever on a Charleston prison ship, declared that he "suffered to the last degree of human misery." Balfour reported that the men on the prison ships were dying in large numbers and that the loss was "truly shocking." A lack of medical supplies and a food shortage that plagued the British army throughout 1780 and forced cuts in the rations to British troops worsened the situation; these were accompanied by reductions of the prisoners' already smaller rations.[89]

With the possibility of a prisoner exchange unlikely, British officials grappled with the problem of the Charleston prisoners. Proposals to relocate them were rejected since the captives would have to be fed and guarded wherever they were held, draining Britain's scarce resources. The best option, officers decided, was to accelerate efforts to recruit the Americans. Now that France and Spain had joined the war, Britain's colonies in the West Indies were threatened, and their garrisons were in dire need of reinforcements. Governor John Dalling of Jamaica, therefore, sent the former royal governor of South Carolina, Lord Charles Montagu, and several officers to Charleston to enlist prisoners.[90]

Arriving at Charleston in early 1781, Montagu obtained Balfour's permission to begin recruiting. Both Clinton and Cornwallis were skeptical of the measure, but Balfour, who had to deal with the captives and worried that many of the men might not survive much longer in confinement, acted as he thought best. Montagu had an advantage because he could promise recruits they would serve only against the French or Spaniards; most captives had shown great reluctance to fight against their former comrades in the American forces. However, France and Spain had been considered foes of the colonists for decades, so the prisoners were more willing to fight "against their ancient enemies." Eventually, Montagu and his officers enlisted 527 men for their new regiment, and additional prisoners chose to join the Royal Navy. Some of the recruits blamed Congress and the American generals for leaving them no alternative but to enlist with the British because of their refusal to arrange a prisoner exchange.[91]

---

88. Borick, 14–15, 17.
89. Borick, 17, 18–19.
90. Borick, 27, 28–29.
91. Borick, 32–33, 36, 37, 39.

Despite American leaders' reluctance to negotiate, a few exchanges were made in New York in 1780. Congress obtained the release of 200 officers and 500 enlisted men held on Long Island. The Royal Navy's severe lack of sailors caused Sproat to agree to release three thousand Americans from the prison ships in exchange for 2,200 British seamen held by the Americans. Admiral George Rodney halted exchanges in September 1780 because the Americans still owed the British 800 men from the earlier agreement. Sproat also worked to alleviate the navy's manpower shortage by trying to recruit more prisoners for British service. As an incentive for prisoners to enlist, Sproat crowded 1,100 men aboard the *Jersey* and reduced their food and water rations.[92]

Silas Talbot, one of the prisoners, described conditions on the *Jersey*: "Dysentery, fever, phrenzy and despair prevailed . . . and filled the place with filth, disgust and horror. The scantiness of the provisions, the brutality of the guards, and the sick, pining for comforts they could not obtain," created "one of the greatest scenes of human distress and misery ever beheld." He estimated that in good weather about 10 men died each day, with the number climbing with increased heat or cold.[93]

Exchanged prisoners brought reports of the horrifying conditions they had experienced, prompting Congress to order Washington to undertake an investigation. Washington's inquiry caused the British to launch one of their own that, not surprisingly, found that the captives were well treated. Sproat denounced the accusations of cruelty as false propaganda. Congress remained unconvinced, and a committee that collected evidence from former prisoners concluded in June 1781 that "contrary to the usage and custom of civilized nations," the British had undertaken "deliberately to murder their captives in cold blood."[94]

Major General Nathanael Greene, who had taken command of the Continental Army in the South in December 1780, took it upon himself to negotiate an exchange, gained Cornwallis's consent, and meetings between American officers and their British counterparts began in March 1781. An agreement was reached in May that covered all the Continental soldiers held by the British, as well as the militia members of both sides. Each side released its captives during the summer. By that time, only 740 Continentals remained at Charleston. At least 800 had died aboard the "pestilential tubs" in the harbor, while 950 had joined the British army or navy. An estimated 1,000 had escaped, and the fate of 400 was unknown. Borick believed these men probably "died or escaped," which would raise the total number of deaths.[95]

The American victory at Yorktown in 1781 produced a shift in British policy as efforts to subdue the rebellion were abandoned. Parliament repealed the 1777 law governing

---

92. Burrows, *Forgotten Patriots*, 153–54, 167.

93. Burrows, 168.

94. Burrows, 175–77.

95. Borick, *Relieve Us*, 76, 77, 79; Middlekauff, *Glorious Cause*, 451.

the treatment of American prisoners in March 1782 and reclassified the captives as prisoners of war rather than traitors or pirates. The change had no immediate effect on conditions for the captives, but legitimated exchanges, which began in the summer and by February 1783 had repatriated nearly all the prisoners held by both sides.[96]

The number of Americans who died in British captivity cannot be calculated with certainty. An estimate that first appeared in April 1782 gave a figure of 11,644 of those confined aboard prison ships in New York. A second calculation produced by Thomas Jefferson in 1786 arrived at a remarkably similar total of 11,000. This number, historian Edward G. Burrows observes, "averages out to around 230 per month, fifty to sixty a week, or between seven and eight per day. That falls comfortably in line with contemporary testimony." Burrows estimated that at least 4,575 Americans held on land in New York also perished, so the total lost in the city was between 15,575 and 18,000, plus an additional 1,000 prisoners captured and held in Savannah, Charleston, and other locations. This would mean that of the roughly 35,800 Americans believed to have died during the Revolution, half perished while in captivity, compared to some 6,800 who died of battle injuries and 10,000 of disease.[97] Neither Loring nor Sproat were ever held accountable for their brutality. Both left New York for Britain in 1783; Loring settled in England, where he died in 1798, while Sproat returned to his family's home in Scotland, residing there until his death in 1799.[98]

British prisoners held by the Revolutionaries generally fared better than captured Americans. Except for the approximately 1,000 prisoners taken at Trenton in December 1776, the Americans did not capture a significant number of British soldiers until October 1777, when Burgoyne surrendered his army at Saratoga, New York. Under the terms of the capitulation, Burgoyne's 3,200 troops were to be marched to Boston, where they would sail to Britain on the condition that they did not serve again in America. The Continental Congress, however, repudiated the agreement on the grounds that the return of the prisoners would free an equal number of troops in Europe for duty in the colonies. The captives were eventually marched to Virginia, later moved to Maryland, then Pennsylvania, and at last back to Massachusetts. Conditions during the marches were harsh, with food often in short supply and no shelter. Nevertheless, few prisoners died, and many were able to escape. Captives were routinely permitted to perform farm labor near their place of confinement, which gave them the opportunity to earn money and purchase food and clothing. Many prisoners chose to remain in America, and some enlisted in the Continental Army.[99]

---

96. Burrows, *Forgotten Patriots*, 180, 195.

97. Burrows, 197, 198–99, 200–201.

98. "Joshua Loring," RevWarTalk, https://www.revwartalk.com/joshua-loring/ (accessed Mar. 16, 2020); Philip Ranlet, "Tory David Sproat of Pennsylvania and the Death of American Prisoners of War," *Pennsylvania History* 61, no. 2 (April 1994): 201.

99. John S. Pancake, *1777: The Year of the Hangman* (Tuscaloosa: University of Alabama Press, 1977), 190; Burrows, *Forgotten Patriots*, 188, 190; Borick, *Relieve Us*, 116; Charles Royster,

Captured Loyalists, considered traitors by the Revolutionaries, suffered harsher treatment than British prisoners. Many were jailed simply because of their political opinions, even though they had taken no action to assist the British. New York confined Loyalists in prison ships on the upper Hudson River, and Virginia and Connecticut also utilized prison ships. Connecticut authorities used the abandoned mine at Simsbury to hold dozens of Loyalists under terrible conditions. Loyalists captured in battle often suffered brutal treatment. Most of the 600 Loyalists captured at King's Mountain, South Carolina, in October 1780 managed to escape, but not before 9 were hanged, and many others were shot while trying to escape or because they could not keep up as they were marched from the battlefield. After a battle in North Carolina in February 1781, an American soldier recalled hearing "some of our men cry out, 'Remember Buford,'" as they attacked six Loyalist prisoners who "were immediately hewed to pieces with broadswords." Unlike their British counterparts, Washington, Greene, and other American generals denounced such cruelty even if they were not always able to prevent it.[100]

Conclusion

World War I saw a change in the attitude of the United States toward Britain, and this was reflected in a change in the way American history was written. Propelled on one side by America's 1917 entry into the war in support of Britain and blocked on the other by fear of prosecution under the federal Espionage Act passed that year and the Sedition Act of 1918, "in books, pamphlets, lectures, and college classrooms, leading academic historians encouraged Americans to see that their ancient animosity for the British stemmed from 'ignorance and prejudice.' Publishers scrambled to 'correct' the nation's history texts accordingly."[101] Failure to comply with the correct version of history brought severe consequences, as film producer Robert Goldstein learned when he released *The Spirit of '76* shortly after the United States entered the war. The movie glorified the American Revolution, but because Goldstein depicted British soldiers committing atrocities against Americans, he was arrested and charged with "fomenting 'hatred of England and England's soldiers,' interfering with the draft, inciting mutiny in the armed forces, and conspiracy to commit treason." Goldstein was found guilty on all counts except the charge of conspiracy, fined $5,000, and sentenced to ten years in prison, later commuted to three years. All prints of the movie

A Revolutionary People at War: The Continental Army and American Character, 1775–1783 (New York: W. W. Norton, 1981), 133.

100. Burrows, *Forgotten Patriots*, 189; Borick, *Relieve Us*, 116–17; Jim Piecuch, *Three Peoples, One King: Loyalists, Indians, and Slaves in the Revolutionary South, 1775–1782* (Columbia: University of South Carolina Press, 2008), 199–200; John T. Hayes, *Massacre: Tarleton and Lee, 1780–1781* (Fort Lauderdale, FL: Saddlebag Press, 1997), 97–98.

101. Burrows, 244–45.

were confiscated, and none is known to have survived.[102] The lesson was clear. When Eugene Armbruster undertook a study of the prison ships that was published in 1920, he found little evidence of "intended cruelty" by the British, only misfortune and "unavoidable circumstances." Armbruster's estimate of American deaths was 7,000. Furthermore, he charged that American accounts of the horrors of imprisonment were outright lies.[103] The work laid the foundation for later historians who argued that both sides were equally guilty of mistreating prisoners and, therefore, neither had the moral high ground to level criticism.[104] With seemingly little further to be said on the subject, the story of the American prisoners faded into relative obscurity. However, new studies of battles and commanders relied heavily on earlier works in which atrocity stories were standard. These accounts could not be ignored, especially given their alleged grounding in primary documents and lopsided casualty figures. As a result, tales of British brutality on the battlefield were often presented in a more nuanced manner or with some attempt at justification, but in many cases, were simply restatements of the previous accounts.

An excellent example of the more balanced approach to the subject is found in the work of Matthew Spring, who recognized that unnecessary violence probably occurred and examined the factors that contributed to such bloodshed. He explained that the high casualties suffered by Americans when British soldiers attacked with bayonets should not be surprising because "when one considers the mechanics of the bayonet charge, it is hardly remarkable that blood was sometimes spilled unnecessarily." Advancing soldiers "who saw rebel musketry pluck down their comrades . . . were keyed up into a state of acute stress. They were hardly liable to halt calmly and accept the surrender of enemies who . . . belatedly threw down their empty weapons" and ceased resisting.[105] The same situation applied to British cavalry, who at the Waxhaws found themselves amid a larger number of American troops and had to depend on quick action with their sabers for survival.

When the false accounts of British massacres, such as those at Paoli and Wyoming, are examined and dismissed as untrue, and the exaggerated tales of the slaughter of Baylor's troops near Old Tappan and Buford's soldiers at the Waxhaws are revised in accordance with demonstrable facts, it becomes clear that only a small number of Americans were deliberately and unjustifiably killed by British soldiers on the battlefield. The propaganda that circulated about these events, however, overcame the truth. Also, in each alleged massacre, American officers were guilty of serious lapses in caution and tactics; they ignored warnings of impending attacks, failed to secure camps adequately, and made poor command decisions in directing their troops. Publicizing

---

102. Burrows, *Forgotten Patriots*, 244–45.

103. Burrows, 245.

104. Burrows, 247.

105. Spring, *Zeal and Bayonets*, 235.

such failures would have undermined Revolutionaries' faith in their cause as well as in their leaders. If the errors of officers like Wayne and Buford became widely known, Americans might question the wisdom of members of Congress and high-ranking generals who appointed such men and retained them in command despite obvious flaws in their leadership. Portraying the British as cruel murderers masked American errors and better served the cause of independence.

For similar reasons, during much of the twentieth century, it was more convenient for Americans to ignore evidence of sexual assaults against women by British soldiers (along with women's participation in the Revolution in general) and downplay the atrocities that occurred aboard British prison ships in favor of promoting wartime alliances with Great Britain. The plight of American prisoners had never received as much attention as the battlefield "massacres," so having already faded from public memory, it was easier to erase. Thus, the deaths of approximately 19,000 American prisoners remain largely shrouded in obscurity, while the myth that British soldiers wantonly slaughtered large numbers of Americans on the battlefield persists despite numerous efforts by historians to correct the record.

5. Invisible Participants: Women and Religious Minorities

Jim Piecuch and Jeff W. Dennis

Men whose minds were warmed with the love of liberty, and whose
abilities were improved by daily exercise, and sharpened with a
laudable ambition to serve their distressed country, spoke, wrote,
and acted, with an energy far surpassing all expectations.[1]

—*David Ramsay, 1789*

Women "crowded on board prison ships, and other places of confinement, to solace
their suffering countrymen. . . . On other occasions the ladies in a great measure
retired from the public eye [and] wept over the distresses of their country."[2]

—*David Ramsay, 1789*

Believe me, the Presbyterians have been the chief and principal
instruments in all these flaming measures, and they always do and ever
will act against Government, from that restless and turbulent anti-
monarchical spirit which has always distinguished them every where.[3]

—*Letter from a New York Loyalist, published in London, 1774*

Women and religious minorities are almost invisible in most accounts of the American
Revolution. For nearly two centuries, historians followed the footsteps of David Ramsay
and other early chroniclers of the conflict, lauding the actions and accomplishments of
the men, who, in their opinion, won American independence, while relegating women
to the background as providers of comfort and moral support, too frail to undertake
the difficult tasks required to create a new nation. Religious minorities, long viewed
with suspicion by members of the major Protestant denominations that dominated
in the colonies, were also ignored, except when they became the subject of occasional
rants, such as accusations that Roman Catholics were agents of papal plots or Quakers

---

1. David Ramsay, *The History of the American Revolution*, 2 vols. (Philadelphia: R. Aitken and Son, 1789), 2:316.

2. Ramsay, *The History of the American Revolution*, 2:172–73.

3. Peter Force, ed., "Extract of a Letter to a Gentleman in London, from New York, May 31, 1774," *American Archives: A Documentary History of the English Colonies in North America*, Fourth Series, vol. 1, 301, https://archive.org (accessed July 31, 2022).

used pacifism to disguise Loyalist sentiments. Despite this lack of attention, both groups were significant participants in the Revolution.

Although possessing few legal rights, women frequently played an active if seldom-noticed role, usually as wives and domestic partners: boycotting British goods, managing farms and businesses while their husbands were away, producing supplies and raising funds for American troops, and serving as nurses, cooks, and laundresses to the army. A few women ventured into areas traditionally reserved for men, including Mercy Otis Warren, who wrote political commentaries; Deborah Sampson, the longest-serving soldier among several American women who entered military service; and Lydia Darragh, a spy.

In 1775, British North America was religiously quite diverse. Religious toleration had increased since the early years of colonization but was extended principally to members of the major Protestant denominations: Congregationalists, Presbyterians, Anglicans, Baptists, and Methodists. The colonies had a long history of anti-Catholic and anti-Jewish sentiment. Responses to the Revolution among American religious minority groups varied considerably. Among religious minorities, most Jews and some Roman Catholics believed that assisting the Americans would bring them greater acceptance. However, many Catholics preferred to support the British, who had extended to them a higher degree of religious toleration than many Americans, particularly Congregationalists. The pacifist beliefs of many other religious minorities—such as Quakers, Mennonites, Moravians, and the Church of the Brethren—prevented them from choosing sides in the conflict. While many of these people provided nonmilitary aid to both sides, such as tending the wounded, and a few renounced pacifism to take an active part in the war, the refusal of the majority to support the war effort or pledge loyalty to the Continental Congress and state governments was considered by Revolutionaries to be evidence of tacit support for Britain. As a result, these peace-loving congregations were frequently persecuted.

The Status of Women in the Eighteenth Century

Women occupied a relatively low position in colonial society, largely based on the widely accepted belief that "God assigned women special stations in life where they were to be modest, patient, subordinate, and compliant."[4] Women were also considered less rational, even less intelligent, than men because they were believed to have a greater capacity for emotion and sentiment, traits that drove their actions more than did reason. Consequently, politics and the law were the domains of men, and women possessed few legal and no political rights. Their place was in the domestic sphere as wives and mothers, caring for their families. The lines between masculine

---

4. Gary B. Nash, *The Unknown American Revolution: The Unruly Birth of Democracy and the Struggle to Create America* (New York: Penguin Books, 2005), 133.

and feminine roles and duties were clearly defined and widely accepted by women as well as men. Unmarried women were subject to the control of their fathers and, after marriage, to their husbands. This practice was incorporated into British law as the doctrine of "feme covert," from the French "femme couvérte," meaning "covered woman."[5] In 1765, William Blackstone, the foremost authority on British law, explained the law's application to marriage, writing, "husband and wife are one person in law . . . the very being or legal existence of the woman is suspended during the marriage." A married woman's property, even if it was hers before marriage, came under the control of her husband, as did any property acquired or income earned during the marriage.[6] Women who did not marry were generally marginalized, and even when they possessed the skills to support themselves, they were relegated to a place "near the bottom of the social scale."[7]

In practice, however, women in America often had more opportunities—and suffered fewer restrictions—than the law officially permitted. Frontier conditions required women to work alongside their husbands on farms and in business and to act in their place when husbands were disabled by illness or injury, away tending to commercial matters, or called from home to perform military service. Over time colonial law evolved to consider these situations, giving wives more power to conduct business on behalf of their husbands and greater control over property that had been theirs before marriage. Historian Laurel Thatcher Ulrich described this aspect of women's roles as "deputy husbands."[8] However, such actions were viewed as an extension of women's traditional roles, so women were still barred from politics, the law, and other exclusively male domains.

A handful of men challenged women's second-class status during the political dispute with Britain and the subsequent war. In 1764, James Otis of Massachusetts, in the pamphlet *The Rights of the British Colonies Asserted and Proved*, asked, "Are not women born as free as men?" and declared that if they were, they had the same "natural and equitable right" to participate in politics as men.[9] In August 1775, an anonymous writer noted in the *Pennsylvania Magazine* the difficult situation women faced. Women, he wrote, had "at all times and in all places" been both "adored and oppressed." He declared that man had "always availed himself of their weakness" and acted as a "tyrant" toward them. The writer further asserted that women had the same right to "public esteem" as men; however, he did not address the issue of women's

---

5. Mary Beth Norton, *Liberty's Daughters: The Revolutionary Experience of American Women, 1750–1800* (Boston, MA: Little, Brown, and Co., 1980), xiv.

6. Woody Holton, *Abigail Adams* (New York: Free Press, 2009), ix.

7. Norton, *Liberty's Daughters*, 41–42.

8. Laurel Thatcher Ulrich, *Good Wives: Image and Reality in the Lives of Women in Northern New England, 1650–1750* (New York: Vintage Books, 1980), 36.

9. Nash, *Unknown Revolution*, 204.

social and political equality.[10] In his December 1776 essay, *The American Crisis, Number 1*, Thomas Paine called on women to support the Revolutionary cause. Lamenting the panic that struck Americans after a series of British military victories and, after reminding his readers of the story of Joan of Arc delivering France, Paine wrote: "Would, that Heaven might inspire some Jersey maid to spirit up her countrymen, and save her fair fellow-sufferers from ravage and ravishment!"[11] New Jersey did not bring forth a Joan of Arc, but earlier in 1776, when the state legislature wrote a constitution, it granted the right to vote to "all freeholders and householders" with a net worth of £50; this right allowed unmarried women and widows owning at least that amount of property to vote in state elections; however, the state constitution was amended in 1807 to restrict voting rights to men.[12]

The New Jersey legislature's action was a rare case. The Revolution placed women in unprecedented situations even as men expected women's status to remain unchanged. The historian Linda K. Kerber noted the paradox, writing that in the conflict with Britain, "women were challenged to commit themselves politically and then to justify their allegiance," yet "the most radical American men had not intended to make a revolution in the status of their wives and sisters."[13] Republicanism, the political philosophy embraced by many Revolutionaries, also worked against women's advancement. The virtues attributed to good republicans, such as morally upright behavior, manly courage, and patriotic self-sacrifice, were contrasted with weaknesses identified with women: effeminacy, timidity, and dependence.[14]

Women and Colonial Resistance

During the decade-long dispute over British policy that preceded the Revolution, the colonists' most powerful weapon was the boycott. Refusing to purchase British goods put economic pressure on manufacturers in the parent country, who in turn pressed the government to alter its policies. Because producing items at home and choosing which goods to buy in the market fell within women's domestic sphere, their participation became crucial to the success of any boycott. Christopher Gadsden of South

---

10. "An Occasional Letter on the Female Sex," Teaching American History, https://teachingamericanhistory.org (accessed Sept. 21, 2021). Although the source given here lists Thomas Paine as the author of this anonymous essay, some scholars argue that Paine did not write the piece, e.g., Frank Smith, "The Authorship of 'An Occasional Letter on the Female Sex,'" *American Literature* 2 (November 1930): 277–80.

11. Thomas Paine, *The American Crisis, Number 1*, December 19, 1776, in *Common Sense and Related Writings*, ed. Thomas P. Slaughter (Boston, MA: Bedford/St. Martin's, 2001), 127.

12. Nash, *Unknown Revolution*, 289.

13. Linda K. Kerber, *Women of the Republic: Intellect and Ideology in Revolutionary America* (New York: W. W. Norton, 1986), 9.

14. Kerber, *Women of the Republic*, 31.

Carolina, a leading opponent of British taxation, admitted that boycotts could not succeed without women's support. In Boston, organizers circulated agreements to boycott British products and pressed women (as well as men) to sign. Through these protests, women were drawn, at least marginally, into the political realm.

Many women went a step further. Some joined men in harassing merchants who ignored boycotts. Greater numbers of women worked to produce cloth in the colonies to replace the large quantities normally imported from Britain. Individually and in organized groups, women spun and wove cloth from American-raised plants and livestock, manufacturing large quantities of linen, cotton, and wool fabric. Production and participation were highest in the colonies from Pennsylvania northward, where the population was larger and more people lived in cities and towns, making collaboration easier. Although white women in the South produced some cloth, that patriotic task was most often assigned to enslaved women.[15]

On October 25, 1774, women gathered at a home in Edenton, North Carolina, where they signed a pledge to participate in the Continental Congress's boycott of British tea and other products. Their action was ridiculed in Britain. *A Society of Patriotic Ladies, at Edenton in North Carolina*, mezzotint by Philip Dawe. London: Printed for R. Saye & J. Bennett, March 25, 1775. British Cartoon Collection, Library of Congress.

One of the most significant protest actions taken by women, later known as the "Edenton Tea Party," occurred on October 25, 1774, in Edenton, North Carolina. Penelope Barker, the wife of the provincial treasurer, organized the event and invited a large number of women to attend. Rather than drink tea, the women drafted, and at least forty-seven signed, a document supporting the provincial congress's boycott of British tea and cloth. The women announced their determination "to give memorable proof of their patriotism" and to demonstrate to the women of Britain "how zealously and faithfully, American ladies follow the laudable example of their husbands, and what opposition your matchless [British] Ministers may expect to receive from a people thus firmly united against them."[16] The women's statement received exten-

---

15. Norton, *Liberty's Daughters*, 155; Nash, *Unknown Revolution*, 143–44.

16. Troy L. Kickler, "Edenton Tea Party: An American First," North Carolina History Project, https://northcarolinahistory.org (accessed Aug. 8, 2022).

sive publicity in London, where the press published denunciations, accompanied by satirical illustrations, of the women's behavior.

Political Activism

Although they were denied any official role in politics, a few women recognized that the Revolution could provide opportunities for them to participate. Abigail Adams is the most famous of these women; however, she kept her efforts private and made no headway. Mercy Otis Warren and Phillis Wheatley were more overtly active and helped shape American opinion while demonstrating that women indeed possessed the intelligence and ability to express political opinions.

Abigail Adams

As her biographer, Woody Holton, observed, "Abigail Adams lives in the American memory as the most illustrious woman of the founding era."[17] In 1776, she sent her husband John a letter in which she urged him to "Remember the Ladies" and press for more rights for women in the new government to be created when the colonies declared independence.[18] This letter earned her a reputation in today's media as an early advocate for women's equality. But because her letter was written in private and produced no positive public results—"As to your extraordinary Code of Laws, I cannot but laugh," John Adams replied—many historians have downplayed her importance.[19] Yet, Abigail Adams's role in demanding improvements in the status of women encompassed more than a single letter; she corresponded with many people on the subject and attempted to assert her individuality within the Adams household. Even if she failed to shape public opinion, she did call attention to women's discontent with their status, inspiring other women to continue the struggle toward equality.

Born in Massachusetts in 1744, Abigail Smith, like most women, received only a limited education, a circumstance that troubled her throughout her life. As early as 1763, her correspondence demonstrated her interest in women's place in society and her dissatisfaction with existing gender roles. In 1764, she married John Adams, who later became a prominent figure in the Revolutionary movement. Abigail Adams met Mercy Otis Warren in 1773, and Warren's political activities encouraged Adams to express her own views on current affairs, denouncing in private letters the Tea Act of 1773 while praising the colonial opposition.[20]

---

17. Holton, *Abigail Adams*, xi.

18. Abigail Adams to John Adams, March 31–April 5, 1776, Massachusetts Historical Society, https://www.masshist.org (accessed Sept. 27, 2021).

19. John Adams to Abigail Adams, April 14, 1776, Massachusetts Historical Society, https://www.masshist.org (accessed Sept. 27, 2021).

20. Holton, *Abigail Adams*, 1, 7, 9–10, 33, 50–51, 53.

Adams supported resistance to royal authority and, at times, took political positions that were more radical than those of most people, such as advocating independence in the spring of 1776, when many Americans still sought reconciliation.[21] In June 1782, Adams wrote another well-known letter to her husband lamenting that women still lacked a political voice and were "obliged to submit to those Laws which are imposed upon us," even though women had demonstrated great patriotism throughout the Revolution.[22] Adams clung to her views regarding the status of women, even as First Lady during John's presidency (1797–1801), but was never able to convince her husband or other men to institute the changes she sought. In 1811, she did, however, express satisfaction that women had made significant gains in access to education.[23]

Mercy Otis Warren

Mercy Otis Warren was arguably the most important and influential woman of the Revolutionary era. She earned the praise of John Adams, who called her "the most accomplished Lady in America," and Thomas Jefferson, who praised Warren's "high station in the ranks of genius," yet she remains an obscure figure.[24] Born into a prominent Massachusetts family, Mercy Otis desired the same opportunity to learn as her brothers, who were schooled by a local minister. She was eventually permitted to join her brothers in their studies and thus received an excellent education, a rarity for women in that era. She also came to realize that women were the intellectual equals of men. In 1754, she married James Warren, the son of another important Massachusetts family. During the 1760s, Mercy's brother James Otis was a leader of the colony's opposition to British policy until mental instability and a severe beating from a political adversary in 1769 curtailed his activities. Convinced that the actions of the British government threatened American liberty, Warren began writing on political topics in the early 1770s.

Warren was thoroughly acquainted with the issues involved in the dispute between Britain and the colonies, not only from interacting with her brother and husband— James Warren was active in the colonial opposition—but also from participating in discussions with visitors to her home, including John Adams and Samuel Adams. Her first work, the satirical play *The Adulateur*, was serialized in a Boston newspaper in March and April 1772. (Longstanding Puritan laws forbade performing plays onstage.) Its "fictional" characters were easily recognizable, with the corrupt and tyrannical villains representing Massachusetts's royal governor Thomas Hutchinson,

---

21. Holton, 85, 94–95, 99–103, 126–28.

22. Holton, 172.

23. Holton, 159, 298, 363.

24. Rosemarie Zagarri, *A Woman's Dilemma: Mercy Otis Warren and the American Revolution* (Wheeling, IL: Harlan Davidson, 1995), xv.

During the Revolutionary era, women were denied a voice in politics. However, Mercy Otis Warren of Massachusetts wrote several important political works advocating resistance to British policy that were published anonymously. After the war, she published a history of the conflict under her own name. Photo by Alfred J. Andrea. John Singleton Copley. Museum of Fine Arts in Boston.

Lieutenant Governor Andrew Oliver, and Chief Justice Peter Oliver. In the play, their chief opponent, a character based on James Otis, led his patriotic followers in defense of liberty. Because she was a woman, Warren kept her authorship anonymous, sharing the fact with only her husband and a few friends.[25] Despite believing in the intellectual equality of women and men, Warren, noted one historian, "accepted the subordination of women to men, believed in separate spheres for each sex, and supported

---

25. Zagarri, *A Woman's Dilemma*, 43, 56–57; Nancy Rubin Stuart, *The Muse of the Revolution: The Secret Pen of Mercy Otis Warren and the Founding of a Nation* (Boston, MA: Beacon Press, 2008), 48–49.

the division of occupations based on gender. She never advocated a public role for women."[26]

In her second play, *The Defeat* (1773), many of the same heroes and villains reappeared, with the Hutchinson character defeated and repentant at the play's conclusion. On March 21, 1774, Warren's poem "The Squabble of the Sea Nymphs" appeared in the *Boston Gazette*, employing mythological figures to celebrate the Boston Tea Party and praising women's heroism in refusing to drink tea. In June 1774, another poem, published in the *Royal American Magazine*, criticized the vanity of those women in Massachusetts who ignored the colonial boycott of British goods and purchased imported luxury items such as gowns and lace. Warren's third play, *The Group* (1775), attacked the greed and lack of honor of Loyalists who supported the military government imposed on Massachusetts by the Coercive Acts. Warren predicted that war was imminent and that the defenders of liberty would triumph.[27] "Still more audacious," Warren biographer Nancy Rubin Stuart wrote, "was *The Group*'s secondary theme, a pro-female message that lamented the personal hardships of war forced upon women" by husbands who greedily pursued wealth and power.[28] A partial version of the play appeared as a pamphlet in New York, and the complete play was printed as a pamphlet in Boston.

In October 1778, Warren published the poem, "The Genius of America Weeping the Absurd Follies of the Day," in the *Boston Gazette*, condemning the greed and corruption of many Americans who, she believed, had abandoned the patriotic virtue of sacrifice in favor of luxuries and the pursuit of pleasure. In 1784, she continued to address such issues when she published, for the first time under her own name, a piece in *Boston Magazine* warning of the moral risk of buying European luxury goods. Warren's "Observations on the New Constitution" (1788) opposed ratification of the U.S. Constitution because she believed the federal government created by the Constitution was too powerful. In 1805, Warren published the *History of the Rise, Progress and Termination of the American Revolution*, a massive three-volume work that she had begun writing during the war.[29] While it is impossible to measure the influence of her political commentary, historians have noted the impact of pamphlets and newspapers in shaping public opinion during the Revolutionary era; Warren certainly made significant contributions in that regard, and her works were widely read.

---

26. Zagarri, *A Woman's Dilemma*, 162.

27. Zagarri, *A Woman's Dilemma*, 60, 63, 67–69; Stuart, *Muse of the Revolution*, 51, 55–56, 57, 68.

28. Stuart, *Muse of the Revolution*, 67.

29. Stuart, *Muse of the Revolution*, 103–4, 136–37, 175, 187, 245; Zagarri, *A Woman's Dilemma*, 98, 121–22.

Phillis Wheatley

Brought to Boston from Africa on a slave ship in 1761, a seven-year-old girl was purchased by the Wheatley family and named Phillis. She quickly learned English, and the Wheatleys taught her to read. In less than two years, Phillis had not only mastered reading the Bible but also demonstrated great skill as a writer, composing poems and passages that reflected her strong religious faith. Wheatley's first poem, written when she was eleven, was published in the *Newport Mercury*, a Rhode Island newspaper. As the dispute between Britain and the colonies intensified, she began to write on political matters. In 1767, she composed a poem praising King George III for the repeal of the Stamp Act. Later Wheatley took an even stronger political stance in a poem that honored Christopher Snider, a twelve-year-old boy killed in February 1770 when Ebenezer Richardson, an informer who aided customs officials in Boston, fired at a crowd of protesters outside his home. In her poem, Wheatley eulogized Snider as the first martyr of the colonial cause. In 1772, Wheatley also subtly linked her own opposition to slavery with Americans' defense of their rights in the poem, "To the Right Honorable William, Earl of Dartmouth."[30] Her ability to combine support for colonial rights with antislavery themes made Wheatley "a significant player in the intertwined politics of slavery and Revolution."[31]

Wheatley's achievement resulted from her knowledge of the Greek and Roman classics that were a key part of many colonists' republican political beliefs. The writings of Homer, Virgil, and others featured many characters who were slaves, women, or both and often proved themselves more intelligent and capable than their masters. Her use of classical references indirectly reminded readers of slaves' humanity and abilities, a point she also made by employing Christian principles to undermine racist beliefs regarding people of African descent.[32] Linking these varied elements with colonial opposition to British policy, Wheatley was able "to criticize slavery, participate in the Anglo-American conversation about liberties, and seem very, very discerning as well as polite."[33]

In 1773, Wheatley traveled to London for the publication of her book *Poems on Various Subjects, Religious and Moral*, a project subsidized by the Countess of Huntingdon. A devout Christian like Wheatley, the countess took a special interest in helping people marginalized by society. Shortly after her return from England, Wheatley's owners freed her. She continued to support the Americans as the Revolution began and, in

---

30. Nash, *Unknown Revolution*, 137, 138.

31. David Waldstreicher, "Women's Politics, Antislavery Politics, and Phillis Wheatley's American Revolution," in *Women in the American Revolution: Gender, Politics, and the Domestic World*, ed. Barbara B. Oberg (Charlottesville: University of Virginia Press, 2019), 147.

32. Waldstreicher, "Women's Politics, Antislavery Politics," 149, 152–53, 156.

33. Waldstreicher, 157.

1776, wrote a popular poem titled "His Excellency General Washington,"[34] in which she acclaimed:

> In bright array they seek the work of war,
> Where high unfurl'd the ensign waves in air.
> Shall I to Washington their praise recite?
> Enough thou know'st them in the fields of fight.
> Thee, first in peace and honors—we demand
> The grace and glory of thy martial band.
> Fam'd for thy valour, for thy virtues more,
> Hear every tongue thy guardian aid implore![35]

Wheatley increasingly linked the Revolutionaries' fight for independence to African Americans' struggle for freedom, and she corresponded with several people on the subject of abolition. Although forced to work at menial jobs for her income, she continued to write poetry. Unfortunately, she was unable to find a publisher for a second book of poems, and most of those Wheatley wrote for the planned volume were lost. In 1784, Wheatley's writing career was cut short by death at the age of thirty-one.[36] Her unique status as a woman, an African American, and a writer on political issues earned her considerable fame. Revolutionaries, including Washington, praised Wheatley for her patriotism, and she was also embraced by members of the growing antislavery movement in New England.

Army Women, Soldiers, and Spies

Some women, by desire or necessity, joined the Revolutionary effort by supporting the Continental Army in camp and even on the battlefield. Thousands of women followed their husbands and other male relatives or companions who entered military service, traveling with the army and assisting in a variety of ways, including replacing men injured in battle. A few women disguised themselves as men and tried to enlist as soldiers, while others acted as spies.

Army Women

One of the least noticed and most misunderstood groups of the Revolution consisted of women who accompanied the armies in camp and on operations. Although they

---

34. Waldstreicher, "Women's Politics, Antislavery Politics," 139; Debra Michals, "Phillis Wheatley," National Women's History Museum, https://www.womenshistory.org (accessed Sept. 14, 2021).

35. Phillis Wheatley, "His Excellency General Washington," 1776, Poets.org, https://poets.org (accessed Sept. 14, 2021).

36. Michals, "Wheatley."

have often been dismissed as prostitutes, the vast majority were not. Many wives and female partners of soldiers chose to stay with men who enlisted in the army, especially when they lived in areas occupied by the British. Often these women brought their children with them. Because eighteenth-century armies had little in the way of support services, army women provided essential assistance by procuring supplies, nursing sick and wounded soldiers, cooking, and doing laundry. Equally important, their presence created a sense of community and formed the "social networks" that historian Holly A. Mayer has noted, "sustained the military even as they complicated its operations."[37]

Upon taking command of the Continental Army, George Washington opposed allowing women to follow the army even though this had long been common practice with the British forces. Washington feared that women would be expensive and disruptive; however, he and other American commanders eventually came to accept their presence after recognizing that their work promoted cleanliness and better health while also helping to prevent desertion. Men often left the army without permission out of concern for their wives and families, so having these women and children present kept many soldiers in the ranks. Officers nevertheless continually strove to maintain some level of control over army women, accommodating those who were beneficial to the troops and trying to rid the army of those they considered harmful, particularly prostitutes.[38]

The army established a set of policies to identify the women with the army and ensure that they had reason to be there. Officers compiled lists of women and children with each regiment, verified their relationships with soldiers in the unit, and allocated rations to women whose presence was approved; children were allotted half-rations. Providing food to these women indicated recognition of their value to the army, as American forces were frequently short of supplies. At the same time, the commanders expected that by accepting rations, women also tacitly accepted the authority of officers to regulate their behavior. Therefore, when nurses were needed to tend to the sick and wounded, and too few camp women volunteered, officers would order women to perform that duty, threatening to withhold rations from those who did not comply.[39]

Most orders concerning women were intended to regulate routine behavior. When the army marched, women were almost always ordered to accompany the baggage wagons though they were usually forbidden to ride on them. Orders also frequently specified the type of work women were to do and the circumstances under which they might receive payment, in addition to rations. Theft was forbidden, and offenders

37. Holly A. Mayer, "Wives, Concubines, and Community: Following the Army," in *War & Society in the American Revolution: Mobilization and Home Fronts*, ed. John Resch and Walter Sargent (DeKalb: Northern Illinois University Press, 2007), 236.

38. Mayer, 237–38, 239, 240.

39. Mayer, 239, 240–41.

were subject to trial and punishment. Punishments for women, however, were less severe than those for men. Whereas the latter could be whipped or even executed for violating orders, women, though sometimes threatened with whipping, rarely, if ever, received such punishment; the most severe penalty imposed was being permanently barred from the army's camp.[40]

As Washington feared, women could sometimes cause disruptions affecting entire units. In July 1780, one notable incident occurred in the army's camp at Ramapo, New York. One Mrs. McLane, an army woman, claiming she had been abused by another, Mrs. Margaret Batten, sought revenge and assaulted Batten. A third woman, Mrs. McLachlan, wife of the regiment's sergeant major, joined the fight. Private John Batten intervened to aid his wife; Colin McLachlan did the same and, in the fracas, struck the private. A captain managed to break up the melee, hitting Mrs. McLachlan in the process. Two trials resulted in Mrs. Batten's expulsion from the army and the acquittal of Mrs. McLane, Mrs. McLachlan, Private Batten, and Sergeant Major McLachlan. With Mrs. Batten gone, some degree of harmony was apparently restored, as there were no further incidents reported among those who remained.[41]

Over the course of the war, an estimated 20,000 women accompanied the Continental Army. At any given time, there was approximately one woman for every thirty to thirty-five soldiers in the ranks. In January 1783, Washington, having overcome his initial objections to women in camps, acknowledged that it had been worthwhile to provide for them and their children, as their presence had allowed the army to retain some of its best troops who might otherwise have been lost through desertion. It was a limited admission of the importance of women to the army but demonstrated that their contributions, if not effusively praised, had not gone wholly unnoticed.[42]

An Army Woman and Warrior: The Elusive Molly Pitcher

One famous legend involving army women is the story of "Molly Pitcher," the woman who took her husband's place after he was injured by enemy fire while loading a cannon. In actuality, there was no single "Molly Pitcher," as many women took such action during the war. One woman known to have joined an artillery crew in action was Margaret Cochran Corbin at the Battle of Fort Washington, New York, on November 16, 1776. When Corbin's husband, John, enlisted in the Continental Army, she accompanied him. He was part of an artillery crew at Fort Washington, and Margaret joined him in helping to load the cannon during the British attack. When John Corbin was killed by British fire, Margaret continued

---

40. Mayer, 242–43.
41. Mayer, 243–44.
42. Mayer, 241, 246, 258.

to work with the gunners until she was severely wounded. After the Americans surrendered, she was taken prisoner and released on her promise not to fight again unless exchanged for a British prisoner. Corbin eventually recovered and, despite having lost the use of her left arm, served until the end of the war as a nurse in the American post at West Point. Congress recognized her service by granting her a pension.[43]

One of the few widely acknowledged women participants in the Revolution was the legendary "Molly Pitcher," who was said to have taken the place of her wounded husband in the crew of an American artillery piece during a battle. In fact, several women acted in the role of "Molly Pitcher" during the conflict. *Molly Pitcher at the Battle of Monmouth, June 1778*, engraving by James C. Armytage after Alonzo Chappel, 1931–1932. National Archives, College Park, MD.

While Corbin fits the description of the legendary "Molly Pitcher," the name was first applied to a woman who participated in the Battle of Monmouth, New Jersey, on June 28, 1778, when American and British forces engaged in a lengthy exchange of artillery fire. The woman traditionally believed to be the "Molly Pitcher" of this battle was Mary Hays, the wife of artilleryman William Hays. Continental soldier Joseph Plumb Martin wrote that he watched a woman helping her husband load a cannon

43. Debra Michals, "Margaret Cochran Corbin," National Women's History Museum, https:// www.womenshistory.org (accessed Sept. 2, 2021).

and that when she took a long stride to reach for ammunition, "a cannon shot from the enemy passed directly between her legs without doing any other damage than carrying away all the lower part of her petticoat." Martin said the woman showed no fear and simply joked that it was lucky the shot was not aimed higher. Some later versions of the story reduced Molly Pitcher's role to carrying water for the men in the gun crew.[44]

Hays may not have been the only woman to have served a cannon at Monmouth. An account written five days after the battle described a woman at a different place on the battlefield whose male partner had been wounded and who took his place in the artillery and "fought with astonishing bravery, discharging the piece with as much regularity as any soldier present." This unnamed woman and Mary Hays were likely only two of several women who worked with artillery crews, bringing water and ammunition during the battle.[45]

Enlisting in the Ranks: Cross-Dressing Female Soldiers

Occasionally women attempted to enlist for military service. Given the limited records available, it is impossible to determine if the practice was widespread. In 1822, a New York newspaper reported that "it was not an unusual circumstance to find women on the ranks disguised as men." Most women recruits were quickly discovered, discharged, and sometimes punished for enlisting. Deborah Sampson, however, succeeded in serving undetected for seventeen months and became a minor celebrity afterward.[46]

Women known to have enlisted include Ann (or Nancy) Bailey, a Boston widow who joined a Massachusetts regiment in February 1777 under the name "Sam Gay." Shortly after her promotion to corporal, her secret was discovered, and she tried to flee but was arrested and charged with two crimes: cheating the state of the enlistment bounty she had received under false pretenses and impersonating a man. Convicted, she was fined and sentenced to at least two months in prison. In spring 1782, another Massachusetts woman, Anne Smith, enlisted as "Samuel Smith" but was quickly discharged when an officer's examination revealed that she was a woman. Like Bailey, she was jailed. Both were at least spared the humiliation inflicted upon an unnamed young woman who enlisted in 1778 in New Jersey. Ordered to bring her commanding officer a drink, she momentarily forgot she was pretending to be a man and curtsied when she delivered the beverage. A second officer, under the pretense of

---

44. Mark Edward Lender and Garry Wheeler Stone, *Fatal Sunday: George Washington, the Monmouth Campaign, and the Politics of Battle* (Norman: University of Oklahoma Press, 2016), 327–28.

45. Lender and Stone, *Fatal Sunday*, 329–30.

46. Alfred F. Young, *Masquerade: The Life and Times of Deborah Sampson, Continental Soldier* (New York: Alfred A. Knopf, 2004), 7.

examining her, opened her clothing and exposed her breasts; compounding the insult, she was then forced to walk out of camp, probably in front of the male soldiers, while drummers tapped out a tune called the "Whore's March."[47]

Anna Marie Lane of Virginia avoided punishment, and state officials recommended she be awarded a pension because she was "very infirm having been disabled by a severe wound which she received fighting as a common soldier" at the Battle of Germantown in 1777. She may have fought alongside her husband, as a John Lane was granted a pension at the same time.[48] The cases of other female soldiers are not as well documented. Elizabeth Gilmore of Pennsylvania is said to have served with her husband in a ranger unit on the frontier, and Sally St. Clair allegedly served in a South Carolina regiment and was killed in action at Savannah, Georgia, in October 1779. An unnamed woman, apparently an escaped slave, was reported to have been a drummer in a Virginia regiment.[49]

Deborah Sampson's male impersonation proved far more successful. Born in Massachusetts in 1760, around 1765, she and her siblings were placed in other people's homes by her poverty-stricken mother. Sampson lived with several families before becoming a servant in the Thomas household in 1770, where she performed various tasks, including farm labor. In 1778, upon reaching the age of eighteen, she became independent and spent the next three years working as a spinner, weaver, and teacher, having educated herself while a servant. Then, in the spring of 1782, she attempted to enlist in the Continental Army using the name "Timothy Thayer." Sampson was discovered, and though she avoided criminal prosecution, she was harshly rebuked by members of her Baptist congregation. Undeterred, she traveled to Bellingham and, on May 20, enlisted again as "Robert Shurtliff." Her reasons for joining the army are unclear, and Sampson herself offered two different explanations: that she enlisted from a sense of patriotism and that she wanted to avoid an arranged marriage to a man she disliked.[50]

Sampson joined some fifty other recruits at Worcester, Massachusetts, and marched to West Point. There she was assigned to the light infantry company of the 4th Massachusetts Regiment. The light infantry, considered an elite force, were the most active soldiers at that point in the war, scouting, skirmishing with British units, and battling Loyalist guerrillas in the Hudson River Valley. Sampson fought in several such skirmishes and was wounded twice, the second time at Tarrytown, New York. Later, she was assigned to noncombat duty as an orderly to General John Paterson. In summer 1783, she was sent with other soldiers to Philadelphia to suppress a mutiny of Pennsylvania troops. While there, she became seriously ill, and the doctor treating

47. Young, *Masquerade*, 7; Marjy Wienkop, "Women Soldiers in the American Revolution," *The Continental Line*, https://www.continentalline.org/CL/article-000202/ (accessed Sept. 14, 2021).
48. Wienkop, "Women Soldiers."
49. Wienkop, "Women Soldiers"; Young, *Masquerade*, 8.
50. Young, *Masquerade*, 24, 29–30, 34, 37, 75, 84.

her discovered that she was a woman. She returned to West Point afterward as Robert Shurtliff, though by then, Paterson and other officers had apparently learned of her deception. Nevertheless, she was not punished and received an honorable discharge on October 23, 1783, likely because she had proven her value as a soldier during her lengthy service. She successfully petitioned for unreceived pay in 1792, was the subject of a biography two years later, and in 1802–1803 made a lecture tour of New England and New York speaking of her military experiences, probably the first such tour by an American woman.[51]

Patriot Spies

Spying could be as dangerous as combat for men since soldiers captured in civilian clothes were frequently executed. Women, however, were less likely to be suspected of espionage and less likely to be executed for that crime, so several women served as spies for both sides. Two notable spies for the Americans were Lydia Darragh of Philadelphia and Anna Strong of Long Island. Darragh, a Quaker, put aside her pacifist beliefs to assist the Americans. After the British occupied Philadelphia in September 1777, officers used the Darragh home for meetings because of its proximity to General Sir William Howe's headquarters. Darragh would conceal herself, listen to the discussions, and send reports to Continental officers outside the city. Her most significant success occurred in December after she overheard the British planning an attack on American forces at Whitemarsh. Darragh obtained a pass to leave Philadelphia to procure flour at a nearby mill, then proceeded to a tavern, where she found an American officer and informed him of the British plan. Her information enabled Washington to prepare to meet the British forces; Howe's intended surprise attack resulted in only inconclusive skirmishing.[52]

Anna Strong was a member of the Culper Spy Ring, a network of informants established in 1778 by Washington's chief of intelligence, Major Benjamin Tallmadge. The group operated for five years in the British-occupied area in and around New York City without being detected. Agents moved through the region, gathering information about British positions and plans from conversations overheard at taverns, coffee shops, businesses, and social gatherings. Important intelligence was recorded using a numerical substitution code or in lemon juice that functioned as an invisible ink, revealed when the paper was heated. The coded messages were brought to Abraham Woodhull's Long Island farm, and his neighbor Anna Strong would hang clothing on a line, the colors indicating a message needed to be retrieved and where American agents should land; Caleb Brewster watched for

---

51. Young, 88, 97–98, 114, 138, 146, 155, 156, 159, 184, 197.

52. Debra Michals, "Lydia Darragh," National Women's History Museum, https://www.womenshistory.org (accessed Oct. 4, 2021; article since removed from site).

Strong's signals from the safety of American-held Connecticut, then crossed Long Island Sound to the indicated location, collected the messages, and passed them to Tallmadge. Information obtained by the Culper Ring enabled Washington to undertake maneuvers that thwarted a planned British attack on Rhode Island in 1780 and contributed to the revelation of Benedict Arnold's plot to surrender the post at West Point to the British in 1781.[53]

Domestic Contributions

The war affected everyone in the newly founded United States as demands for manpower and supplies, along with the disruption and damage that resulted from military operations, forced people to adapt to the new circumstances. Women, regardless of their political views, took charge of farms and family businesses while men were away, often providing crops and goods for the armies while struggling to minimize the direct consequences of the conflict within their homes.

Women's activities occasionally extended beyond the limits of their households. Throughout the war, Americans were plagued by high inflation and shortages of goods. Sometimes merchants took advantage of the situation by withholding items from the market, waiting for prices to rise even further. Women, who were responsible for feeding their families and often having to do so alone when their husbands were away on military service, occasionally stepped outside the law to obtain by force what they could not purchase fairly in the market. In July 1777, one such instance occurred in Boston. Wealthy merchant Thomas Boylston, an avowed supporter of the Revolution, kept large quantities of coffee and sugar in his warehouse, expecting that creating scarcity would allow him to reap higher profits. When he refused requests to sell the coffee at affordable prices, a crowd of as many as one hundred women confronted him and demanded the keys to his warehouse. When he refused, the women threw him into a cart, at which point he surrendered the keys and fled while the women carried off the coffee they needed. That November, another mostly female crowd in Beverly, Massachusetts, struck at hoarding merchants, took control of their sugar supply, and assigned a woman to sell it at a fair price.[54]

Other women who broadened the boundaries of their domestic sphere were Esther de Berdt Reed and Sarah Franklin Bache of Philadelphia. Both were members of prominent families: Reed's husband, Joseph, was the president of Pennsylvania's governing Supreme Executive Council, and Bache was Benjamin Franklin's daughter. In spring 1780, upon learning that Washington's soldiers were suffering from a lack of food, clothing, and money to pay them, Reed organized a group of women who called

---

53. Victoria Williams, "Culper Spy Ring," George Washington's Mount Vernon, https://www.mountvernon.org (accessed Oct. 4, 2021).

54. Nash, *Unknown Revolution*, 232, 237.

at the homes of Philadelphians and residents of nearby towns seeking donations for the troops.[55] To explain the women's action, on June 10, 1780, Reed wrote an anonymously published broadside, "The Sentiments of an American Woman," which was widely distributed. She stated that the women were "animated by the purest patriotism," and if they could not "march to glory" in battle as men did, they could "at least equal, and sometimes surpass them in our love for the public good." Reed asserted that a man "cannot be a good citizen who will not applaud our efforts for the relief of the armies which defend our lives, our possessions, our liberty."[56]

The women eventually raised over $300,000, two-thirds in paper currency and the remainder in gold and silver coins. Reed planned to convert the entire amount to coins and pay each soldier $2, but Washington demurred, believing that it would cause the troops to resent receiving their regular pay in paper money. He instead proposed that the funds be used to purchase cloth and make shirts for the soldiers. Reed died in September, and Bache took over the project. The women sewed 2,200 shirts, which were delivered to the army in December 1780. Reed's example inspired women in Maryland, New Jersey, and Virginia to undertake similar efforts.[57]

Religion and Revolution

Historians have routinely underrepresented American religion in their accounts of the Revolution in recent decades, a myth of omission reflective of the nation's increasingly secular milieu. Yet eighteenth-century Americans were acutely religious people informed by passionate religious convictions. Few, if any, would have welcomed the concept of a "wall of separation" between church and state. Religion played an integral role in the coming of independence.

Outside academia, many Americans, including a substantial number of present-day evangelicals, take the opposite view and exaggerate the era's religious unity, insisting the United States originated as a "Christian nation." Prescribed by biblical precepts and achieved through divine favor, the founding then becomes a morally upright event imbuing a morally upright people. Such exceptionalism reflects mythic storytelling from the earliest years of the republic. "The religion of the colonists also nurtured a love for liberty," assured David Ramsay in his 1789 *History of the American Revolution*. "Though there were a variety of sects, they all agreed in the communion of liberty, and all reprobated the courtly doctrines of passive obedience, and non-resistance."[58]

---

55. Rosemary Plakas, "Sentiments of an American Woman," Library of Congress, https://guides .loc.gov (accessed Oct. 1, 2021).

56. [Esther de Berdt Reed], "The Sentiments of an American Woman," June 10, 1780, New-York Historical Society, https://wams.nyhistory.org (accessed Oct. 1, 2021).

57. Plakas, "Sentiments"; Nash, *Unknown Revolution*, 417–18.

58. Ramsay, *History of the American Revolution*, 1:29.

Other early national voices (e.g., George Banning) concurred: the Revolution was a uniquely Protestant-Christian experience setting America apart from the corruption of Old World religious and political establishments.

The actual record of American religion and its relationship with independence appears considerably less uniform and far more contested than commonly believed. First, a multitude of American Protestants rejected the Revolution, refusing to rebel against religiously ordained state authorities. Some were active Loyalists, and others maintained principled neutrality. Second, Catholics and Jews provided vital contributions on behalf of the United States. Indeed, the Revolution might have failed, but for the American alliance with Catholic France and assistance from Catholic Spain.

Still, Patriots diminished or denied non-Protestant contributions and suppressed Protestant voices of opposition or pacifism. Any moral or biblical reasoning that questioned the Revolution would not be countenanced. Self-anointed committees of safety and other "guardians of liberty" regularly targeted suspected religious opponents. They barred Loyalist ministers and neutralist laity from public expression, appropriated their places of worship, confiscated personal property, halted their livelihoods, and sometimes ended their lives altogether. In short, even as the Revolutionaries sermonized indignantly upon the alleged tyrannical actions of Britain, they themselves behaved with unmistakable tyranny against religious nonsupporters of independence.[59]

"A Presbyterian War"

"Call this war . . . by whatever name you may, only call it not an American Rebellion," insisted a Hessian officer stationed in Pennsylvania during 1778. "It is nothing more or less than an Irish-Scotch Presbyterian Rebellion." Independence was chiefly the goal of "Congregationalists, Presbyterians, and Smugglers," echoed Joseph Galloway, a former Continental congressman.[60] Fellow Loyalist Thomas Smith agreed that "the whole was nothing but a scheme of a parcel of hot-headed Presbyterians."[61]

Similar sentiments were held across the Atlantic. In March 1775, Edmund Burke warned Parliament how American religion, particularly in the Congregationalist and Presbyterian northern colonies, represented "a refinement on the principle of

---

59. Gregg L. Frazer, *God against the Revolution: The Loyalist Clergy's Case against the American Revolution* (Lawrence: University Press of Kansas, 2018), 25–26.

60. Mark A. Noll, *Christians in the American Revolution* (Vancouver: Regent College Publishing, 2006), 52–53.

61. Richard Gardiner, "The Presbyterian Rebellion?" *Journal of the American Revolution*, September 5, 2013, https://allthingsliberty.com (accessed May 22, 2022).

resistance," "the Protestantism of the Protestant religion."[62] As the conflict developed, royal officers and officials became steeped in intelligence that indicated variously how dissident Protestantism was "at the bottom" of the war. "Cousin America has run off with a Presbyterian Parson," quipped politician Horace Walpole. George III particularly despised those "whigs and Presbyterians," who he held responsible for his imperial imbroglio.[63]

To be sure, colonial America provided fertile ground for religious independence. The Great Awakening of the 1720s to 1760s gave rise to "spiritual democracy" as common-class, popularly established "Separate" congregations directly challenged the state-supported churches. Religion became more personal, emotional, and comprehensive, and Americans viewed subsequent political events through Awakened eyes. Many interpreted the Stamp Act and other imperial taxes that followed the Seven Years' War as evidence of a growing tyranny, which, if left unchecked, would eventually strip the colonists of their religious as well as political freedoms. The old Reformation formulation of the supposedly autocratic papacy as "Antichrist" was then extended to any variety of perceived oppression, governmental or ecclesiastical.

An Anglican effort in the 1760s to appoint a bishop for North America offered further evidence of supposed imperial decadence. New England Congregationalists despised the "Catholic" practices of the Church of England and worried that an American bishop would serve as a prelude to the commandeering of their churches. As early as 1750, Boston minister Jonathan Mayhew issued a widely distributed sermon condemning the Church of England as the "kingdom of the Antichrist."[64]

Most alarming among imperial measures was the Quebec Act of 1774. This directive reassigned all lands north of the Ohio River and west of the Appalachian Mountains to predominantly Catholic Canada. It also guaranteed religious freedom for Canadian Catholics. American responses bordered on hysteria. The act was cited widely as proof the Crown and its minions meant to inculcate "popery" throughout the colonies. In New York, a young Alexander Hamilton castigated the law as an "atrocious infraction" of "dark designs" against religious and political freedom. For many American clerics, the Quebec Act proved the breaking point. "Sedition flows copiously from the pulpits," complained British general and Massachusetts military governor Thomas Gage.[65]

A plethora of clerical voices endorsed militancy at the opening of the Revolution. Although the large majority were Presbyterians or Congregationalists, Baptists and other clerics also lent support. God was for America, liberty, and independence,

---

62. Thomas S. Kidd, *God of Liberty: A Religious History of the American Revolution* (New York: Basic Books, 2010), 75–76.

63. Gardiner, "The Presbyterian Rebellion?"; Charles H. Metzger, *Catholics and the American Revolution: A Study in Religious Climate* (Whitefish, MT: Literary Licensing, 2011), 136.

64. Kidd, *God of Liberty*, 60.

65. Kidd, 69, 71.

they asserted, and He would favor the colonists in their "unquestionably righteous Cause."[66] College presidents Ezra Stiles (Yale), John Witherspoon (Princeton), and James Madison (William & Mary), joined by a host of prominent evangelists, helped lead the Patriot mission. In January 1776, Lutheran pastor Peter Muhlenberg delivered one particularly dramatic appeal. Quoting from the book of Ecclesiastes, he preached that "to everything there is a season . . . a time of war, and a time of peace." Closing the homily, Muhlenberg allegedly shed his parson's robe to reveal a uniform underneath. As many as 300 of his congregants were said to have enlisted that day.[67]

Faith and the Founding Fathers

While most Revolutionary laity adhered to traditional Christian theology, many of their elite-educated spiritual and political leaders quietly practiced "theistic rationalism," a sort of halfway-house between evangelicalism and deism, a worldview in which past revelation (i.e., the Bible) mattered, but was not allowed to trump contemporary reason. Adherents acknowledged a universal Being at once rational and accessible, potent and kind, a personal God who honored the virtuous prayers of all people—Christian and otherwise. Jesus was regarded as a great moral authority (though not divine, per se). Unbounded happiness awaited those dedicated to beneficence and morality, while limited punishment would be the lot of the iniquitous.[68]

George Washington, a steady believer in Providence and prayer, secured the employment of more than a hundred chaplains to help instill morality within the Continental Army. With his forces largely comprised of amateur soldiers, the American commander sensed that they must not also be amateur Christians. Congregationalist Abiel Leonard was ranked as the general's favorite chaplain. Quoting from the book of Psalms, Leonard implored: "Teach I pray thee, my hands to war, and my fingers to fight."[69]

Patriot politicians and publicists similarly appreciated the importance of religion. Patrick Henry, who modeled his fiery oratorical style after Presbyterian evangelist Samuel Davies, bespoke "the holy cause of liberty" in his famed "liberty or death" address. John Adams, who believed American independence to be divinely ordained, extolled the Bible as "the most Republican Book in the World." Harmonized friend Benjamin Rush, a "Christian cannot fail of being a republican." Benjamin Franklin promoted the motto "Rebellion to Tyrants is Obedience to God." And, as advised by Rush and Franklin, even the deist Thomas Paine ably employed biblical exposition

---

66. Noll, *Christians in the American Revolution*, 153.

67. Kidd, *God of Liberty*, 115.

68. Gregg L. Frazer, *The Religious Beliefs of America's Founders: Reason, Revelation, and Revolution* (Lawrence: University of Kansas Press, 2012), 19–22.

69. Kidd, *God of Liberty*, 120.

with "the rhetoric of evangelical dissent" in shaping his hugely influential *Common Sense.*[70]

"Remember that there can be no political happiness without liberty; that there can be no liberty without morality; and that there can be no morality without religion," admonished David Ramsay.[71] Indeed, the perceived need for spiritual virtue continued long after the Revolution. Presidents Washington and Adams called forth national days of prayer. A biblical skeptic, Thomas Jefferson nonetheless praised America's "benign religion" in his First Inaugural Address, viewing it as an indispensable footing for the republic.[72] His draft for the Declaration of Independence (subsequently fortified through Congressional edit) relocated Divine Rights with the people: "We hold these truths to be sacred & undeniable; that all men are created equal & independent, that from that equal creation they derive rights inherent & inalienable."[73] Another key Jefferson composition was the Virginia Statute for Religious Freedom, a precursor to the First Amendment's federal guarantee. Altogether, while the American Revolution set into motion the disestablishment of religion, it never aimed to maim or destroy Christianity—as would be attempted in Revolutionary France.

Religious Minorities: The Principled Pacifists

An appreciable number of Americans refused on religious grounds to take up arms on behalf of any belligerent. Most were congregants of Quaker or German pietist communities. These people also became targets of the Patriots. Their unwillingness to support military operations, insisted the vituperative Thomas Paine, constituted nothing more than "crypto-Toryism," a particularly insidious variant of Loyalism.[74]

Since its Quaker founding, Pennsylvania had served as a refuge for the marginalized among America's religious practitioners. Here resided perhaps 5,000 German pietists at the time of the Revolution. Mennonites, a devout, long-persecuted Anabaptist group, accompanied William Penn in the colony's initial settlement. They staunchly opposed slavery as well as state-mandated religion and public schools. Moravians were spirited missionaries with a streamlined doctrine centered upon the instruction and life lessons of Jesus. From their headquarters at Bethlehem, they ministered to Pennsylvania's indigenous Lenape people; Moravian Indian missions also opened in New York and North Carolina. The Church of the Brethren similarly strove to

---

70. Kidd, *God of Liberty*, 76, 88, 111, 213; James P. Byrd, *Sacred Scripture, Sacred War: The Bible and the American Revolution* (New York: Oxford University Press, 2013), 10, 47.

71. Ramsay, *History of the American Revolution*, 2:356.

72. Kidd, *God of Liberty*, 242.

73. "Declaring Independence: Drafting the Documents," Library of Congress, https://www.loc.gov/exhibits/declara/ruffdrft.html (accessed Dec. 28, 2022).

74. Noll, *Christians in the American Revolution*, 133.

internalize Christ's teachings and personal example. Many colonists knew them as the "Dunkers," referring to their particular manner of baptism, a "threefold, face-forward immersion."[75]

Each of the German pietist groups suffered for their pacifism. At Upper Saucon, Pennsylvania, eleven Mennonite families were stripped of nearly every scrap of food, fuel, and property—even their Bibles. Renowned Dunker Christopher Saur, the proprietor of America's most successful publishing operation, gently accepted arrest, physical abuse, and imprisonment. His press destroyed, Saur lived out his final years in poverty. The Moravians lent peaceful assistance to the Patriots only to endure heart-wrenching tragedy in 1782 when American militia brutally murdered nearly one hundred of their Indian converts at the Gnadenhutten mission.

Among conscientious objectors, Quakers constituted by far the most numerous and the most consistently maltreated group. Founded in mid-seventeenth-century England by people who rejected elaborate religious ritual and formal clergy and called themselves the Religious Society of Friends, Quakers were social radicals, accepting all people as equals, including women, Indians, and slaves. As did German pietists, they sought to honor the lessons and ministry of Jesus. "[Christ] positively enjoins us, to love our enemies, to bless them that curse us; to do good to those that hate us, and pray for them which despitefully use and persecute us," reminded Philadelphia's Anthony Benezet. But "war requires of its votaries that they kill, destroy, lay waste, and to the utmost of their power distress and annoy, and in every way and manner deprive those they esteem their enemies."[76]

In their annual meetings, the Friends formally refused to support violence in any way, whether through active service, material contribution, or oath of loyalty. Paying others to kill, they recognized, would yield the same results as directly taking life. Unable in good conscience to support the raising of militia, Pennsylvania Friends largely abdicated from political authority during the French and Indian War. Nevertheless, many colonists remained envious of their wealth and suspicious of their motives. Beyond Pennsylvania, appreciable Quaker communities were present in New Jersey, Delaware, Rhode Island, and the Carolinas.

The Revolution actuated systemic hostilities against the Friends. Thousands were penalized in property, lands, and repeated fines. Many were beaten or jailed, and some were killed. The experiences of Philadelphia's Henry and Elizabeth Drinker illustrate these travails.[77] Henry, a prosperous merchant, considered appointment as a British tea agent in 1773. Stunned by the ensuing public furor, he declined the commission but remained the target of rebel rabble-rousers. In 1777, a document surfaced, patently fraudulent, claiming clandestine Quaker collusion with the enemy.

---

75. Noll, 125.

76. Noll, 143–44.

77. See Richard Godbeer, *World of Trouble: A Philadelphia Quaker Family's Journey through the American Revolution* (New Haven, CT: Yale University Press, 2019).

Patriot authorities arrested Henry with eighteen other Friends, imprisoning them at Winchester, Virginia. No charges were tendered, and no evidence was presented. That autumn, Philadelphia fell under British control. Elizabeth was forced to share her home with a royal officer and his boisterous coterie. She missed her husband terribly. Ominous news arrived in spring 1778: several Quaker prisoners had died. With Henry also reported gravely ill, Elizabeth joined a group of women that met with Martha and George Washington. The women were received kindly, and at the general's urging, Henry and his surviving fellow Friends were released after eight months of internment. Somehow, he recovered. That summer, Philadelphia returned to Patriot control. For the war's remainder, the Drinkers endured recurrent fines, theft, and destruction of their property. They witnessed the closing of Quaker schools and the public execution of two Friends for suspected treason. Henry's brother John was abducted repeatedly and badly beaten. Philadelphia's self-avowed "Guardians of Liberty," Elizabeth confided in her diary, were in truth, most "unfeeling men" and "cruel persecutors."[78]

Most Quakers maintained strict pacifism across the Revolution. In Christian love, some cared for the hungry, wounded, and ill, or buried the dead without prejudice to either the British or Patriot cause. Very few became Loyalists, while perhaps one in five aligned with the Revolutionaries. Disowned by orthodox Quakers, the latter faction reorganized as "Free Quakers." Most prominent among these dissidents were Nathanael Greene and Thomas Mifflin. By Ramsay's estimation, the services of these two generals "made some amends for the embarrassment which the disaffection of the great body of their people occasioned."[79]

Religious Minorities: "Papist Patriots" and "Unrecognized Patriots"

Two small religious groups, Roman Catholics and Jews, stood conspicuously outside the Protestant majority. About 25,000 Catholics resided in the thirteen colonies at the time of the Revolution, approximately 1 percent of the population. Two-thirds of that total were concentrated in two counties of Maryland, where Catholics had opened the colony's development in the 1630s. Most remaining Catholics lived in or near Philadelphia, mostly German Americans, accepted through the aegis of Quaker authority. Jews accounted for a scant 0.001 percent of the American population in 1775, about 2,000 people, principally enclaved at port cities such as New York, Philadelphia, Newport, and Charleston.

Colonial Catholics and Jews were common targets of pejorative language and prejudicial treatment. Since the time of the Reformation, Protestants had disparaged Catholics as agents of the "Antichrist," with American "papist" phobia peaking just

---

78. Godbeer, *World of Trouble*, 6.

79. Ramsay, *History of the American Revolution*, 2:313–14.

prior to the Revolution. Religious attacks against Jews dated from much earlier in Western history. Jewish American mercantile success further stoked colonial resentment and abuse.

Remarkably, disproportionate numbers from each of these religious minorities actively supported the Patriot cause. Certainly, Maryland Catholics believed their faith was better served by American than British authorities. Altogether, nearly 80 percent of Maryland's Catholic men appear to have sworn fidelity and to have donated or militarily served in the Revolutionary cause—twice the percentage of American Protestants.[80] Many hundreds engaged in privateering, in Continental service, and in Maryland's "Flying Camp" (i.e., strategic reserve) militia. Among the state's political elite, Catholic Thomas Sim Lee won the election for governor in 1779. Charles Carroll, a tactful and popular advocate of religious freedom who signed the Declaration of Independence, was nationally known. During 1776, Charles and his brother John, a Catholic priest, helped lead a congressional commission to Montreal in hopes of rallying Revolutionary support from largely French-Catholic Canada. The mission failed as *les Canadiens* reckoned their provincial status vis-à-vis the Que-

Members of religious minorities were generally ignored in many histories of the Revolution, which often emphasized Protestant beliefs as an important factor contributing to the rebellion. However, Jews, Roman Catholics, and people belonging to small Protestant sects frequently played essential roles. Charles Carroll of Maryland was the only Roman Catholic to sign the Declaration of Independence and later joined the effort to win support for the Revolution among Catholics in the British province of Quebec. *Charles Carroll, Barrister, Member of the Continental Congress*, print by Albert Rosenthal, 1885. Thomas Addis Emmet Collection, New York Public Library.

bec Act preferable to open rebellion alongside longstanding outsiders.[81]

Pennsylvania's Catholic community had less universal sympathy for the Revolutionary cause. A sizeable number chose Loyalism, some serving in Alfred Clifton's "Roman Catholic Volunteers," organized in New York in 1778. That regiment soon disbanded, although eighty recruits continued service with the "Volunteers of

---

80. Maura Jane Farrelly, *Papist Patriots: The Making of an American Catholic Identity* (New York: Oxford University Press, 2012), 242.

81. Holly A. Mayer, "Canada and the American Revolution," Museum of the American Revolution, https://www.amrevmuseum.org (accessed Dec. 28, 2022).

Ireland."[82] Stephen Moylan ranked highest among the state's Catholic Patriots. Early in the Revolution, he served variously as Washington's aide-de-camp, quartermaster general, and personal secretary. After that, he raised and commanded a regiment of Continental dragoons, emerging from the war with the rank of brigadier general. Other prominent Pennsylvania Patriots included George Meade, grandfather of the famed Civil War general, and Thomas Fitz Simmons, who helped shape an apprecia-tive "Address of Catholics" to George Washington. John Barry was the state's out-standing Catholic in naval service. Barry was the first person selected to command an American warship in 1775. His forces captured a host of enemy vessels, comman-deering gunpowder and other essentials. Barry earned the sobriquet "Father of the American Navy," an honor shared with John Paul Jones and John Adams.

Jewish Americans also contributed notably to the Patriot cause. Francis Salvador was elected to South Carolina's provincial congress in 1775, where he issued an early call for independence. In Paul Revere-like fashion, during 1776, Salvador rode thirty miles to rally militia against a Cherokee attack. He was among the first killed in action soon afterward. From Charleston's King Street neighborhood, more than twenty-five men enlisted in Captain Richard Lushington's "Jews Company," which fought in Georgia as well as South Carolina during 1779 and 1780.[83] One well-known mem-ber of Lushington's unit, Jacob Cohen, rose to command a cavalry company that participated in the 1781 victory at Yorktown. The greatest number of Jewish recruits came from Pennsylvania. Here Solomon Bush commanded militia from 1776 until the war's end, reaching the rank of lieutenant colonel. Fellow Philadelphian David S. Franks served as a Continental major and liaison officer for the Count D'Estaing. Later, as aide-de-camp to Benedict Arnold, Franks was exonerated of any knowledge or role in his commander's West Point conspiracy.

Some Jewish entrepreneurs engaged in privateering, including the wealthy and highly generous Patriot contributor Isaac Moses. Haym Salomon compiled the most remarkable resume among Jewish businessmen. Between 1776 and 1778, Salomon helped arrange escapes for American prisoners in New York. He even attempted to convince Hessian officers to resign. After these actions necessitated flight to Pennsyl-vania, Salomon conducted his most important Revolutionary service as the leading broker for foreign loans under U.S. Superintendent of Finance Robert Morris.

A small fraction of American Jews actively sided with the Loyalist cause. Isaac Touro of Rhode Island's Newport community was outspoken in his support for Britain. He relocated to New York during the Revolution and eventually died in Jamaica. Choco-late producer Abraham Wagg of New York sought to consult British policymakers following the entry of France into the war in 1778. He left for England the following year, never to return.

---

82. Metzger, *Catholics and the American Revolution*, 249.

83. Samuel Rezneck, *Unrecognized Patriots: The Jews in the American Revolution* (Westport, CT: Greenwood Publishing, 1975), 46.

Patriot narrators downplayed the significant contributions to independence performed by Jewish and Catholic Americans in favor of a more idiosyncratic Protestant account. The title of Samuel Reznecks seminal work, *Unrecognized Patriots*, indicates the longstanding myth that Jewish Americans contributed little to independence. Maura Jane Farrelly's *Papist Patriots* intimates with its title the irony that an impressive number of Catholics, a people long associated with papal and foreign tyranny in Protestant America, served with Revolutionary distinction.

Conclusion

Ultimately, whether they supported or opposed independence, women and members of religious minorities failed to experience significant gains in the immediate aftermath of the Revolution.

For American women, change came slowly. As Linda K. Kerber observed, "for many women the Revolution had been a strongly politicizing experience, but the newly created republic made little room for them as political beings."[84] Those few alterations in women's status that did occur were confined to the domestic sphere. Many American clerics called for greater affection for and appreciation of women within the marital relationship, and morality and propriety became more explicitly identified as female virtues. This encouraged a shift in attitudes toward women's role in politics. Because mothers were both guardians of virtue within the family and educators of male children who needed to be taught the principles of republicanism so that they could practice civic virtue as adult citizens, women were expected to teach and model this political morality for their children, a concept that Kerber termed "Republican Motherhood." Yet, while conditions changed in the private sphere, American women remained largely segregated from public life, legally subordinate to their husbands, and politically veiled.[85]

Drafted in 1787, the U.S. Constitution made no mention of women, and the only reference to religion was a statement in Article VI that banned religious qualifications for federal office. Four years later, the First Amendment was ratified, ensuring that the federal government would not establish a taxpayer-supported religion and guaranteeing citizens freedom of worship. Virginia had already taken such a step, having adopted Jefferson's "Statute for Religious Freedom" in 1786. Several other states, however, chose to retain established churches; New Hampshire did not end state support of the Congregational Church until 1817, Connecticut followed a

---

84. Kerber, *Women of the Republic*, 11.

85. Kerber, *Women of the Republic*, 11; Linda K. Kerber, "The Republican Mother and the Woman Citizen: Contradictions and Choices in Revolutionary America," in *Women's America: Refocusing the Past*, ed. Linda K. Kerber, Jane Sherron De Hart, and Cornelia Hughes Dayton (New York: Oxford University Press, 2011), 147–53.

year later, and Massachusetts became the last state to abandon official support of the Congregational Church in 1833. Longstanding prejudices against Catholics and Jews, and Revolutionary-era hostility toward Quakers and other pacifist denominations, persisted and acted as informal restrictions on these groups' ability to worship freely and participate in civil society.

The Revolution thus laid a foundation for allowing women to participate, albeit indirectly and within the household, in political affairs and for greater religious freedom and tolerance. It would take more than a century before the Nineteenth Amendment granted women the right to vote (1920), while anti-Catholic prejudice remained an issue during John F. Kennedy's presidential campaign in 1960. Largely deaf to women's voices, openly hostile toward conscientious objectors, and further opposed to other American minorities, the Revolutionaries compromised much-exhorted virtue and appreciably slowed the arrival of freedom's full promise—which many would argue has yet to be wholly realized.

6. The Myth of Merciless Indians and Apathetic Slaves

Jeff W. Dennis

He has excited domestic insurrections amongst us, and has endeavored to bring on
the inhabitants of our frontiers, the merciless Indian Savages, whose known rule
of warfare, is an undistinguished destruction of all ages, sexes and conditions.
—*Declaration of Independence, 1776*

Though degrading freemen to the condition of slaves, would, to many, be
more intolerable than death, yet Negroes who have been born and bred
in habits of slavery, are so well satisfied with their condition, that . . .
emancipation does not appear to be the wish of the generality of them.
—*David Ramsay, 1789*[1]

Whose History Is It?

The American Revolution housed multiple movements among America's multiple
peoples. Each of these founding stories deserves consideration. Native Americans
and African Americans contributed vitally to Revolutionary ideas, activities, and outcomes. Whether allied with or adversarial to the Patriot cause, they fought deter-
minedly to extend freedom and independence.

Early American narrators diminished Native and Black peoples in relating the
inception of the United States. "Merciless" Indians had opposed the Revolution, they
argued, while "well satisfied" slaves were oblivious to it. Neither people, therefore,
merited much mention in the tale of independence. The founding resulted, they
insisted, from the heroism of virtuous Euro-American men, despite Native belliger-
ence and Black indolence.

This view prevailed in popular as well as much of professional thinking for most
of two centuries. Perspectives shifted dramatically, however, with the arrival of the
civil rights movement in the mid-twentieth century. Indians and Black people then
became credited as noteworthy contributors to the nation's creation. Indeed, some
narrators went so far as to argue that democracy in the United States was attributable
principally to Native American or African American involvement.

---

1. David Ramsay, *The History of the American Revolution*, 2 vols. (Philadelphia: Aitken & Son,
1789), 1:24.

During the late 1970s and 1980s, a small group of authors shaped what became known as the "Iroquois influence thesis." The view asserts that the Iroquois, or Six Nations (for the number of tribes comprising their confederacy), exerted "a profound impact on American notions about unity, territorial expansion, the origins of sovereignty in the people, and universal suffrage." Six Nations headmen are said to have "lectured to colonial and revolutionary leaders" who "respected and used" the counsel received to help script the Albany Plan of Union, Declaration of Independence, and the U.S. Constitution and Bill of Rights.[2]

A consensus of historians who examined the thesis found it insufficient in evidence and plausibility.[3] Even so, the theory excited public attention, as it served to support the nation's growing appreciation and concern for Native America. In 1988, the thesis achieved official recognition through a U.S. congressional resolution. Subsequently, it was adopted into the curriculum of some public schools and even gained acknowledgment from the *Harvard Law Review*.[4]

Far larger in the public mind is the 1619 Project. Inaugurated in August 2019 through a *New York Times* one-hundred-page report, the project seeks to recast America's past as one forged more from slavery and race than liberty and independence. Accordingly, the founding of the United States may not date so much from the Declaration of 1776 as from the initial arrival of African slaves at Jamestown in 1619. The Revolution, in this view, was a strategy by many American elites to secure slavery against fears that Britain otherwise would end that most undemocratic of institutions. "Some might argue that this nation was founded not as a democracy but as a slavocracy," stressed Nikole Hannah-Jones, lead author for the project. Consequently, "black Americans, more than any other group, embrace the democratic ideals of a common good."[5]

The 1619 Project operates within a potent climate of painful memory for centuries of injustice dealt to Black Americans. It holds further appeal for many minority students who long have sensed little personal connection with the traditional American narrative. Equipped with materials available from the Pulitzer Center on

2. Donald A. Grinde Jr. and Bruce E. Johansen, *Exemplar of Liberty: Native America and the Evolution of Democracy* (Los Angeles: American Indian Studies Center, 1991), xx, xxii, xxiv, 177.

3. See, e.g., Elisabeth Tooker, "The United States Constitution and the Iroquois League," *Ethnohistory* 35 (1988): 305–36; Samuel B. Payne Jr., "The Iroquois League, the Articles of Confederation, and the Constitution," *William and Mary Quarterly* 53, no. 3 (1996): 605–20; Philip A. Levy, "Exemplars of Taking Liberties: The Iroquois Influence Thesis and the Problem of Evidence," *William and Mary Quarterly* 53, no. 3 (1996): 588–604.

4. Erik M. Jensen, "The Harvard Law Review and the Iroquois Influence Thesis," *British Journal of American Legal Studies* 6 (2017): 225–40, https://papers.ssrn.com (accessed July 19, 2021).

5. Nikole Hannah-Jones, "1619 Project," *New York Times Magazine*, August 14, 2019, 16, 26, https://pulitzercenter.org (accessed July 19, 2021).

Crisis Reporting, by the close of 2020, more than 4,500 public school teachers were employing the 1619 curriculum.[6]

The high-profile message of the 1619 Project soon elicited a high-profile academic and public response. Renowned historians Gordon Wood (the Revolution), Sean Wilentz (Jacksonian America), Victoria Bynum (Southern history), James Oakes (abolitionism), and James McPherson (the Civil War) challenged much of the project's narrative and conclusions.[7] The most aggressive censures, however, came from the political realm, including a Florida state ban on the teaching of "critical race theory" (which is not part of the 1619 Project) and a U.S. Congressional bill to halt federal funds for schools using 1619 materials.[8]

Apart from these critiques, a number of prominent professionals and public officials expressed appreciation for the project. In 2020, Columbia University honored Nikole Hannah-Jones with its Pulitzer Prize for Commentary. Among academics, Leslie Harris, a highly regarded scholar of slavery, praised the project's large-scale reframing of American history, even as she rejected its contention that the Revolution was waged on behalf of slavery. Although "it is easy to correct facts," Harris noted, "it is much harder to correct a worldview that consistently ignores and distorts the role of African Americans and race in our history."[9]

As our nation redefines what America is, we reinterpret what America was. The founding generation of Patriot historians essentially narrated white male Protestant republicanism. The Indian influence thesis and 1619 Project have broadened the discussion of democracy in America, despite the criticism they have received. The outcome should inspire a more supple national story, reinforced with heightened nuance and paradox.

The United States is and always has been a remarkable confluence of peoples, visions, and actions. This chapter investigates the quite real and courageous contributions made by Native Americans and African Americans on both sides of the Revolution. No diminution or exaggeration is necessary. These peoples were patriots and revolutionaries, too, creators and champions of pragmatic strategies for liberty, opportunity, and autonomy.

---

6. "The 1619 Project in Schools," 2020 Annual Report, Pulitzer Center on Crisis Reporting, https://pulitzercenter.shorthandstories.com (accessed July 19, 2021).

7. Adam Serwer, "The Fight Over the 1619 Project Is Not about the Facts," *The Atlantic*, December 23, 2019, https://www.theatlantic.com (accessed Dec. 28, 2022).

8. Sarah Ellison, "How the 1619 Project Overtook 2020," *Washington Post*, October 13, 2020, https://www.washingtonpost.com (accessed Dec. 28, 2022); Leah Asmelash, "Florida Bans Teaching Critical Race Theory in Schools," CNN, June 10, 2021, https://www.cnn.com (accessed Dec. 28, 2022).

9. Ellison, "How the 1619 Project Overtook 2020"; Leslie M. Harris, "I Helped Fact-Check the 1619 Project. The Times Ignored Me," *Politico*, March 6, 2020, https://www.politico.com (accessed Dec. 28, 2022).

"Merciless Indian Savages"

No Patriot myth appears more virulent or self-justifying than the Declaration of Independence's "merciless Indian Savages." Yet evidence indicates that Americans—far more than Native peoples—qualified as savage in their Revolutionary conduct. From before the Revolution opened until well after it ended, American troops exercised remarkable ferocity upon the frontier. They murdered many hundreds of noncombatant women, children, and the elderly. They torched thousands of Indian homes, confiscated or destroyed Indian food supplies, plowed up Indian fields, and cut down Indian orchards. They targeted neutralist headmen, assassinated peace emissaries, and massacred pacifist "praying Indians." The birth of the United States included a tragic agenda of aggression against Native peoples.

Two decades earlier, colonists resisted "the Enemies of America" in the French and Indian War. Now, Britain was portrayed as having replaced France in its collusion with Indian interests.[10] It was advertised as a noble "War for Independence," but the Revolution could just as well have been called the "British and Indian War," and it included some markedly ignoble actions undertaken by the Patriots.

The United States was largely a fictive term in 1776. The thirteen colonies lacked sufficient commonalities and unity with respect to history, livelihood, and religion. It is honorable that the founding generation defined their new nation as a champion for republicanism and universal human rights. But the Patriots also founded the country through contradistinction from the "other," that is, identifying themselves by who they were not. Indians long had represented the consummate enemy for many Americans. These non-white, non-Christian, "uncivilized" peoples were in possession of many millions of acres of highly arable land. Particularly for more westerly ambitious Americans, appeals to Indian-hating and Indian warfare strongly reinforced the Revolution.

Well in advance of Lexington and Concord, the first salvos in the Revolution were discharged along the Ohio River in 1774, as Virginians assailed the Shawnee nation in the thinly justified "Lord Dunmore's War." Disregarding a Crown directive, the colonists used their campaign to pry Kentucky open to American settlement. Indian fighting continued across the Revolution, and tellingly, it amplified with the coming of independence. In asymmetric response to warrior raiding upon the frontier, during the summer and autumn of 1776, American armies from four states launched invasions against a heavily outnumbered and under-munitioned Cherokee people. Patriot militias systematically destroyed the nation's towns and provisions. They left

10. Henry Laurens to John Lewis Gervais, in *The Papers of Henry Laurens*, 16 vols., ed. Philip M. Hamer, George C. Rogers, David R. Chesnutt, et al. (Columbia: University of South Carolina Press, 1969–2003), 9:391.

thousands of villagers to face the coming winter without food or shelter, scalped fallen warriors to collect £75 bounties, and killed noncombatants unable to flee.[11]

The 1776 campaign against the Cherokees played well with many in the American audience. Patriot David Ramsay claimed, "some well-meaning people could not see the justice or propriety of contending with their formerly protecting parent State; but Indian cruelties, excited by royal artifices, soon extinguished all their predilection for the country of their forefathers."[12] To secure peace, in 1777, the Cherokees were forced to pay a massive indemnity in territory, more than five million acres, in treaties concluded with South Carolina and Virginia. Much praised in Patriot propaganda, the Cherokee War of 1776 would serve as a model for subsequent Revolutionary invasions into Indian country.

The thirst for land has been downplayed in the traditional story of the Revolution. It does not fit well with the Patriots' vaunted stance against British tyranny or their bold insistence upon republican rights, such as "no taxation without representation." Still, land factored significantly in the coming of independence. In the largely agricultural world of the eighteenth century, land meant wealth, status, and opportunity.

George III's Proclamation Line of 1763 did little to stem incursions upon areas west of the Appalachian Mountains. Even so, it sent a clear message that the Crown wished to preserve Native lands, if for no other reason than to avoid repetition of large-scale frontier conflict such as what occurred in Pontiac's War (1763–1766). Additionally, two royal superintendents were appointed during the 1760s to imperialize Indian relations. These actions, which signaled at least some consideration for Native peoples, did not sit well with many Americans. Squatters and itinerants migrated west in open defiance of the royal fiat. Elite gentlemen, including such notables as George Washington, Benjamin Franklin, and Thomas Jefferson, bristled at the lack of western estate available for their ambitious speculations. For some prominent Americans, the break with Britain came in 1774 with the Quebec Act. Thereby, London reassigned all lands north of the Ohio River and west of the Appalachian Mountains to Catholic Canada—a measure "equally iniquitous & impolitic," as assayed by South Carolina merchant-turned-planter Henry Laurens.[13]

---

11. "Arthur Fairies' Journal of an Expedition Against the Cherokee Indians," transcribed and annotated by Will Graves, *Southern Campaigns of the American Revolution Magazine* 2 (October 2005): 20–34.

12. David Ramsay, *History of South Carolina, from Its First Settlement in 1607 to the Year 1808*, 2 vols. (Spartanburg, SC: Reprint Company, 1959), 1:162.

13. Henry Laurens to James Laurens, July 21, 1774, in Hamer et al., *Papers of Henry Laurens*, 9:518.

Patriots and Indians

A powerful, if subtle, myth perpetuated by the Patriots (as they designated themselves) is that they constituted America's true patriots, in contrast to others who actively opposed independence or sought to avoid the conflict altogether. In truth, numerous Black people qualified as Patriots, as did many Native peoples who demonstrated uncompromising devotion to their communities and sacred lands. "If patriotism was the subordination of private interests to the common good," John Murrin once opined, "the most heroic patriots of the period were Indian warriors—and also Indian women."[14]

Despite two centuries of disease, displacement, and war, on the eve of the Revolution, more than 150,000 eastern woodlands peoples lived in proximity to British America. They remained a vital concern within the strategic and commercial calculus of the Crown and its colonies. The conclusion of the Seven Years' War in 1763, however, reshaped intercultural relations to British advantage. With France exiled from North America and Spain a relatively peripheral presence in Louisiana, most eastern woodland peoples could no longer play one European colonizer off another. Pontiac's War persuaded the British Crown to provide at least some protections for Indian peoples and lands. Yet never again would the northern nations enjoy the mutually affirming "middle ground" of Native-French liaison.

Social and cultural distancing grew conspicuously between Indians and Euro-Americans during the final colonial years, even as geographic distancing along the frontier diminished. Trade, the principal "path" connecting the two worlds, was roughly trod upon as colonists became increasingly enamored with acquiring western lands. Alcohol was used to help run up Native debts in anticipation of acreage as payoff. Traders who purchased valuable goods such as beaver furs and deer hides from Indians routinely began a transaction by serving rum to Native hunters. When the Indians became intoxicated, sometimes traders convinced them to trade their pelts for more rum instead of needed items such as cloth and gunpowder, which the traders would then supply to their customers on credit, charging exorbitant sums. On other occasions, traders took advantage of the situation to undervalue Indians' furs or steal them outright if a Native lost consciousness. Afterward the trader would feign sympathy and provide goods on credit. In subsequent years the same methods would be employed, driving Indian hunters and trappers deeper into debt until tribal leaders were forced to sell land to colonial governments at bargain prices; the governments would in turn sell the land to settlers and compensate the traders from the proceeds. The Iroquois at Fort Stanwix in 1768 and the Cherokee nation at Lochaber in 1770

---

14. John Murrin, "Self-Interest Conquers Patriotism: Republicans, Liberals, and Indians Reshape the Nation," in *The American Revolution: Its Character and Limits*, ed. Jack P. Greene, (New York: New York University Press, 1987), 225.

finally did consent to sell some contested territory. But the cessions did little to stem the pressures on their peoples and lands.

Another persistent Patriot myth is that Indians were naive and foolish, readily manipulated at the bargaining table, or worse, easily deluded into barbarous action by British intrigue. Recalling the Cherokee War of 1776, David Ramsay opined: "The unfortunate misled Indians, finding themselves attacked on all sides, sued in the most submissive terms for peace. They had not the wisdom to shun war, nor the cunning to make a proper choice of the party with whom they made a common cause."[15]

The actual Native American story that emerges from the era of the Revolution is intriguingly complex. With innovations in trade and diplomacy, ritual and religion, alliance and warfare, accommodation and relocation, Indian Patriots waged their own campaigns for independence with firm commitment to their people, civilization, and lands. That no Native efforts ultimately could halt American expansion does not dim the creativity reflected.

Indian Independence

While many Revolutionaries maligned Indians as inherently malevolent or foolish, some observers, particularly New Englanders, lauded Indians as symbols of freedom and independence. The most famous instance occurred in December 1773 when some of Boston's Tea Party participants garbed themselves in Indian attire. For these "Sons of Liberty," Native Americans represented a people fiercely independent as well as distinctive in appearance from the Old World. The image of the "noble savage" has long paralleled the stereotype of Indians as heathen rogues. Both icons, of course, are much imbued with myth.[16]

British authorities became flustered when Native allies disregarded the royal cause. "All of our Rhetorick could no longer diswade them from taking up the Hatchet," grieved British Deputy Superintendent Alexander Cameron on the eve of the 1776 Cherokee War.[17] Indian warriors followed their own lead, prioritizing their own agendas and employing their own tactics. Where Crown and Native interests coincided, Indians fought with impressive audacity alongside the British. When interests conflicted, warriors readily ignored the demands of imperial officials. This failure to understand Indian independence constituted a particular difficulty for British strategists, as it would result in a series of "what if" lost opportunities.

---

15. Ramsay, *History of South Carolina*, 1:160.

16. Paul Jentz, *Seven Myths of Native American History* (Indianapolis, IN: Hackett Publishing, 2018), 1–52.

17. Alexander Cameron to John Stuart, July 9, 1776, *Records of the British Colonial Office, Class 5 Files*, Part I: Westward Expansion, 1700–1783 (Frederick, MD: University Publications of America), reel 7, vol. 77, microfilm, 456.

"A Matter Which Does Not Concern You"

Addressing the Cherokees in August 1775, British Indian Superintendent John Stuart implored: "There is a difference between the White people of America, this is a matter which does not concern you: they will decide it among themselves."[18] At the opening of the Revolution, many eastern woodland peoples would just as soon have remained free of the fray. Cherokee, Creek, and Iroquois towns, among others, accommodated appreciable neutralist factions. But peace did not appear practical for many. Stuart's premise was flat wrong. The Revolution was a matter that greatly concerned Indians. Well before 1775, they had become dependent on the frontier trade, especially in guns and munitions, essential goods subject to constant interruption and interception during the war. Too, with inexorable pressures already upon their lands and with Dunmore's War before them as a test case, Indians knew full well what would develop if Americans successfully overcame British authority.

In Native communities across eastern North America, villagers debated and selected courses of action. For the first year, the majority remained neutral, partly through the influence of women and older men less eager for war. After that, most eastern woodland peoples adopted varying degrees of belligerency. The largest number of militants fought as allies of the British, although a few smaller nations supplemented the Patriot cause. In many instances, younger warriors, determined to forcibly halt American expansion, openly ignored their elders and traditional tribal polity to take up arms. Nations fissured deeply in the process, often with certain factions establishing new communities distanced from traditional homelands as well as from white settlement.

Cherokee warriors launched the first considerable Indian attack against the Americans in the Revolution. Led by Dragging Canoe, groups of young militants set off to punish the southern frontier in the early summer of 1776. Viewing themselves as the Aniyunwiya (real people), they rejected counsel from the British and tribal elders and instead welcomed a war belt proffered by Shawnee emissaries. The Aniyunwiya departed from the remaining Cherokee nation the following year, appalled at their people's 5,000,000-acre accommodation for peace. Relocating near present-day Chattanooga, they became known as the Chickamauga nation. Dragging Canoe and his forces continued militancy for most of the next two decades. They often raided frontier settlements. Sometimes they assisted British offensives. Sometimes they accompanied young warriors of other nations, including the Shawnee and Delaware (Lenape) of the North and Choctaw and Creek (Muskogee) of the South.

Just as the Revolution partitioned colonists among Whig (anti-British), Loyalist (pro-British), and neutralist camps, it divided Native communities. Dragging Canoe was the son of the venerable headman Attakullakulla, one the greatest diplomats of

---

18. John Stuart to Cherokee Chiefs and Warriors, August 30, 1775, *Records of the British Colonial Office*, vol. 76, microfilm, 288.

the eighteenth century. Both men were authentic Cherokee Patriots. Yet they bitterly disagreed on what was best for their nation. A microcosm of what happened across much of Indian America, the father followed faith in diplomacy and trade, while the son trusted hunting and war. In such a manner, families, villages, and peoples were broken.

Beyond the Cherokee nation, Creeks, Choctaws, and Chickasaws constituted formidable southern peoples in proximity to American settlement. Creek country was divided geographically between its Upper Towns (in present-day Alabama) and Lower Towns (in southwest Georgia). The Lower Towns pursued neutrality during the war, for they were more vulnerable to Patriot attacks and needed American goods. In contrast, the Upper Towns could operate with greater impunity from Revolutionary reprisal and enjoyed better access to British support. The massive Patriot invasion of Cherokee lands in 1776 initially quelled Creek militancy. In subsequent years, however, multiple outrages committed by settlers against villagers, augmented by a scant American trade, moved many warriors to action. Led by the young métis (person of mixed-descent) Alexander McGillivray, by the summer of 1778, some 800 Creek militants were engaged against the Americans. The British capture of Savannah that December further emboldened Creek participation in the war, and their support proved critical in the Crown's defense of Augusta in September 1780.

British authorities particularly relied upon Chickasaw and Choctaw assistance to help secure key Mississippi posts and Gulf ports against attack. Superintendent John Stuart expressed surprise that Chickasaw allies would prioritize their seasonal hunt over Crown objectives. More disconcerting, while most Choctaw villages aligned with imperial interests, some towns colluded with Spain (America's ally as of June 1779). The British command never accepted that southern Indians were independent actors, not mercenaries. Major General John Campbell complained in September 1780, "I sincerely regret the Necessity of ever employing Savages, or being obliged to court them in War."[19] The following spring, 1,000 warriors, having been denied basic supplies and respect, vacated Campbell's defenses at Pensacola. The post fell after that to the Spanish siege, and British West Florida was lost.

"Total War in Indian Country"

Historian Colin Calloway designated the Revolution as "a total war in Indian country."[20] During 1776, Revolutionaries launched an all-out assault against the Cherokees (with more violence against the Cherokees to follow). During 1779,

---

19. Ethan A. Schmidt, *Native Americans in the American Revolution: How the War Divided, Devastated, and Transformed the Early American Indian World* (Santa Barbara, CA: Praeger, 2014), 113.

20. Colin G. Calloway, *The American Revolution in Indian Country: Crisis and Diversity in Native American Communities* (Cambridge, UK: Cambridge University Press, 1995), 46.

Iroquois villagers were targeted with a full-scale attack. Atrocities also would be enacted against the peoples of the Ohio country. Generous allotments of Indian land were absorbed in the process.

Once esteemed among the most fearsome and indomitable Native peoples, the Iroquois confederacy fractured critically during the Revolution. Here too, older sachems and women strove unsuccessfully to preserve traditional unity and consensus. Onondagas, Cayugas, and Senecas desired neutrality, albeit with a positive predisposition toward the Crown. Mohawks, the "Keepers of the Eastern Door," openly favored the British. Their neighbors, the Oneidas and Tuscaroras, leaned toward the Americans. Six Nations' neutrality became compromised in May 1776 when Oneidas and Tuscaroras formally aligned with the Patriots. This maneuver repositioned the two nations "out

During the Saratoga campaign, Mohawk Indians scouting for British General John Burgoyne's army killed twenty-five-year-old Jane McCrea on July 27, 1777, as she attempted to reach her fiancé, a Loyalist officer. Americans publicized the incident to inflame sentiments against "barbarous" Indians and their British allies. *The Death of Jane McCrea*, oil painting by John Vanderlyn, 1804. Wadsworth Atheneum, Hartford, CT.

from under the shadow of their Mohawk brethren."[21] Americans barely could provision their new allies, however, with little to nothing to spare for other Six Nations peoples. In response, Mohawk headman Joseph Brant mobilized belligerents in support of the British. Besides accessing imperial goods, Brant strategized that this service could secure royal protection for Iroquois lands. Indians, principally Mohawk and Seneca warriors, constituted the bulk of British support at the Battle of Oriskany in August 1777. They faced off against an American corps bolstered by Oneidas. The Iroquois confederacy was, for the time being, broken.

Mohawks supported Loyalists under Colonel John Butler in attacks upon the Wyoming Valley of Pennsylvania and Cherry Valley of New York during 1778. American propagandists insisted that Indians committed great "inhuman barbarities" in these campaigns. In fact, little evidence exists to indicate that any noncombatants were killed in the first battle, while the thirty-two innocent victims killed in the second engagement likely served as retribution for recent murders committed against villagers. In destroying the town of Oquaga, Patriot forces were reported as having discovered several small children hiding in a cornfield, whom they ran through with bayonets before displaying their writhing bodies as they died. Very likely, "Brant and his men exercised more restraint" than did Americans on the New York frontier.[22]

Beyond providing mythological fuel for the "merciless Indian savages," Brant's campaigns threatened to cut access to corn and wheat essential to the Continental cause. During 1779, General Washington decided upon a punitive operation against British-aligned Iroquois, stating in his order: "The immediate objects are the total destruction and devastation of their settlements . . . to ruin their crops now in the ground and prevent their planting more."[23] As early as 1753, Indians addressed Washington as "Town Destroyer" (Caunotaucarious), an appellation subsequently personified by his actions against Iroquois villagers in the Revolution.[24]

Despite enduring significant deprivation during the coming winter, Iroquois' resolve to resist the Americans only hardened. During 1780, Brant led attacks against the divided Oneida, neutralizing remaining support for the Patriots. Iroquois warriors assailed the New York frontier almost unopposed in 1781 until halted by an imperial ministry desperate to curtail expenses.

---

21. Schmidt, *Native Americans in the American Revolution*, 131.

22. Schmidt, 134–36.

23. Schmidt, 137.

24. Glenn F. Williams, *Year of the Hangman: George Washington's Campaign against the Iroquois* (Yardley, PA: Westholme, 2005), x.

"A Spirited Resistance"

The title of a monograph by Gregory Dowd, "a spirited resistance" aptly describes the ingenious manner in which trans-Appalachian prophets and diplomat-warriors promoted unprecedented intertribal collaboration across Native America during the era of the Revolution. The emergent message was that "all Indians were of a single people, separately created and required to perform special duties." Through shared religious and strategic practice, white encroachment might be halted from the tip of Michigan all the way to the Gulf of Mexico.[25]

That such a markedly unconventional effort met, at least for a generation, with no little success, belies the traditional portrayal of Indian societies as tribal cliques. "The striking fact," Dowd remarked, "is that Native Americans themselves, unlike many of their historians, could think continentally."[26] What they undertook and accomplished during the era of the Revolution was extraordinary, given the overwhelming threats, including ongoing smallpox epidemics, that confronted these peoples.

College and university faculty often find the need to challenge the dismissive, erroneous perception of Indians as primitives. Perhaps they did not possess or perhaps they had not once needed European-style technology. But civilization is far more than that. With respect to women and children, personal freedom and civic responsibility, tolerance of religious beliefs, regard for the natural world, and even personal hygiene, Native American civilization likely equaled or surpassed standards within Western culture. Observed the eighteenth-century traveler-ethnographer William Bartram: "If we consider them with respect to their private character or in a moral view, they must, I think, claim our approbation. . . . As moral men they certainly stand in no need of European civilization."[27]

"The West" to Americans in 1776 primarily meant the region west of the Appalachian Mountains and east of the Mississippi River. Along the Ohio Valley resided the Shawnee, Miami, Mingo (western Iroquois), and western Lenape peoples. They recognized clearly the colonists' Revolutionary intention: "To deprive us entirely of our whole Country."[28] Militants within these nations saw the war as an opportunity to halt and even push back white settlement. Yet division developed in the West, too. Each of these peoples entertained strong neutralist as well as pro-British factions. A modicum of pro-American sentiment was evident in some towns as well.

---

25. Gregory Evans Dowd, *A Spirited Resistance: The North American Indian Struggle for Unity, 1745–1815* (Baltimore, MD: Johns Hopkins University Press, 1992), xiii–xiv, xvii–xx.

26. Dowd, *Spirited Resistance*, xv.

27. William Bartram, *William Bartram on the Southeastern Indians*, ed. Gregory A. Waselkov and Kathryn E. Holland Braund (Lincoln: University of Nebraska Press, 1995), 114.

28. Schmidt, *Native Americans in the American Revolution*, 141.

Militancy in the Ohio country eventually won out, in no small part because of American targeting and killing of neutralist headmen. Included among the slain were the beloved Shawnee Cornstalk in 1777 and the venerable Delaware White Eyes in 1778. Americans purposely murdered Native peace advocates to foment a war that might liberate millions of acres from Native possession. West of the Appalachians, it seems, the Revolution operated at its most ignoble, often with little agenda other than to kill Indians and extract real estate. The most infamous episode occurred in March 1782 at the Christian mission of Gnadenhutten, north of the Ohio River. Here, American militia methodically clubbed to death nearly one hundred pacifist Indians, mostly women and children. Lenape and other militants hit back hard, crushing an American invasion force that June and ritually executing its commander, Colonel William Crawford, a close personal friend of George Washington. Still, nothing seemed to deter the entry of more squatters across the Appalachians. Ohio Valley villagers who continued to cling to neutrality were left with little choice but to abandon their traditional homelands and remove farther west.

Although cruelties were committed on both sides of the western frontier, Americans appear again to have exceeded Natives in aggression. George Rogers Clark's exploits, much celebrated in Patriot publicity, were something short of glorious. In an exchange with British commandant Henry Hamilton, Clark boasted that "he would never spare man, woman, or child of them [the Indians] on whom he could lay his hands." American militia fulfilled this genocidal promise many times by the Revolution's end.[29]

"We Are Not Yet Conquered"[30]

When British chief minister Lord North heard of Lord Cornwallis's surrender at Yorktown in October 1781, he reportedly uttered: "Oh God. It's all over."[31] And for the British effort to recover the thirteen colonies, it was. Faced with mounting debts and a plethora of enemies, Parliament voted to quit the war in North America early in 1782. Funding for imperial military initiatives evaporated. The Americans waited and then won a lopsided peace at Paris in September 1783. Among other stipulations, the settlement granted the United States the Ohio country and Great Lakes region

29. Gary B. Nash, *The Unknown American Revolution: The Unruly Birth of Democracy and the Struggle to Create America* (New York: Penguin Books, 2005), 351.

30. Dragging Canoe, in a speech to northern Indians, July 12, 1779, quoted in E. Raymond Evans, "Dragging Canoe," *Journal of Cherokee Studies* 2 (1977): 176–89, 184.

31. Alan Gilbert, *Black Patriots and Loyalists: Fighting for Emancipation in the War for Independence* (Chicago: University of Chicago Press, 2012), 177.

(formerly assigned to Canada). No consultation with or provision for any of Britain's Indian allies was included. In short, the treaty "gave them nothing."[32]

The Native American war for independence did not wind down after Yorktown. It did not conclude with the Paris Treaty. It continued for another decade and was subsequently reinvigorated during the War of 1812. Determined to protect their peoples and lands, warriors continued collective operations. Led by the Miami headman Little Turtle and the Shawnee war chief Blue Jacket, an extensive confederacy emerged north of the Ohio River during the 1780s. Resistance continued to the south as well, as facilitated by Dragging Canoe's Cherokee operatives in liaison with Creek militants associated with Alexander McGillivray.

The United States operated under the Articles of Confederation for most of the 1780s. That government held little authority, which emboldened Britain and Spain to extend posts into American territory from which they equipped the Indians. Undeterred, Confederation diplomats foisted a series of treaties aimed at wrenching away large tracts of land from the Iroquois, Great Lakes, and Ohio Valley nations. These negotiations were concluded with but rump representations from among these peoples, as Americans insisted upon the right of conquest. Supposedly, when Britain abandoned the war, their Indian allies also had been vanquished. Keeping with previous Patriot protocol, Native forfeiture of extensive estate was expected.

Conquest theory was pure myth, a fallacy for which Americans would pay dearly. For more than a decade after Yorktown, some 250 Kentuckians were killed each year in Indian raids, including the grandfather of Abraham Lincoln. In 1790, Little Turtle's warriors drove back an American army of 1,500 troops under the command of General Josiah Harmar. A year later, the Miami confederation annihilated a second invading force into Ohio, this one led by General Arthur St. Clair. Only 24 men out of more than 1,100 soldiers and camp followers escaped unharmed. Nearly one-third of the entire federal army was extinguished. Not until General Anthony Wayne's victory at Fallen Timbers in August 1794 did militant resistance in the northwest subside.

America's Indian Allies

A limited number of Indian nations assisted the Revolutionary cause. In a myth of omission, Americans largely downplayed or ignored these peoples' contributions at the war's close. To quote Colin Calloway: "Though Indian people laid down their lives in the cause of freedom, they could not enjoy the benefits of freedom once it was won."[33]

Among southern Indians, the Catawbas, with their land reserve surrounded by white settlement, threw in their lot with the Patriots shortly after the opening of the

---

32. Dowd, *Spirited Resistance*, 93.
33. Calloway, *American Revolution in Indian Country*, 85.

Revolution. Much reduced through generations of smallpox and war, the Catawbas could field only about fifty warriors in 1775. Still, the nation proved of real value to the Americans. Among other services, during 1776, warriors provided reconnaissance in the Patriot invasions against the Catawbas' longtime enemy, the Cherokees. During 1780, Catawba Town provided bivouacs and cattle for General Thomas Sumter's spent partisan forces at a critical point in the southern Revolution. Subsequently, the nation was forced to flee northward as British operatives retaliated by decimating their homes and fields. Finally able to return home to South Carolina in 1781, the Catawba people were welcomed with state cash and corn in compensation for their sacrifice. The last Indian people to maintain title within the state, Catawbas nonetheless lost all but 12 of their 225-square-mile reserve by the Revolution's end. In a two-volume state history published in 1809, David Ramsay never mentions the Catawbas' important role in the Revolution, only attesting that the nation was "fast sinking into insignificance."[34]

Small enrollments of northern Indians also served with the Patriots, including warriors from the Penobscot and other New England nations. Perhaps most singular here were the Stockbridge Indians. Led by sachem Daniel Ninham, a community of Wappinger and Mahican refugees at Stockbridge, Massachusetts, pledged their support in 1775. Similar to the Catawbas, the Stockbridge Indians joined, hoping to secure their community, which was already fully surrounded by American settlement. Some forty warriors enlisted. Half of that force was lost in a single engagement against British cavalry in 1778. Yet those who survived fought on to the close of the war. Largely ignored after that, the Stockbridge people eventually joined the Oneida.

The Oneida nation ranked as the most numerous among America's Indian allies in the Revolution. Preferring tribal autonomy over Iroquois neutrality and in rapport with the American missionary Samuel Kirkland, in May 1776, a sizeable Oneida cohort declared for the Patriots. Some Tuscaroras joined in as well. About sixty Oneidas were with American troops at the Battle of Oriskany in 1777. During 1779, Oneida and Tuscarora warriors performed reconnaissance for the Patriot invasion of Iroquois homelands. Joseph Brant responded with an offensive that leveled several of their towns. Faced with disaster, an appreciable number of warriors from the two nations changed alignment to the British before the war's end. America's Oneida allies were dispossessed after the Revolution and relocated to Wisconsin and Ontario. Those Tuscaroras who did not join the British continued a tenuous presence in upstate New York.

"Well Satisfied" Slaves

From today's perspective, no Patriot myth appears more patently absurd than that of David Ramsay's "well satisfied" slave. Indeed, the South Carolina Revolutionary went

---

34. Ramsay, *History of South Carolina*, 1:113.

so far as to assure readers that "life is often more pleasantly enjoyed by the slave, than his master."[35]

The gifted poet Phillis Wheatley, herself a slave, would not agree: "In every human Breast, God has implanted a Principle, which we call Love of Freedom; it is impatient of Oppression and pants for deliverance."[36] Scores of American slaves who sued in northern courts and petitioned assemblies for freedom would have agreed with Wheatley. So would the more than 20,000 slaves who enlisted for service alongside British or American forces during the Revolution. And so would perhaps as many as 100,000 people who simply took leave of their masters during the War for Independence. Many of these runaways departed to British lines, and others joined maroon communities of former fugitive slaves. Altogether, as historian Gary Nash summed it, the Revolution constituted the "first mass slave rebellion in American history."[37] One-in-four slaves escaped during the crisis, and no doubt many more would have if the opportunity had become available to them.

Ramsay's head-in-the-sand view that American slaves liked being slaves persisted long after the Revolution, even well after the Civil War. Writing near the close of the nineteenth century, Harvard historian John Fiske assured readers that "relationships between the master and slave in Virginia were so pleasant that the offer of freedom fell upon dull, uninterested ears."[38] Today's historians know better, of course, and a rich literature has emerged. Even so, many Americans still hold little awareness of the critical roles performed by free Blacks and slaves in the Revolutionary era.

Black people in 1775 constituted approximately 20 percent of the American population. Included were nearly half-a-million slaves (far more numerous in the South) and perhaps 40,000 free Blacks (most conspicuous in the North). Four-in-ten people in the Chesapeake and six-in-ten people in the Lower South were held as chattel. These regions constituted "slave societies" as compared to "societies with slaves" farther north.[39] Slaves, in fact, outnumbered white people more than fifteen-to-one in some coastal precincts of South Carolina.

While Patriot narrators targeted Native Americans as a defining enemy for the Revolution, they quite purposefully downplayed the presence of Black Americans

---

35. Ramsay, *History of the American Revolution*, 1:24.

36. Phillis Wheatley, Letter to Samson Occum, February 11, 1774, in *Black Americans in the Revolutionary Era: A Brief History with Documents*, ed. Woody Holton (Boston, MA: Bedford/St. Martin's, 2009), 51.

37. Gary B. Nash, "The African Americans' Revolution," in *The Oxford Handbook of the American Revolution*, ed. Edward G. Gray and Jane Kamensky (New York: Oxford University Press, 2013), 250–72.

38. Gary B. Nash, *The Forgotten Fifth: African Americans in the Age of Revolution* (Cambridge, MA: Harvard University Press, 2006), 5–7.

39. Judith L. Van Buskirk, *Standing in Their Own Light: African American Patriots in the American Revolution* (Norman: University of Oklahoma Press, 2017), 37.

altogether. Conflict with Indian peoples would free up western lands. But conflict with slaves would cripple the American labor force. Worse, such battles would not be confined largely to the frontier and military campaigns. Slave insurrection would occur at the family hearth, perhaps without warning or opportunity for defense. In Patriot reckoning, both Native and Black peoples qualified as the "other." The first could be treated as an alien "other" whereas the second could not. Slaves were not "savages" but "my people," "well satisfied" members of the extended plantation family. As such, they were not concerned with matters beyond the master's household.

The "Two Revolutions"

The era of the American Revolution occasioned a variety of meanings for a variety of peoples. Historian Alan Gilbert particularly analyzes "two revolutions." One was the struggle for American independence. The other was an effort to emancipate slaves. Freedom and equality were at the heart of both movements, and their dual contexts were inextricably linked. Even so, during the Revolution, many who sought independence rejected slave emancipation, while others who sought emancipation rejected American independence. The first revolution succeeded in creating the United States, yet fell short of its founding pledge to universally honor "life, liberty, and the pursuit of happiness." The second revolution succeeded in making emancipation inevitable, yet fell short of its immediate goal, leaving many years to follow of struggle toward Black freedom and equality.[40]

African Americans contributed essentially to each of the two revolutions. Black people in New England most often supported both causes. Helping secure American independence, they believed, would help secure freedom for all. Black people in the Mid-Atlantic, Chesapeake, and especially the Lower South, more commonly sided against independence, believing that Britain offered the faster, surer way to the end of slavery. Overall, the Revolution brought African Americans together in collaboration as never before. The networks and organizations they founded would continue the struggle for freedom long after Yorktown. The Revolution forever changed Black America, even as Black America forever changed the Revolution.

Somerset Decision and Dunmore's Proclamation

Euro-American talk of freedom inevitably inspired African American talk of freedom. During the last colonial years, Black Americans, too, began to call for liberty. In January 1765, Henry Laurens recorded "a peculiar incident" at Charleston, South Carolina, when slaves, "apparently in thoughtless imitation" of earlier Stamp Act

---

40. Gilbert, *Black Patriots and Loyalists*, viii–ix, 6.

By His Excellency the Right Honorable JOHN Earl of DUNMORE, His
MAJESTY's Lieutenant and Governor General of the Colony and Dominion of
VIRGINIA, and Vice Admiral of the same

A PROCLAMATION.

AS I have ever entertained Hopes, that an Accommodation might have taken Place between GREAT-BRITAIN and this Colony, without being compelled by my Duty to this most disagreeable but now absolutely necessary Step, rendered so by a Body of armed Men unlawfully assembled, firing on His MAJESTY's Tenders, and the formation of an Army, and that Army now on their March to attack His MAJESTY's Troops and destroy the well disposed Subjects of this Colony. To defeat such treasonable Purposes, and that all such Traitors, and their Abettors, may be brought to Justice, and that the Peace, and good Order of this Colony may be again restored, which the ordinary Course of the Civil Law is unable to effect; I have thought fit to issue this my Proclamation, hereby declaring, that until the aforesaid good Purposes can be obtained, I do in Virtue of the Power and Authority to ME given, by His MAJESTY, determine to execute Martial Law, and cause the same to be executed throughout this Colony; and to the end that Peace and good Order may the sooner be restored, I do require every Person capable of bearing Arms, to resort to His MAJESTY's STANDARD, or be looked upon as Traitors to His MAJESTY's Crown and Government, and thereby become liable to the Penalty the Law inflicts upon such Offences; such as forfeiture of Life, confiscation of Lands, &c. &c. And I do hereby further declare all indented Servants, Negroes, or others, (appertaining to Rebels,) free that are able and willing to bear Arms, they joining His MAJESTY's Troops as soon as may be, for the more speedily reducing this Colony to a proper Sense of their Duty, to His MAJESTY's Crown and Dignity. I do further order, and require, all His MAJESTY's Leige Subjects, to retain their Quitrents, or any other Taxes due or that may become due, in their own Custody, till such Time as Peace may be again restored to this at present most unhappy Country, or demanded of them for their former salutary Purposes, by Officers properly authorised to receive the same.

GIVEN under my Hand on board the Ship WILLIAM, off NORFOLK, the 7th Day of NOVEMBER, in the SIXTEENTH Year of His MAJESTY's Reign.

DUNMORE.

(GOD save the KING.)

Some British officials openly sought African American support in suppressing the rebellion. On November 7, 1775, Virginia's royal governor Lord Dunmore issued a proclamation that offered freedom to all slaves who would fight for the British, provided the slaves were owned by people who supported the Revolution. Although hundreds of Blacks responded to Dunmore's call, American historians later downplayed the fact, insisting that slaves preferred bondage to serving in the military. Dunmore's Proclamation, issued November 7, 1775, published November 14, 1775. Library of Congress.

protesters, "began to cry 'Liberty.'" The city was placed on lockdown for a week as more than one hundred slaves went missing.[41] In March 1770, an imposing Black sailor named Crispus Attucks led a group of disgruntled Massachusetts men to threaten a squad of occupying British soldiers. Attucks was one of five people killed in the ensuing gunfire, dubbed the "Boston Massacre" in the colonial press.

The *Somerset* decision of June 1772 further inspired African Americans to action. Here British chief justice Lord Mansfield ruled slavery to be "so odious, that nothing can be suffered to support it, but positive law."[42] Although the decision only restricted slavery in England, the precedent was set for the remainder of the British realm. At some point, the decision intimated moral law, which disqualifies slavery, must supplant existing positive law, which allows slavery.

News of the *Somerset* ruling spread rapidly across Black as well as white America. In the Lower South, during 1773, numerous groups of slaves departed for maroon communities. In Massachusetts, the leading crucible in the coming of the Revolution, Black activists repeatedly petitioned legislators to abolish slavery. Abigail Adams numbered among white observers well disposed to their cause. She wished that "there was not a slave in the province," for it seemed the height of hypocrisy to "fight ourselves for what we are daily robbing and plundering from those who have as good a right to freedom as we have."[43]

When Massachusetts was ordered under martial law in 1774, some Black Bostonians approached General Thomas Gage, offering their services in the event of war. No doubt, this was done in anticipation of a general British emancipation. The following April, as conflict loomed between Britain and the colonies, slaves approached the royal governor of Virginia, Lord Dunmore. Dunmore thereupon informed London of his aim "to arm all my own Negroes, and receive all others that will come to me whom I shall declare free."[44] Accordingly, on November 14, 1775, Dunmore issued a proclamation that offered freedom to slaves and indentured servants owned by Revolutionaries in exchange for British military service.

The announcement greatly encouraged American slaves even as it greatly offended American slaveholders. In short order, at least 800 Black men, along with several hundred women and children, managed to elude slave patrols and make it behind Dunmore's lines. Garbed with sashes that read "Liberty to Slaves," Dunmore's "Ethiopian Regiment" was said to have fought "with the intrepidity of lions." In many places across the South, a mass exodus began, including some of George Washington's people. Lund Washington, the general's cousin and caretaker at Mount Vernon,

---

41. Nash, *Unknown American Revolution*, 61.

42. Edward Countryman, *Enjoy the Same Liberty: Black Americans and the Revolutionary Era* (Lanham, MD: Rowman & Littlefield, 2014), 132–33.

43. Nash, "African Americans' Revolution," 253.

44. Nash, "African Americans' Revolution," 254.

reported that "there is not a man of them but would leave us, if they could make their escape. . . . Liberty is sweet."[45]

Dunmore's pronouncement helped activate the southern Revolution. According to *Forced Founders* author Woody Holton, the "informal partnership" forged by Black people and British authorities "infuriated white colonists" to independence.[46] David Ramsay later recalled how white Americans "were struck with horror" by the proclamation, fearing general slave insurrection as well as an enormous loss of property.[47]

Dunmore's corps scored impressive success against superior numbers in an engagement at Kemp's Landing in November 1775. The following month, however, they were defeated at the Battle of Great Bridge. Smallpox subsequently decimated the regiment. Only 300 Black soldiers were able to accompany Dunmore upon his embarkation from Virginia in August 1776. The regiment then participated in General Sir William Howe's campaign that repeatedly humbled the Continental Army in New York.

Black Patriots

Whereas southern slaves banked on British backing, many northern free Blacks and slaves forwarded freedom in liaison with the Patriots. Black minutemen were present at Lexington and Concord in April 1775. That June, 150 Black Patriots participated at Bunker Hill, where freeman Peter Salem was credited with killing British commander John Pitcairn. George Washington assumed Continental command at Boston in July 1775. He was stunned to see African American troops and how easily they mingled with white New England soldiers. Initially, slaveholding Washington tried to stem further Black enlistment. He soon reversed course, however, acknowledging the need for these recruits. Indeed, African American soldiers "fought harder and served longer"[48] than any other Patriot cohort. They fought not only for freedom from Britain but also for freedom for themselves and for their people.

Black Patriots may well have saved the Revolution following the disastrous American defeat on Long Island in August 1776. Trapped between the sea and British forces, Washington's army was evacuated in small boats under cover of fog and night by hundreds of skilled Black and white oarsmen. African American sailors also proved indispensable that Christmas, helping ferry Washington's strike force across the Delaware River for the surprise attack against the Hessians at Trenton. That victory, combined with another success at Princeton the following week, again salvaged the Patriot cause,

---

45. Nash, "African Americans' Revolution," 259.

46. Woody Holton, *Black Americans in the Revolutionary Era: A Brief History with Documents*, ed. Woody Holton (Boston, MA: Bedford/St. Martin's, 2009), 2.

47. Ramsay, *History of the American Revolution*, 1:250.

48. Gilbert, *Black Patriots and Loyalists*, 28.

despite General Howe's mockery of the rebels' "motley crew," which he branded as "the strangest that was ever collected: old men of 60, boys of 11, and Blacks of all ages and ragged for the most part."[49]

During 1776, Black Patriots were heartened by the unalterable, universal precepts pledged within the Declaration of Independence: "We hold these truths to be self-evident, that all men are created equal, that they are endowed by their Creator with certain unalienable Rights, that among these are Life, Liberty and the pursuit of Happiness." Interestingly, Jefferson's original draft of the Declaration included a long passage that indicted the Crown for the transatlantic slave trade as well as for "now exciting those very people to rise in arms among us, and to purchase that liberty of which he has deprived them." Slavery was wrong. But Britain was to blame, not America, for this unnatural institution birthed through an "assemblage of horrors."[50]

Congress balked. After days of feverish editing, all that remained concerning Jefferson's assault upon slavery was that the king had "excited domestic insurrections amongst us." The founders were reluctant to tackle slavery head-on, even though they knew it was dreadful. (Genetic evidence reveals Jefferson's own deeply problematic relationship with the institution.) Directly addressing slavery in the context of the language of liberty would have all but required some immediate emancipatory response. Better to

Despite efforts by some American leaders to prevent African Americans from performing military service, many Black men joined the Continental Army in hopes of obtaining freedom. Organized in 1778, the 1st Rhode Island Regiment was composed of African American enlisted men led by white officers and noncommissioned officers. After the war, most historians ignored or minimized the actions of Black participants. *American Soldiers at the Siege of Yorktown*, watercolor by Jean-Baptiste-Antoine DeVerger, 1781. Library of Congress.

49. Gilbert, 64.

50. Countryman, *Enjoy the Same Liberty*, 62.

downplay the matter, decided the Declaration's signatories, rather than forfeit personal "property" and raise the wrath of American slaveholders.

Some contemporary voices dismiss the founders' statements on universal equality and freedom as mere hyperbole with respect to non-white peoples.[51] Yet private correspondence, as well as public discourse, reveals that many Patriot leaders seem to have meant what they said. Patrick Henry summed slavery "as repugnant to humanity as it is inconsistent with the Bible and destructive to liberty." "I cannot justify it." Even so, Henry faltered to free his slaves because of "the general inconveniency of living without them." No doubt, he reassured himself, "a time will come when an opportunity will be afforded to abolish this lamentable evil."[52] Thomas Jefferson, Henry Laurens, James Madison, and George Mason, among other leading Patriot slaveholders, expressed similar discomfort. Robert Carter, Virginia's largest slaveholder, actually freed all 452 of his people—a deed repeated by George Washington in his will. Temporarily, at least, slavery appeared out of vogue in the world of the Revolution.

Steeped in Enlightenment and Great Awakening ideals, the Revolutionaries, explained historian Nicholas Guyatt, "couldn't easily conclude that non-white people were different from or permanently inferior to themselves." Most founders wished for an end to slavery even as they simultaneously rejected Black citizenship. Freed people might be shipped to Africa, wished Jefferson and others, where they could advance in civilization without impeding or being impeded by white liberty. In short, Guyatt concluded, the Revolutionaries were segregationist more than blindly racist, trusting that separation eventually would yield equality.[53]

Black Patriots became increasingly numerous after 1776. In all, perhaps 9,000 African Americans enlisted on behalf of the Revolution. The largest number of Black men were in the Continental service, with many continuing for the duration of the war. Most were northern free Blacks or bondsmen promised liberty in exchange for their service. Some Chesapeake free men and slaves also served with the Patriots. So did many Black women who assisted in army camp life.

As the Continental Army's white enlistment lagged in 1777, Congress advised the states to meet their quotas "by drafts, from their militia, or in any other way."[54] Consequently, a practice arose whereby slaves often served in place of their drafted masters. New York awarded slaveholders western land bounties in exchange for slave soldiers, who would receive freedom at the war's conclusion. Most Black enlistments

---

51. See, e.g., Hannah-Jones, "1619 Project," 16.

52. Simon Schama, *Rough Crossings: The Slaves, the British, and the American Revolution* (New York: HarperCollins, 2006), 14; Nash, *Unknown American Revolution*, 118.

53. Nicholas Guyatt, *Bind Us Apart: How Enlightened Americans Invented Racial Segregation* (New York: Basic Books, 2016), 8, 323.

54. Robert A. Selig, "The Revolution's Black Soldiers," AmericanRevolution.org, https://www.american-revolution.org/blk.php (accessed July 21, 2021).

were integrated within white units; dozens of Black soldiers, for instance, were present in each Virginia regiment at Valley Forge. Still, Massachusetts and Connecticut assembled all-Black companies, while more than half of Rhode Island's 1st Regiment were African Americans.

Commanded by Colonel Christopher Greene, the 1st Rhode Island acquitted itself well, crushing a Hessian attack on Fort Mercer in October 1777. Impressed by this service, the following February, Rhode Island issued a Slave Enlistment Act, declaring all Black recruits "absolutely FREE" with compensation to be provided to owners.[55] Truly revolutionary, the law energized independence and presaged further emancipation to come. The 1st Regiment proved instrumental at the Battle of Rhode Island in August 1778, preserving the American line against two "furious" enemy advances. A grateful George Washington commended the regiment as "well intitled to a proper share of honor of the Day."[56]

Light infantry led by Lieutenant Colonel John Laurens was among the American forces relieved by "the Black Regiment" during the Battle of Rhode Island. Early in 1779, Laurens, scion of one of South Carolina's wealthiest slaveholding families, forwarded a plan to enroll southern slaves for Continental service. Similar to Rhode Island's legislation, the measure proposed freedom for all who served for the war's duration with compensation provided to their masters. The plan received support from Henry Laurens, John's prominent father, as well as other South Carolinians serving at Philadelphia. That March, Congress approved a measure for raising 3,000 Black soldiers.

The principal theater of the Revolution relocated to the Lower South during 1779. Savannah had fallen into British possession, and Charleston would be targeted next. Laurens's strategy to infuse the fight for independence with emancipation could have enlivened flagging Patriot morale in the South and stymied British advance. If approved, it would have arrested American slavery at the very heart of slave country. But Governor John Rutledge and the South Carolina legislature would have none of it. They rejected Laurens's proposal outright in 1779 and again in 1780, even as British forces bore down on Charleston. The state instead decided to offer slaves captured from Loyalists as bounties for white recruitment. Sad to say, but in the Lower South, many Americans would have preferred to lose the war than to lose their slaves. Thundered Rutledge, "religion & humanity had nothing to do" with slavery; "interest alone is the governing principle with Nations."[57]

---

55. Michael Lee Lanning, *Defenders of Liberty: African Americans in the Revolutionary War* (New York: Citadel Press, 2000), 205–6.

56. Robert Geake, *From Slaves to Soldiers, The 1st Rhode Island Regiment in the American Revolution* (Yardley, PA: Westholme, 2016), 39–40.

57. Lawrence Goldstone, *Dark Bargain: Slavery, Profits, and the Struggle for the Constitution* (New York: Walker Publishing, 2005), 191.

Black Loyalists

Two related myths served in tandem with the Patriot chimera of the well-contented slave: first, that slaves were gullible, simple-minded people, readily misled by British intrigue; and second, those Black people who did participate in the Revolution really did not contribute much value anyway.

Perhaps above all else, the Revolution provided African Americans with *choices*:[58] whether to continue in normal routine or to resist it; whether to stay or run away; whether to join a maroon community or ally with the colonists or the British; whether to embrace or reject American independence as the better route to freedom. As Sylvia Frey sees it, the Revolution generated a "triagonal war,"[59] wherein Black Americans could operate between, alongside, or against white belligerents. The range of choices available varied from place to place and from time to time. But African Americans had choices, some of which served as steps toward freedom. The specific choices made by free Blacks and slaves during the Revolution were highly logical given local, specific circumstances. African American men and women sought the best options available for themselves and their families. In general, the best hope for freedom meant alliance with independence in New England and abeyance or active opposition to independence in the Mid-Atlantic and South.[60]

Black Loyalists, just as did Black Patriots, contributed significantly during the Revolution. About 15,000 escaped men, as well as thousands of refugee women, lent service to the British. In all, perhaps as many as 100,000 slaves ran away, while many who remained resisted labor, further crippling the southern economy. Among active recruits, there were Black infantrymen, Black dragoons, Black foragers and guerrilla fighters, and Black pioneers (guides and spies). Most African Americans who joined British ranks, however, were assigned as laborers.

Probably the best-known Black Loyalist operative was "Colonel Tye." Tye (Cornelius Titus) escaped from slavery in New Jersey in 1775 to join Dunmore's Ethiopian Regiment. He later returned to New Jersey and in 1779, began conducting a series of successful raids, ransacking Patriot properties and capturing a number of prominent American leaders. Tye's "Black Brigade" further extended guerrilla operations during 1780, often in coordination with white Loyalists of the "Queen's Rangers." When Tye died late that summer from an infected wound, even Patriot enemies expressed admiration for his exceptional abilities.

Quamino Dolly was another Black Loyalist of note. He helped the British snare Savannah in December 1778, leading troops along an undetected route behind

---

58. Countryman, *Enjoy the Same Liberty*, xxv; Van Buskirk, *Standing in Their Own Light*, 19.

59. Sylvia R. Frey, *Water from the Rock: Black Resistance in a Revolutionary Age* (Princeton, NJ: Princeton University Press, 1991), 108.

60. Douglas R. Egerton, *Death or Liberty: African Americans and Revolutionary America* (New York: Oxford University Press, 2009), 68, 88.

American lines. A Franco-American task force bolstered by 500 Black Haitians tried to retake the city the following October. British defenses held, though, thanks in no small part to more than 600 Black Loyalist troops and support personnel, among them guides who directed reinforcements along hidden approaches, helping break the siege.

On June 30, 1779, British commander-in-chief Sir Henry Clinton issued a proclamation promising every slave "who shall desert the Rebel Standard, full security to follow within these Lines, any Occupation which he shall think proper." Subsequently advertised by Clinton as "freedom and a farm," the declaration accelerated an already prodigious Black flight, with many thousands of men, women, and children refugees soon overtaxing imperial supplies.[61] The British had undertaken what South Carolina would not. Devoid of Black recruits, Charleston capitulated in May 1780 in the worst American defeat of the war. More than 5,000 Patriot troops were lost.

It took considerable courage for Black men to enlist alongside the British, especially those who served as raiders. These guerrilla fighters constituted a "second front" of sorts, continually intercepting Patriot communications and confiscating supplies. They were taking "enormous risks" and could expect a "uniquely murderous" treatment if captured by Americans. To hear Patriots such as C.C. Pinckney tell it, the "black Dragoons" daily committed "the most horrible depredations and murder." But in truth, these men's "lack of murderousness" contrasted decidedly from the "barbarism" practiced by many southern Revolutionaries.[62]

Black Loyalists accomplished a good deal in service to the Crown. Much more could have been done had British authorities committed to a general emancipation. They were reluctant to do so for fear of offending Loyalist slaveholders, as well as from concern of how such a measure might impact Britain's lucrative Caribbean plantations. Taken as a whole, the Crown's approach toward manumission exhibited "a notoriously patchwork quality."[63] Attested historian Jim Piecuch, "victory in the South was well within the British grasp" had imperial authorities "brought every supporter of the king, regardless of race, into action against the rebels."[64]

Yorktown and the Paris Treaty

During 1781, James Armistead, an escaped slave from Virginia, provided another vital African American contribution. Feigning spy service on behalf of the Loyalists,

---

61. Gilbert, *Black Patriots and Loyalists*, 121.

62. Gilbert, 149, 158–59.

63. Gilbert, 131.

64. Jim Piecuch, *Three Peoples, One King: Loyalists, Indians, and Slaves in the Revolutionary South, 1775–1782* (Columbia: University of South Carolina Press, 2008), 334.

Armistead gained access to British headquarters to gather critical details that he delivered to the Marquis de Lafayette. This intelligence helped inform Franco-American operations subsequently employed against Lord Cornwallis's army at Yorktown.

According to some historians, 1,500 Black troops (25 percent of American forces) campaigned with Washington that autumn (other historians believe this figure is too high). Included were members of the 1st Rhode Island, complimented by one foreign officer as being "the most neatly dressed, the best under arms, and the most precise in its maneuvers" among any of the Continental units.[65] Many of the troops arrayed against them were Black soldiers too. By the summer of 1781, about 4,000 African Americans, most in nonmilitary roles, were with Cornwallis's army in Virginia.

The siege lasted three weeks before concluding with a formal British surrender on October 19. With supplies nearly exhausted, during the operations, Cornwallis forced from his defenses thousands of slaves, many of whom were afflicted with smallpox. A Hessian officer grieved over this abandonment of "our black friends," who soon would "face the reward of their cruel masters." Perhaps Cornwallis thought his order might provide these people a chance to escape. Perhaps he was attempting germ warfare. Perhaps there was no motive other than conserving supplies. Whatever the rationale, Yorktown proved a disaster for thousands of African American men, women, and children who had risked everything to reach British lines.[66]

Yorktown, of course, was a disaster for the British cause as a whole. Cornwallis lost his entire army of more than 7,000 men. London was done. In 1782, Lord Dunmore tried to renew imperial interest in the war, conveying to Parliament South Carolina Loyalist John Cruden's call for 10,000 new Black recruits. General Sir Guy Carleton, the new commander-in-chief for British North America, showed no interest.

In 1782, Patriots likewise eschewed further Black recruitment. To shove the British from Charleston, General Nathanael Greene urged South Carolina to consider once again Colonel Laurens's plan to create four regiments of slave soldiers who would be freed following the war. It would be wise, Greene argued, for the state to take advantage of its "natural strength" and thereby "secure the fidelity" of its Black population.[67] For the third time in three years, South Carolina's answer was a flat "no." Brave to a fault, John Laurens fell in a skirmish at the Combahee River that August. Ironically, it was a Black Loyalist soldier who killed the young emancipationist.

Henry Laurens was one of four American diplomats appointed in 1782 to conclude peace with Britain. His principal contribution at Paris was to add an article to

---

65. Gilbert, *Black Patriots and Loyalists*, 174–75.
66. Nash, *Unknown American Revolution*, 338–39.
67. Van Buskirk, *Standing in Their Own Light*, 169–71.

the treaty that required the return of slaves who had fled to the British. Here the father "betrayed his son."[68] British commanders largely ignored the order. By 1784, perhaps 15,000 slaves had embarked with Loyalist masters from Lower South ports. More than 3,000 freed people boarded at New York, the scene of the largest British evacuation. Many of these individuals were shipped to Nova Scotia, others to East Florida, the Caribbean, and England. Subsequently, 1,200 of the Canadian émigrés relocated to Sierra Leone in West Africa in a sort of "reverse diaspora."[69]

"To Begin *Their* World Anew"

A long-acclaimed myth is that the founders really could not have done much more concerning slavery than they did, and the nascent republic was just too fragile to attempt otherwise. Excising the lesion of slavery at that time would have killed the United States.

Gary Nash found this argument "odious," a surrender to "inevitability, almost always in historical writing a concept advanced by those eager to excuse mistakes and virtually never by those writing on behalf of victims of the mistakes." The real issue, Nash contended, was a lack of leadership, a want for determination or courage, not the lack of opportunity.[70] Perhaps some type of Revolutionary fatigue was at work. Whatever the case, many decisions rendered during the early republic do not reflect well on the traditional heroes in America's creation story.

From his Parisian post in 1787, Thomas Jefferson extolled the Constitutional Convention as "an assembly of demigods" who would devise a "good and wise" plan for government.[71] But the work completed at Philadelphia that summer was not "good and wise" with respect to African Americans. The Convention, in fact, became morally compromised through compliance with slavery. A series of awkward settlements were brokered, including the three-fifths compromise, a truly bizarre variety of virtual representation for slaves, and the slave-trade compromise, which prohibited any national ban on the importation of Africans for twenty years.

Virginia slaveholders James Madison and George Mason, among other Convention luminaries, chafed at conceding to the infamous Middle Passage. South Carolina and Georgia delegates insisted upon it, however. Otherwise, South Carolina delegate John Rutledge promised they would not join the new union. That was an idle threat.

---

68. Gilbert, *Black Patriots and Loyalists*, 167.

69. Nash, "African Americans' Revolution," 263–64.

70. Nash, *Forgotten Fifth*, 70, 90–91.

71. From Thomas Jefferson to John Adams, 30 August 1787, *Founders Online*, National Archives, https://founders.archives.gov (accessed July 22, 2021). [Original source: *The Papers of Thomas Jefferson*, vol. 12, *7 August 1787–31 March 1788*, ed. Julian P. Boyd (Princeton, NJ: Princeton University Press, 1955), 66–69.]

For strategic as well as economic reasons, Lower South states had no choice but to approve the Constitution. Yet the premium was on consensus, and no one called the bluff.[72] The Atlantic slave traffic would be permitted until 1808, with an interstate fugitive slave clause to boot.

Frankly, "the framers were embarrassed by slavery."[73] They should have been. In the world of the Revolution, they knew better. The word itself never appears in the Constitution, only a series of clunky euphemisms. As the era of the Revolution closed, Black Americans would have to continue the struggle for freedom within an official atmosphere of adversity and ambiguity. There remained helpful white allies, to be sure. Still, they would have to do most of the heavy lifting. They would have "to begin *their* world anew."[74] From their Revolutionary experiences, African Americans shaped networks and institutions that continued to champion liberty. In northern states, they did so through Black churches, Black mutual aid societies, Black businesses, and Black newspapers and publications. In southern states, they did so within the slave quarters and the "invisible church," as well as through informal communication networks ("the Word"), and innumerable covert and sometimes overt acts of resistance.

Conclusion

Of the founders, George Washington ranks highest and is the most mythologized. It is true that he took honor very seriously, and it was the foundation for his unparalleled reputation and career. Washington treated Indians with honesty during his presidency. Per his secretary of war Henry Knox's plan, the federal government would purchase "excess hunting grounds," leave Indian peoples with a small reserve of their homelands, and provide training toward profitable American livelihood and citizenship. Concerning Black Americans, Washington manumitted his slaves in his will and made financial provisions for those needing assistance.

For the time, those were noble actions. Yet Washington could have done more, much more toward honoring Native peoples and culture and especially by calling out slavery. Even so, he went a good deal further than fellow Virginian Thomas Jefferson, who during his presidency dealt unscrupulously to gain Indian lands, and who encouraged the spread of slavery westward, even as he deluded himself that somehow the institution would become "diluted" in the process.[75]

The Patriots had taken great risks against long odds to secure independence. In the world of the Revolution, anything had seemed possible. Unbounded liberty and equality were divinely ordained, self-evident truths, Jefferson said. But then the

---

72. Nash, *Forgotten Fifth*, 80–85.
73. Countryman, *Enjoy the Same Liberty*, 76.
74. Nash, "African Americans' Revolution," 264.
75. Countryman, *Enjoy the Same Liberty*, 97.

founders fell back. They acquiesced to property and self-interest in abstention of freedom and fairness. Native American land and African American labor were just too important to too many citizens to have it otherwise, they reasoned. Many further rejected the idea of integrating so many "others" into equal society. "Regrettable, but inevitable" became the policy: at least for the foreseeable future, Black people would remain slaves in the South while eastern Indians would be removed to the West.

To help justify this enormous injustice, Patriot narrators worked to repress memory of the many noteworthy Native and Black contributions to independence. These peoples did not really understand the Revolution, they wrote. For the most part, they were unwitting pawns of the British and certainly not in a position to receive any equal portion of the fruits of liberty. In truth, of course, freedom and justice are never zero-sum affairs; they are cherished gifts that all must share. The Revolutionary stories of Native America and Black America remain critical today for informing the fuller meaning of liberty and independence. Relating the founding in proper perspective requires attention to the patriotism, innovation, and sacrifices performed by each of these quintessentially American peoples.

7. THE LOYALISTS

Jim Piecuch

> A Tory is a thing whose head is in England, whose body is in
> America, and whose neck ought to be stretched.[1]
> —*Revolutionary aphorism, 1777*

> Lord Cornwallis was "compelled . . . to conduct, rather than command, a numerous
> band of traitors and robbers . . . decorated with the name of *Loyalists*. This rabble
> preceded the troops in plunder, taking special care never to follow them in danger.
> Their progress was marked by fire, devastation, and outrages of every kind."[2]
> —*Francois Jean de Beauvoir, Marquis de Chastellux, 1787*

Few participants in the American Revolution have been the subject of more misinformation—when their presence is acknowledged at all—than the Loyalists, those colonists who sided with the British during the conflict. As historian Maya Jasanoff noted, members of this "large but little-studied group . . . have long been relegated to the margins of mainstream history; they are often seen as losers, backward, and wrong" when they are not simply forgotten or omitted from historical accounts.[3] Other historians agreed that in American accounts of the Revolution, Loyalists "are disparaged through condescension or want of attention."[4] Neglect of the Loyalists allowed historians to portray "the Revolution simply as the triumph of liberty over tyranny," focusing on heroic Revolutionaries while ignoring those Americans who opposed them.[5]

When historians do mention them, Loyalists are often referred to as "Tories," a derogatory term commonly used by the Revolutionaries. By the early eighteenth century, the word "Tory" had little meaning except as an insult people used against their

---

1. "Tory," The Free Library, https://www.thefreelibrary.com (accessed June 3, 2020).

2. Francois Jean de Beauvoir, Marquis de Chastellux, *Travels in North America in the Years 1780, 1781, and 1782*, trans. Howard C. Rice, 2 vols. (Chapel Hill: University of North Carolina Press, 1963), 2:570.

3. Maya Jasanoff, "The Other Side of Revolution: Loyalists in the British Empire," *William and Mary Quarterly* 65, no. 2 (April 2008): 206.

4. Jerry Bannister and Liam Riordan, "Loyalism and the British Atlantic, 1660–1840," in *The Loyal Atlantic: Remaking the British Atlantic in the Revolutionary Era*, ed. Jerry Bannister and Liam Riordan (Toronto: University of Toronto Press, 2012), 6.

5. Paul H. Smith, *Loyalists and Redcoats: A Study in British Revolutionary Policy* (Chapel Hill: University of North Carolina Press, 1964), vii.

political enemies. Because of the term's negative connotations, Loyalists almost never referred to themselves as Tories. Even historians sympathetic to Loyalists use the term "Tories" and rarely depict them favorably. Paul H. Smith, the author of a detailed account of the Loyalists' military contributions to the British war effort, described Loyalists as "conservative, cautious, abhorring violence. . . . The Loyalist's virtues were military weaknesses. He was generally uncertain of his position, and was disinclined to commit himself boldly. He was more likely to hesitate than to volunteer, to watch on the sidelines than to fight openly."[6] Others similarly criticized the Loyalists for their flawed character, arguing that participation in a revolution demanded boldness and optimism, traits that were lacking in the pessimistic and thus cowardly Loyalists.[7] Many historians have insisted that the Loyalists harbored "some personal deficiency" that prevented them from understanding the importance of the Revolution or foreseeing the better future it would bring, and as a result, have portrayed them "as weak and unimaginative . . . lackeys of the Crown."[8]

Existing alongside this view of Loyalists as timid and passive is the contradictory assertion that Loyalists were wantonly cruel, committing acts of violence that incited retaliation by the Revolutionaries and provoked a bitter, bloody civil war in areas where Loyalists were most numerous, particularly New York, New Jersey, and the Carolinas. This portrayal of the Loyalists was entrenched by the mid-nineteenth century, and historians have continued to repeat the accusation. Don Higginbotham wrote that the Loyalists were "for the most part angry, bitter men" who desired "harsh retribution" against the Revolutionaries; when the British army occupied a region, these "bloodthirsty loyalists" convinced British officers to impose oppressive policies on the populace that provoked retaliation.[9] Walter Edgar took the argument a step further, arguing that the British occupation of the southern states depended on cruelty to succeed. "From Charles, Lord Cornwallis, to the humblest Tory militiaman, the occupying forces believed that fear and brutality would cow the populace," he declared,[10] adding that atrocities "were initiated by British regulars or their Tory allies.

---

6. Smith, *Loyalists and Redcoats*, 58.

7. Quoted in Ann Gorman Condon, "Marching to a Different Drummer—The Political Philosophy of the American Loyalists," in *Red, White, and True Blue: The Loyalists in the Revolution*, ed. Esmond Wright (New York: AMS Press, 1976), 1.

8. Condon, "Marching to a Different Drummer," 2; Ann Gorman Condon, "Foundations of Loyalism," in *The Loyal Americans: The Military Role of the Loyalist Provincial Corps and Their Settlement in British North America, 1775–1784*, ed. Robert S. Allen (Ottawa: National Museums of Canada, 1983), 2.

9. Don Higginbotham, "Reflections on the War of Independence," in *War and Society in Revolutionary America: The Wider Dimensions of Conflict*, ed. Don Higginbotham (Columbia: University of South Carolina Press, 1988), 7, 11, 20–21.

10. Walter Edgar, *Partisans and Redcoats: The Southern Conflict That Turned the Tide of the American Revolution* (New York: William Morrow, 2001), xvi.

Patriot militia bands responded in kind, and the violence escalated into a fury that laid waste entire communities."[11]

Other points of confusion or inaccuracy concerning the Loyalists include where they lived, the occupations they pursued, and even the nature of their political beliefs. The most common view is that the majority of Loyalists lived in coastal cities and that they were either royally appointed officeholders in the colonial governments, clergy of the Church of England, lawyers trained in England, or merchants who profited from trade connections across the British Empire; in short, members of the colonial upper class who based their political allegiance on personal interest.[12] Historians who have acknowledged that some Loyalists were motivated by political opinion tended to dismiss their beliefs as "a sophisticated creed" of royalist politics beyond the comprehension of most colonists.[13]

Some evidence can be found to support the myth that Loyalists were selfish, timid, unpatriotic people who feared change yet also engaged in ruthless violence against the Revolutionaries. However, a close examination of the surviving records provides a far different perspective, demonstrating that the motives and actions of Loyalists have been badly distorted.

Loyalist Numbers and Backgrounds

Perhaps the best-known estimate of the Loyalists' numbers comes from a statement attributed to John Adams that during the Revolution, one-third of Americans supported independence, one-third were Loyalists, and the remaining third were neutral. Repeated in books, classrooms, and documentary films, this statement is widely accepted as fact. There are problems with the assertion, however. First, Adams never made such an estimate. The myth originated in a history of the Revolution published in 1902, in which the author misinterpreted a remark Adams made. Adams was referring to American attitudes toward the French Revolution and surmised that one-third of the people opposed it. There is no evidence that Adams ever attempted to calculate the number of Loyalists during the American Revolution. The second problem with the figure is that it overstates the percentage of the American population that supported the British. While historians often disagree over how many colonists remained loyal to Britain, none of the estimates come close to Adams's alleged 33 percent.[14]

---

11. Edgar, *Partisans and Redcoats*, xvii.

12. Ruma Chopra, *Choosing Sides: Loyalists in Revolutionary America* (Lanham, MD: Rowman and Littlefield, 2013), 2; Gary B. Nash, *The Unknown American Revolution: The Unruly Birth of Democracy and the Struggle to Create America* (New York: Penguin Books, 2005), 238–39.

13. Wallace Brown, *The King's Friends: The Composition and Motives of the American Loyalist Claimants* (Providence, RI: Brown University Press, 1965), 258.

14. Dan Shippey and Michael Burns, "The One Third Myth," The Breed's Hill Institute, www.breedshill.org (accessed June 3, 2020).

Various methods have been employed to determine exactly how many Americans were Loyalists. The calculations are usually limited to colonists of European ancestry, as there is less information available concerning Native Americans and African Americans, and the choices of nearly all the latter were constrained by slavery. Based on the number of Loyalists who entered military service under the British in provincial regiments along with average family size, one study yielded a figure of 513,000, over 25 percent of the thirteen colonies' white population and 20 percent of the total population. Others arrived at a slightly lower number, about 500,000, though the present consensus is that about 20 percent of Americans were Loyalists, while 45 percent actively supported the Revolution. At least 60,000 Loyalists, and perhaps as many as 80,000, left the United States during or at the end of the war to settle elsewhere in the British Empire, while the approximately 400,000 who remained accommodated themselves to the new government.[15]

The number and percentage of Loyalists varied from one colony to another, and these figures are more difficult to determine. Historians seeking such information have relied heavily on the records of the Commission of Enquiry into the Losses, Services, and Claims of the American Loyalists, often referred to as the Loyalist Claims Commission. Created by Parliament in 1783 to compensate Loyalists for the financial losses they had suffered, the five-member board held most of its meetings in London, interviewing claimants in person when possible, and from 1785 to 1789, three members traveled to North America to meet with Loyalists at Halifax, St. John's, Montreal, and Quebec City in Canada and even in New York City. The commission's final report, issued on March 31, 1790, indicated that it had received 3,225 claims and evaluated 2,201; the other 1,024 claims were withdrawn or not examined by the commission for various reasons. The commission approved most of the claims, though some were rejected because the petitioners lacked evidence to prove their financial losses, did not need assistance, or could not demonstrate that they had indeed been loyal to Britain during the conflict.[16]

A study by Wallace Brown, whose findings have been widely accepted as the most accurate analysis of where Loyalists lived and what occupations they pursued, reviewed 2,908 claims and showed New York leading with 38 percent of the claimants, followed by South Carolina (11 percent), Massachusetts (10.7 percent), New Jersey (8.2 percent), Pennsylvania (7 percent), North Carolina (5.3 percent), Connecticut

15. Paul H. Smith, "The American Loyalists: Notes on Their Organization and Numerical Strength," *William and Mary Quarterly* 25, no. 2 (April 1968): 268–69; Shippey and Burns, "One Third Myth"; Jasanoff, "Other Side of Revolution," 206, 208; Rebecca Brannon, introduction to *The Consequences of Loyalism: Essays in Honor of Robert M. Calhoon*, ed. Rebecca Brannon and Joseph S. Moore (Columbia: University of South Carolina Press, 2019), 1.

16. Claude Halstead Van Tyne, *Loyalists in the American Revolution* (1902; repr. Gansevoort, NY: Corner House Historical Publications, 1999), 301–3; Eugene R. Fingerhut, "Uses and Abuses of the American Loyalists' Claims: A Critique of Quantitative Analyses," *William and Mary Quarterly* 25, no. 2 (April 1968): 246–47, 247n.

(5.2 percent), Virginia (4.5 percent), and Georgia (3.5 percent), with less than three percent in the other four colonies.[17]

Brown's effort to determine Loyalist numbers by region led to the conclusion that Loyalism was strongest in Georgia, New York, and South Carolina, with New Jersey and Massachusetts some distance behind. The results, based on calculating the number of claimants as a percentage of each colony's estimated population, matched the majority of assessments of where Loyalists were most numerous.[18]

The study also appeared to support the view that royal officials, merchants, lawyers, and clergy of the Church of England comprised a significant percentage of Loyalists. Over 18 percent of the claimants were described as merchants and shopkeepers, slightly more than 10 percent were classified as officeholders in the colonial governments, nearly 2 percent were lawyers, and more than 2 percent were Anglican ministers. However, the claims showed that Loyalists' occupations were far more varied than generally believed. About 49 percent were farmers, while almost 10 percent were artisans who practiced various trades. Nearly 3 percent were doctors, and the claimants included smaller numbers of other professions, including teachers, innkeepers, and sailors.[19]

Problems with the Loyalist Claims

While the Loyalist claims are valuable records, statistical analysis must be approached with caution. The number of claims filed represents less than 1 percent (.00645) of the total number of Loyalists and are "frequently either too ambiguous or devoid of the data needed" to assess "the economic or social status of the claimants."[20] In addition, the conclusion that most Loyalists lived in coastal cities fails to consider the presence of the British army in many of those locations, which made it easier for nearby Loyalists to seek refuge there, whereas Loyalists living inland could usually make such a journey only with great risk and difficulty. Thus the vast majority of Connecticut's claimants lived close to British-occupied New York City and Long Island. Furthermore, colonists who might have remained neutral or maintained a passive loyalty were more likely to embrace open Loyalism when their towns were in British possession.[21]

Other problems with statistical analysis of the claims are the difficulty of determining a claimant's occupation and the probable underrepresentation of less wealthy

17. Christopher F. Minty, "Reexamining Loyalist Identity during the American Revolution," in Brannon and Moore, *Consequences of Loyalism*, 34; Brown, *King's Friends*, 289.

18. Brown, *King's Friends*, 253, 256.

19. Brown, 263.

20. Fingerhut, "Uses and Abuses of the Loyalists' Claims," 245–46.

21. Fingerhut, 248–49, 249n.

Loyalists. Numerous claimants listed multiple occupations, such as farming and practicing blacksmithing or another trade, so assigning a person to a particular occupation is often arbitrary. Also, the conclusion that most claimants were at least moderately wealthy more likely reflects the circumstances of poorer, occasionally illiterate Loyalists, who lacked documents to verify their financial losses and could not afford to obtain them, and thus they did not submit claims to the commission. Other Loyalists who made claims later in the process, having learned that the board usually reduced the amounts requested by claimants, inflated the value of their property to maximize their compensation. When this practice and the paucity of claims from poor Loyalists are considered, the assertion that Loyalists were wealthier and more likely to be involved in trade than the colonial population as a whole is dubious.[22]

Historians who study Loyalism, examining a broad range of sources, have found that, with the exception of royal officials (who were indeed almost unanimously loyal) and ministers of the Church of England (most of whom maintained their allegiance to Britain), Loyalists differed little from other Americans.[23] Loyalists "comprised native and foreign born, those in backcountry areas as much as in cities, and those who worshipped in Anglican churches as well as those who were Quakers and Congregationalists. The average loyalist might come from any walk of life."[24] Members of some ethnic groups and religious denominations, however, were disproportionately loyal compared to the colonists as a whole. Immigrants from Scotland and the German-speaking European states tended to embrace Loyalism because they believed the British government had been and would continue to be more tolerant of minorities than the predominantly English Revolutionaries; Roman Catholics and members of other religious minorities feared that once free of British restraint, the larger denominations might restrict the freedom of worship enjoyed by smaller sects, or even persecute them as the New England Puritans had done in the previous century.[25]

Loyalist Political Beliefs

Although all Americans who adhered to the British government have been termed Loyalists, their reasons for doing so varied. Some Loyalists held a strong political attachment to the British government and its constitution, while others took a position based on local concerns. Some were conservative, and others desired major

---

22. Fingerhut, 250–51, 252.

23. Nash, *Unknown Revolution*, 238; Chopra, *Choosing Sides*, 2.

24. Chopra, *Choosing Sides*, 1–2.

25. Holger Hoock, *Scars of Independence: America's Violent Birth* (New York: Crown Publishing, 2017), 29; Chopra, *Choosing Sides*, 2; Nash, *Unknown Revolution*, 239; Keith Mason, "The American Loyalist Problem of Identity in the Revolutionary Atlantic World," in Bannister and Riordan, *Loyal Atlantic*, 42.

changes in the colonies' political, social, or economic systems. A few Loyalists based their opinion on complex political doctrine, though most were motivated by simpler forms of patriotism.

The assertion that Loyalism was a "sophisticated creed" was true for some Loyalists, but not all. Most of those who emerged as Loyalist leaders had been prominent and politically active before the Revolution, such as Thomas Hutchinson, the royal governor of Massachusetts, and could defend their views using complex constitutional arguments.[26] Others, like the Reverend Jacob Bailey, also based their decisions to remain loyal to Britain on "sophisticated intellectual reasons."[27] A Harvard-educated Anglican minister serving a parish in Pownalborough, Massachusetts (in present-day southeastern Maine), Bailey's congregation supported the Revolution. However, Bailey concluded that renouncing his oath to the king, who was head of the Church of England, would "be an act of both treason and sacrilege." His reasoning did not impress parishioners, who threatened him, killed his livestock, and eventually forced him to flee to Halifax with his family in June 1779.[28]

The one belief that united prominent Loyalists like Hutchinson with subsistence farmers in the countryside was allegiance to King George III. Many Loyalists also considered participation in the empire essential to the preservation of liberty. They expected that the continued expansion and economic development of Britain's North American territory would create a larger, more powerful, and more prosperous empire, where colonists and Britons shared a commitment to the British government and constitution, and the liberty they provided. Together the king's subjects would enjoy the freedom, economic benefits, and security of this vast empire. Other Loyalists, looking at the present rather than the future, believed that the colonists benefited from their current economic ties to Britain and the protection provided by the British military, particularly the navy.[29]

Despite their characterization as conservatives who feared change, Loyalists envisioned the future in many ways. Some whose Loyalism was rooted in their conservative beliefs held a low opinion of the Revolutionary leaders and "worried about an American future under the reign of power-hungry demagogues who conspired against the true freedoms of the British government." Others feared "the consequences of a disordered society" should the existing political system be overthrown, preferring that reform come from the British Parliament rather than colonial mobs.[30] New Jersey's royal governor, William Franklin, the Loyalist son of Benjamin Franklin, and prominent Pennsylvania lawyer Joseph Galloway were such conservatives who worried that the Revolutionary movement would upset the social order. At the other end of the spectrum, "many of the

---

26. Condon, "Marching to a Different Drummer," 3.

27. Maya Jasanoff, *Liberty's Exiles: American Loyalists in the Revolutionary World* (New York: Alfred A. Knopf, 2011), 9.

28. Jasanoff, *Liberty's Exiles*, 7.

29. Condon, "Marching to a Different Drummer," 2, 4; Jasanoff, *Liberty's Exiles*, 9.

30. Chopra, *Choosing Sides*, 3, 21.

Loyalists were among the most radical proponents of a transformed American society, people who sought a place in the body politic for ordinary people and an overhauled legal system where those in the lower classes could obtain simple justice."[31]

The Break Between Loyalists and Revolutionaries

During the initial dispute between the colonies and the British government over taxation that began with Parliament's passage of the Stamp Act in 1765, no significant internal divisions emerged among the colonists. This unity held for nearly a decade; "the serious division between Whigs and Tories did not materialize until the final crisis following the Boston Tea Party" in December 1773.[32] Even then, large numbers of people who later remained loyal to Britain continued to oppose British policy.[33] It was only between the outbreak of fighting in April 1775 and the adoption of the Declaration of Independence in July 1776 that numerous colonists, faced with a choice of opposing the British government by force or retaining their allegiance to king and country, chose the latter course. Isaac Low, a New York merchant, had led several committees organizing protests against Parliament's taxation, served in the First Continental Congress, pledged to boycott British merchandise, and as late as April 29, 1775, openly denounced King George III as a "tyrant." However, when it became clear later in the year that the imperial dispute was almost certainly going to be resolved by violence, Low decided the opposition to Britain had gone too far and maintained his loyalty to the British government.[34] In Georgia, the Reverend John Joachim Zubly, a native of Switzerland, composed a series of "widely circulated pamphlets" between 1765 and 1775 that provided readers "a compelling rationale for opposition to Parliament's pretensions to power in America."[35] His importance in mobilizing the resistance movement in Georgia was recognized by Georgians, who named him a delegate to the Second Continental Congress in 1775. Yet, Zubly quickly became disenchanted with more radical members of Congress who pushed for a military solution to the imperial dispute. Late in 1775, he left Philadelphia in frustration, and the next year, faced with a choice of taking an oath to Congress or declaring himself a Loyalist, Zubly chose the latter.[36]

The actions of Low, Zubly, and many others demonstrate that Loyalists were not enemies of freedom. Their disagreement with the Revolutionaries was not over the

---

31. Nash, *Unknown Revolution*, 239.

32. Wallace Brown, *The Good Americans: The Loyalists in the American Revolution* (New York: William Morrow, 1969), 32.

33. Brown, *Good Americans*, 33.

34. Chopra, *Choosing Sides*, 4.

35. Randall M. Miller, ed., *Zubly: "A Warm & Zealous Spirit"* (Macon, GA: Mercer University Press, 1982), 6.

36. Miller, *Zubly*, 20–22.

need to preserve freedom but rather "where the real danger to colonial liberty lay." Whereas the Revolutionaries believed that the British government was attempting to strip them of their rights and liberty, Loyalists "perceived that liberty could be threatened from below as well as from above, that a mob . . . could take away property as well as a ministry, that a committee could violate conscience as well as a king." Loyalists, while frequently conceding that the British government had acted in a manner that infringed upon the colonists' rights, believed that king and Parliament were less of a threat to liberty "than the tendencies toward mob rule, enforced conformity, and brutalization" that were becoming "pervasive" in every colony as the Revolutionaries established control.[37] Contrary to the commonly held belief that Loyalists preferred tyranny to freedom, poring through their abundant writings "one looks in vain for Loyalists who were opposed to liberty or the rights" of British subjects.[38]

Large numbers of colonists supported one side or the other due to circumstance rather than political ideology. The presence of British troops induced many people who were uncommitted or lukewarm in their sentiments to declare themselves Loyalists; the opposite occurred when British forces withdrew from an area, forcing Loyalists to choose between going with the troops or remaining at home to face reprisals from the Revolutionaries. In regions controlled by the Revolutionaries, Loyalists faced various forms of harassment that intimidated them into silence. Personal concerns also played a role as individuals chose one side or another to protect their property or family members.[39]

Many Loyalists supported British rule in America because they harbored grievances against local leaders rather than the royal government. People in several colonies, who believed their concerns had been neglected by legislators and prominent individuals who embraced the Revolutionary movement, thought their problems were more likely to be resolved under the British.

In South Carolina, "two distinct societies" existed, the wealthy slave-owning planters along the coast and the more numerous settlers in the backcountry; there was little interaction between the two groups. The colony's opposition to British policy that began with protests against the Stamp Act in 1765 originated among the coastal planters and Charleston residents and did not extend to the interior of the colony.[40] Most backcountry settlers were subsistence farmers, and few owned slaves. They resented the prosperous planters who monopolized political power and whose lack of concern for the welfare of backcountry people was often expressed with thinly disguised contempt. The failure of the planter-dominated colonial government to provide courts and law enforcement in the backcountry gave rise to the Regulator movement of 1767, as frontier settlers meted out their own justice to criminals. The legislature responded by

---

37. Condon, "Marching to a Different Drummer," 6.

38. Brown, *Good Americans*, 66.

39. Chopra, *Choosing Sides*, 3.

40. Lewis Pinckney Jones, *The South Carolina Civil War of 1775* (Lexington, SC: Sandlapper, 1975), 22.

creating six new judicial districts and circuit courts in the interior. However, this did not address the lack of backcountry representation in the legislature, as it left most of the region divided into two extensive electoral districts, making it difficult for most voters to reach a polling place. In the minds of backcountry people, oppressive "taxation without representation" was the policy of the colonial legislature, not the British government, so when the planters assumed leadership of the Revolutionary movement, large numbers of inland settlers declared themselves Loyalists.[41]

Similar situations existed in New York's Hudson River Valley and on Maryland's Eastern Shore. Along the Hudson, landowners grew wealthy from the labor of tenant farmers who worked their vast holdings. Robert R. Livingston, for example, owned 160,000 acres worked by tenants who struggled to eke out a living while most of the crops they produced yielded profits that swelled Livingston's coffers. Thus his "tenant farmers knew almost reflexively" that when Livingston declared his support for the Revolutionaries, "they would take the other side." The tenants refused to take the oath of allegiance to the Continental Congress, resisted serving in the militia, and plotted to unite with the British army since "for them, the tyranny of their landlords was far more injurious than the English tyranny bemoaned by the American patriots."[42] In Maryland, poor farmers on the Eastern Shore likewise opposed the Revolutionary state government because it ignored their desire for expanded voting rights and a greater voice in public affairs. These people "became Loyalists because conservative patriots, with a history of class imperiousness and insensitivity, drove them into the arms of the British."[43]

Passive Loyalists and Revolutionary Persecutors

Some Loyalists were indeed passive, for "it took great courage to express a violently unpopular minority view, to undergo social ostracism, economic ruin, imprisonment, and to face sometimes even physical torture and death, all of which many met with great fortitude."[44] A British officer reported in 1778 that Loyalists had to "disguise their Sentiments, and never will venture to declare for Britain 'till they see a prospect of being placed in Security against their Enemies."[45]

Although the Revolutionaries' harsh, often vicious persecution of Loyalists is well documented, most historians have not challenged the standard accounts that the Loyalists were the perpetrators rather than the victims of violence. Over a century

---

41. Jones, *South Carolina Civil War*, 25–26.

42. Nash, *Unknown Revolution*, 246.

43. Nash, 241.

44. Brown, *Good Americans*, 65.

45. "Remarks on Some Improvements Proposed by an Officer to Be Made in the Plan of the American War," 1778, Jeffery Amherst Papers, War Office 34/110/144, David Library of the American Revolution, Washington Crossing, PA, microfilm.

ago, British historian Sir John Fortescue described the Revolutionaries' treatment of Loyalists as a form of "terrorism" that "degenerated into indiscriminate robbery and violence."[46] More recently, Martha Condray Searcy emphatically declared that the Revolutionaries initiated the violence in the southern colonies and that there was no evidence that Loyalists had retaliated in kind.[47] Despite these efforts to describe the Revolutionaries' cruelty toward Loyalists accurately, "it remains surprisingly controversial in the United States today to count loyalists among the victims of republican chauvinism." Yet there are abundant records of the harassment that Loyalists suffered, from the famous if rare cases of tarring and feathering to legal sanctions that often led to the seizure of their property and banishment from their homes.[48]

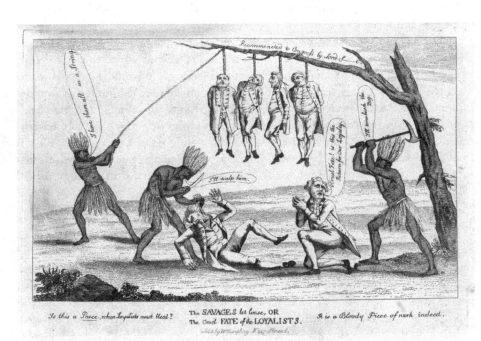

This British cartoon predicted that the Loyalists would suffer torture and execution after the war if left to the cruelty of the Americans, who had already committed many such acts against their neighbors who remained loyal to Britain. The Americans are portrayed as Indians; as in American art, British illustrators often used Indian images to symbolize barbarism and savagery. *The Savages Let Loose, or the Cruel Fate of the Loyalists*, etching published by William Humphrey, London, 1783. British Cartoon Prints Collection, Library of Congress.

46. Sir John Fortescue, *The War of Independence: The British Army in North America* (repr. Mechanicsburg, PA: Stackpole Books, 2001), 259.

47. Martha Condray Searcy, *The Georgia-Florida Contest in the American Revolution, 1776–1778* (Tuscaloosa: University of Alabama Press, 1985), 171.

48. Jasanoff, "Other Side of Revolution," 207.

Persecution of Loyalists began in Massachusetts months before the outbreak of warfare between the Revolutionaries and the British. On September 1, 1774, British soldiers from Boston seized artillery and gunpowder that the Massachusetts provisional government (an unofficial body chosen by colonists who refused to accept the royal governor's authority) had stored near Cambridge in preparation for possible armed conflict. In response, about 4,000 men from Boston and nearby towns assembled the next day at Cambridge's "Tory Row," a neighborhood of luxurious homes on present-day Brattle Street owned by wealthy supporters of the royal government, threatened the lives of the inhabitants, and forced Thomas Oliver to resign from the provincial council. During the next several months, continued harassment drove two of Tory Row's residents, William Brattle, a brigadier general in the militia, and David Phips, a colonel, along with several militia officers in other towns, either to resign their commissions or to take refuge in Boston where the British army could protect them. The provisional congress replaced them with trusted opponents of the royal government, thereby taking control of the colony's militia.[49]

These early attacks on Loyalists were carried out without official sanction, though the situation changed after the First Continental Congress convened in September 1774. Along with approving a boycott of British goods and limiting colonial exports to Britain, the delegates adopted the Continental Association to enforce these actions in every colony. The resolution called for each county and town in the colonies to choose a committee to monitor compliance.[50] All those found violating the trade restrictions or who refused to swear an oath to uphold the Association were to be declared "foes to the rights of *British-America*," their names made "publickly known," and be "universally contemned as the enemies of *American* liberty." What form the condemnation was to take, the Continental Congress did not specify, leaving such decisions to the "committees of safety" organized to carry out the instructions. More than 7,000 people in the colonies were serving on the committees by the spring of 1775.[51]

Among the milder forms of persecution for those who refused to take the oath were public humiliation, damage to an individual's reputation, and economic pressure, such as the inability to obtain credit or difficulty pursuing a trade or running a business because people refused to deal with a Loyalist. More severe punishments included being thrown into the nearest body of water, being forced to sit on a block of ice, beating, whipping, and, in one case, Connecticut Loyalist Peter Guire had the letters "G. R." (for the king's Latin designation, Georgius Rex), branded on his

---

49. Charles Neimeyer, "'Town Born, Turn Out': Town Militias, Tories, and the Struggle for the Control of the Massachusetts Backcountry," in *War & Society in the American Revolution: Mobilization and Home Fronts*, ed. John Resch and Walter Sargent (DeKalb: Northern Illinois University Press, 2007), 23, 27, 28, 30.

50. Hoock, *Scars of Independence*, 28–29.

51. Hoock, 29.

forehead. Doctor Abner Bebee, also of Connecticut, was attacked by a mob, tarred and feathered, then thrown into a hog pen where members of the mob jammed mud and animal waste into his eyes and mouth; the crowd also leveled his gristmill.[52]

The tarring and feathering administered to Bebee was a painful, sometimes deadly form of torture. A Loyalist described the procedure: "First, strip a Person naked, then heat the Tar untill it is thin, & pour it upon the naked Flesh, or rub it over with a Tar Brush. . . . After which, sprinkle decently upon the Tar . . . as many Feathers as will stick to it." In some cases, the feathers were set on fire. The next step was to place a hangman's noose around the victim's neck and ride the person through the streets in a cart to be ridiculed.[53] Another victim of this punishment, John Hopkins of Savannah, Georgia, was accused of having disparaged the Revolutionaries. A mob dragged him from his home and carried him to the town square, where he was tarred and feathered before being forced to ride through the town for three hours, his captors frequently stopping and compelling him to proclaim "Damnation to all Tories and Success to American Liberty" before he was released.[54]

After fighting began in April 1775, the persecution of Loyalists intensified. In Cambridge, Massachusetts, the remaining residents of "Tory Row," fearing for their lives, sought safety within the British lines at Boston. The provisional government confiscated five of the seven properties. In Virginia, John Randolph of Williamsburg, a friend of Thomas Jefferson and political moderate, discovered that his belief that Britain and America together "produced a relationship of far more strength and value than either could achieve separately" was unacceptable to his radical neighbors. Jefferson advised him to leave Virginia, and Randolph did so, traveling with his wife and daughters to England and "leaving behind every belonging they could not easily carry." Difficult as the Randolphs' situation was, Virginia Loyalists who could not afford to leave the colony usually experienced greater hardships.[55] Politicians Ralph Wormeley Jr. and John Tayloe Corbin "were arrested, sent away from their homes, and kept under guard for years." When Wormeley was finally permitted to return home in 1778, he found that his possessions had been looted by both Revolutionaries and Loyalists.[56]

Mobs roamed the streets of New York City, accosting people and demanding that they denounce the king. Those who refused were beaten. Printer James Rivington attempted to keep his newspaper, the *New-York Gazette*, impartial by printing material from Revolutionaries and Loyalists. Eighty men from New York and Connecticut

---

52. Hoock, 32, 34, 35.

53. Hoock, 24.

54. Deposition of John Hopkins, July 25, 1775, in *The Price of Loyalty: Tory Writings from the Revolutionary Era*, ed. Catherine S. Crary (New York: McGraw-Hill, 1973), 63.

55. Taylor Stoermer, "'The Success of Either Lies in the Womb of Time': The Politics of Loyalty in the Revolutionary Chesapeake," in Brannon and Moore, *Consequences of Loyalism*, 30.

56. Stoermer, "'The Success of Either,'" 31.

responded to his balanced approach by destroying his print shop in November 1775; Rivington escaped to a British naval vessel in the harbor. Other printers suspected of Loyalist sympathies suffered lesser harassment, including the burning of pamphlets authored by Loyalists to counter the published writings of their opponents, and soon these printers conformed to the committees' demands, effectively barring Loyalists from communicating their views to the public.[57]

Over one hundred armed men in the South Carolina backcountry confronted Thomas Brown, a recent immigrant from England, to demand that he sign the Continental Association. Brown refused, whereupon he was struck on the head with the butt of a musket, fracturing his skull, and tied to a tree. Tar was then applied to his legs, and his feet were pushed into a fire, causing severe burns and the loss of two toes. Some members of the mob then partially scalped him before he was placed in a cart and driven through towns and settlements, where he was forced to declare his support for the Continental Association. As soon as he was able, Brown escaped to the loyal colony of British East Florida, where he organized other Loyalist refugees into a provincial regiment, the King's Rangers, and began launching raids into Georgia.[58]

Loyalists imprisoned for their political opinions frequently endured harsh conditions. The most notorious prison was a copper mine in Simsbury, Connecticut, where captives were held underground in tunnels carved through the rock. At times the mine held as many as one hundred prisoners, and those considered the most dangerous were chained to wooden benches or support timbers. Some men were placed in iron collars chained to beams. The tunnels were only about five feet high, damp from leaking groundwater, and dark unless a prisoner was fortunate enough to procure candles.[59]

Although women had no political rights and were seldom permitted to express political opinions, Loyalist women were not exempt from harassment. The Revolutionaries "consigned female loyalists to much the same fate as their male relatives." Women whose husbands had fled to avoid arrest or persecution were especially vulnerable. Their property was often plundered, and they were "verbally abused, imprisoned, and threatened with bodily harm even when they had not taken an active role in opposing the rebel cause." Women bold enough to assist the British by aiding prisoners or providing intelligence were frequently subjected to physical abuse.[60] Richard Pearis, a South Carolina Loyalist, was arrested in early 1776 and chained in a Charleston jail for nine months. During his imprisonment, a party of Revolutionary militia appeared at his home. While his wife, two daughters, and son watched, they burned the house and outbuildings and destroyed any other property they could not

---

57. Hoock, *Scars of Independence*, 37, 38–39.

58. Hoock, 41–42.

59. Hoock, 45–48.

60. Mary Beth Norton, "Eighteenth-Century Women in Peace and War: The Case of the Loyalists," *William and Mary Quarterly* 33, no. 3 (July 1976): 398.

carry away. When the destruction was complete, the militiamen "beat and abused my daughters," Pearis wrote, and forced the entire family to walk twenty-five miles in one day without food, after which they were taken another hundred miles from their home in an open wagon. The Revolutionaries then "turned them out to shift for themselves amongst a Parcel of Rebels," and the family spent the next three years subsisting by "their own Industry" and the charity of some sympathetic people "under continual apprehension of being massacred." Pearis made his way to British West Florida on his release from prison and, like Brown, became an officer in a Loyalist military unit.[61]

The Loyalists received no reprieve when state governments were formed in 1776 after the colonies declared independence. Anticipating the decision for independence, the Second Continental Congress defined the crime of treason in June 1776. Anyone who waged war against the United States, retained their allegiance to George III, or assisted the British could be tried and executed for treason. John Adams was pleased with the law, predicting that it would convince "thousands" of Loyalists, who he described as "an ignorant, cowardly pack of scoundrels," to join the Revolutionaries.[62] The new state legislatures followed the example of Congress and enacted laws to suppress and punish Loyalists. These laws required that residents swear an oath of loyalty to the state government; persons refusing to do so were subject to capital punishment as traitors, though some states imposed lesser penalties. In general, these laws were harsher in states where Loyalists were most numerous and posed a greater threat to the Revolutionaries. New Hampshire, which had few Loyalists, only barred people who refused the state oath from holding civil and military offices and practicing law. Rhode Island, also with a small number of Loyalists, ordered state officials to seize all arms and ammunition from people suspected of Loyalism, and prohibited Loyalists from voting in town meetings, using the courts, and holding civil or military offices. In Massachusetts, where Loyalists were more numerous, those who refused to take the state's oath were barred from public office, practicing law, working as a teacher or member of the clergy, and were to be disarmed. Anyone who had joined the British or was suspected of posing a danger to the state was to be arrested and sent into the British lines and faced the death penalty should they return. New Jersey imposed fines on lawyers, educators, and members of juries who did not take the state oath. However, Loyalists who wished to renounce their allegiance to Britain could be forgiven, though they would forfeit all their property to the state. Anyone in North Carolina who took up arms against the United States or even made negative remarks about the United States or the state government was barred from access to the courts and

---

61. Richard Pearis, Loyalist Claim, 1783, Audit Office Papers, 12/49/300.
62. Hoock, *Scars of Independence*, 118.

from buying or transferring real estate and would forfeit all their land to the state government.[63]

The Massachusetts law expelling Loyalists was a banishment act, while the New Jersey and North Carolina legislation taking the property of Loyalists was termed a confiscation act. Seven other states, in addition to Massachusetts, passed banishment acts; all thirteen eventually approved some form of confiscation.[64] Many states combined the banishment of Loyalists and confiscation of their property, as did New York in a 1779 law. The legislation declared that all persons who voluntarily maintained their allegiance to the king were "enemies to this State and the . . . United States" and "forfeited all rights to the protection of this state, and to the benefit of the laws" protecting their property. All persons named in the law "should be immediately hereby convicted" of treason "in order to work a forfeiture of their respective estates, and vest the same in the people of this state." The offenders were to be expelled from the state, and if they were later discovered within its borders, they were to be executed.[65]

New York's law was similar to two measures enacted earlier by South Carolina. The first, passed in 1777, required anyone who refused to swear allegiance to the state to leave within sixty days or as soon after that as it took them to sell whatever property they could and find a means to depart for Britain or a loyal colony. A second measure enacted in 1778 deprived Loyalists of all political rights and the ability to conduct business and legal transactions and added the death penalty for banished persons who returned to the state.[66] The laws resulted in the departure of numerous Loyalists. Revolutionary leader Edward Rutledge boasted that the state had "sent forth Cargoes" of Loyalists into exile, which he considered "a small punishment, tho' apparently severe, for the many Injuries, they have, and the irreparable ones they would have brought on the virtuous part of our Community."[67] Although there are no precise numbers of Loyalists who had their property confiscated, estimates put the figure at tens of thousands. Funds received when state governments sold this property went into the state treasuries.[68]

---

63. Hoock, *Scars of Independence*, 118; Van Tyne, *Loyalists in the Revolution*, 318–19, 321, 325.

64. Hoock, *Scars of Independence*, 118; Chopra, *Choosing Sides*, 33.

65. Quoted in Chopra, *Choosing Sides*, 115.

66. Robert Stansbury Lambert, *South Carolina Loyalists in the American Revolution* (Columbia: University of South Carolina Press, 1987), 60, 62–64.

67. Edward Rutledge to John Adams, July 16, 1778, in *Papers of John Adams*, ed. Robert J. Taylor (Cambridge, MA: Belknap Press, 1983), 6:295.

68. Hoock, *Scars of Independence*, 119.

Loyalists and the British Army

Particularly distressing to Loyalists was their repeated abandonment by the British army. General Sir Henry Clinton, commander-in-chief in America from 1778 to 1782, repeatedly complained that occupying territory and then evacuating it not only demoralized Loyalists in those areas but, when the British left, it either forced Loyalists who had declared their support for Britain to flee as refugees or, if they chose to remain, exposed them to retaliation at the hands of the Revolutionaries.[69] General James Murray agreed, writing that "Our Evacuation of places, & leaving" Loyalists "to the vengeance of the Rebels, have rendered many of them hitherto Cautious." The British could not expect the Loyalists to make vigorous exertions on their behalf given "the disgusting Experience they have of Us," which included arrogant, condescending behavior toward Loyalists by army officers.[70] Joseph Galloway, an exile in London, echoed these views, urging that the British government, "Instead of rejecting the loyal force of the country, and daily sacrificing to the savage barbarity of rebellion, *enjoin our Generals to embrace it with zeal and cordiality.*"[71]

On other occasions, Loyalists attempting to unite with British forces suffered disastrous defeats that sapped the morale of Loyalists everywhere when the news became known. After the British captured Savannah in December 1778, Loyalist colonel James Boyd left the army to recruit a force in the southern backcountry. He quickly raised over 700 men from North and South Carolina, then moved southward to unite with the British. The Loyalists, pursued by Revolutionary militia, were attacked by about 400 Revolutionaries at Kettle Creek, Georgia, on February 14, 1779. Boyd was killed, and most of his recruits were captured or dispersed; only 270 finally reached the British.[72] Boyd's defeat proved "disastrous for Tory hopes in the southern backcountry. Many were now arrested, tried for treason, and harassed by their Whig neighbors and authorities. From then on they would be more cautious."[73]

Two years later, North Carolina Loyalists experienced a similar crushing disappointment. When a British army under Lieutenant General Charles, Earl Cornwallis, entered the state in early 1781, Dr. John Pyle raised some 400 fellow Loyalists. He set off to join the British, who were camped at Hillsborough. Cornwallis sent his cavalry,

---

69. Andrew Jackson O'Shaughnessy, *The Men Who Lost America: British Leadership, the American Revolution, and the Fate of the Empire* (New Haven, CT: Yale University Press, 2013), 220–21.

70. James Murray to George Townshend, September 1, 1782, Sol Feinstone Collection, David Library of the American Revolution, Washington Crossing, PA, no. 992.

71. Joseph Galloway, *Fabricius: Or, Letters to the People of Great Britain; On the Absurdity and Mischiefs of Defensive Operations Only in the American War; and on the Causes of the Failure in the Southern Operations* (London: G. Wilkie, 1782; repr. in *Selected Tracts,* by Joseph Galloway [New York: Da Capo Press, 1974]), 3:1044.

72. Rod Andrew Jr., *The Life and Times of General Andrew Pickens: Revolutionary War Hero, American Founder* (Chapel Hill: University of North Carolina Press, 2017), 63–66.

73. Andrew, *Andrew Pickens,* 68.

commanded by Lieutenant Colonel Banastre Tarleton, to find Pyle and bring him to camp. Unfortunately for Pyle and his men, on February 25, they encountered the American troops of Lieutenant Colonel Henry Lee's Legion, who wore green uniform coats almost identical to those worn by Tarleton's troops, causing Pyle to mistake Lee for Tarleton. Lee realized his advantage, and pretending to be Tarleton, he ordered Pyle to form his Loyalists alongside the road while the cavalry passed. When the two columns were side-by-side, Lee's men turned on the Loyalists with swords. Shocked and unprepared, the Loyalists were slaughtered. About 90 were killed, a few were captured, and most of the remainder were wounded and fled. The Revolutionaries did not suffer a single casualty.[74] Andrew Pickens, who with his militia had participated in Lee's attack on Pyle's Loyalists, informed General Nathanael Greene that the victory "has been of infinite Service. It has knocked up Toryism altogether in this part" of the state.[75]

The British army also alienated large numbers of Loyalists by mistreating them and seizing their property. British soldiers did not specifically target Loyalists. However, in their desire to punish rebellious Americans—or merely to take desired goods—they rarely discriminated between allies and enemies. Plundering civilians occurred for a variety of reasons. Some British troops wished to punish the treasonous colonists. Others sought to retaliate for the Revolutionaries' practice of guerrilla warfare. Perhaps most often, soldiers were simply hungry after arduous marching and fighting or wanted fresh food after long periods of receiving rations of salted meat and dry biscuits. The British army's pursuit of George Washington's retreating soldiers across New Jersey in the fall of 1776 was marked by extensive looting that converted neutral Americans into Revolutionaries and angered Loyalists when they became victims of such behavior. Both General Sir William Howe, commander of British forces at the time, and his successor, General Clinton, issued orders against plundering and inflicted harsh punishments on soldiers caught violating these regulations, but with limited success.[76] As the Revolution drew to a close, Lord George Germain, secretary of state for the American Department and responsible for directing military operations, wrote that "the great mischief Complain'd of in the prosecution of this war is that relaxation of discipline which disgraces the army and has alienated the Affections of the inhabitants [of America] from the Royal Cause."[77]

---

74. John S. Pancake, *This Destructive War: The British Campaign in the Carolinas, 1780–1782* (Tuscaloosa: University of Alabama Press, 1985), 173.

75. Andrew Pickens to Nathanael Greene, February 26, 1781, in *The Papers of General Nathanael Greene*, ed. Richard K. Showman (Chapel Hill: University of North Carolina Press, 1994), 7:358.

76. Gregory J. W. Urwin, "'To Bring the American Army under Strict Discipline': British Army Foraging Policy in the South, 1780–81," *War in History* 26, no. 1 (January 2019): 5, 7, 8, 9, 11; Stephen Conway, "'The Great Mischief Complain'd of': Reflections on the Misconduct of British Soldiers in the Revolutionary War," *William and Mary Quarterly* 47, no. 3 (July 1990): 377, 378, 379.

77. Quoted in Conway, "'Great Mischief Complain'd of,'" 370.

Loyalist Military Support for the British

The most compelling evidence that large numbers of Loyalists were neither passive nor timid is the extent of military support they provided to the British. In the face of numerous obstacles, some 19,000 Loyalist volunteers served in provincial regiments during the conflict, while thousands more did so in local militia and irregular units, bringing the number of Loyalists who performed some type of military service to at least 30,000.[78]

From the beginning of the war, British officials intended to utilize Loyalists to augment the Crown's regular troops. However, when hostilities began, Loyalists found themselves at a disadvantage because they lacked organization. In contrast, the

Numerous accounts insist that Loyalists were few and too timid to take an active role in support of the British. Yet, thousands of American Loyalists enlisted and served in provincial units. Among these were the Queen's Rangers, organized in 1776, one of many Loyalist regiments that proved themselves the equal of British regular troops. "A Light Infantry Man and Huzzar [Hussar] of the Queen's Rangers," watercolor, 1900, artist unknown, from John Graves Simcoe's *Military Journal*.

78. Chopra, *Choosing Sides*, 29.

Revolutionaries could rely on groups formed over the previous decade, including local chapters of the Sons of Liberty, provincial congresses, and committees of safety, for leadership. These institutions had rendered royal government in the colonies almost powerless and unable to organize a coherent Loyalist resistance. Most Loyalists, therefore, waited for direction from royal authorities before taking action.[79]

In a few instances, Loyalists attempted to oppose the Revolutionaries with little or no British assistance and without success. General Thomas Gage, the British commander in Boston, encouraged Massachusetts Loyalists to resist the Revolutionaries and sent arms to 300 Loyalists in Bristol County; they were no match for the 2,500 Revolutionary militia who dispersed them in April 1775 before the battles at Lexington and Concord. Once fighting had begun and large numbers of refugees sought safety in Boston, Gage authorized the creation of Loyalist units, though enlistments were few, and Gage devoted little attention to planning how to employ Loyalist recruits.[80] South Carolina Loyalists, acting on their own initiative, assembled 2,000 men in the backcountry. They surrounded a slightly smaller Revolutionary force in November 1775 and negotiated a temporary suspension of hostilities, only to see the treaty ignored by Revolutionary leaders in Charleston who sent additional militia the following month to arrest Loyalist leaders and disperse and disarm the Loyalists who gathered to oppose them.[81] Governor Josiah Martin of North Carolina encouraged recent immigrants from the Scottish Highlands to take action, but the 1,500 Loyalists were defeated by Revolutionary militia in February 1776.[82]

Loyalist activities in the Carolinas, despite their lack of success, confirmed the belief of officials in the British government that Loyalists would play a crucial role in suppressing the rebellion. Yet, the government never formulated detailed plans to recruit and employ them alongside the British army. As a result, "the Loyalists never occupied a fixed, well-understood place in British strategy."[83] Responsibility for implementing the government's intentions to create Loyalist military units was left in the hands of army officers in America, who did so when and if they believed it would be beneficial rather than as part of a coherent plan. Most Loyalist units organized in the early years of the war were created through the initiative of prominent Loyalists

---

79. Smith, *Loyalists and Redcoats*, ix, 7, 10.

80. Smith, *Loyalists and Redcoats*, 11, 12–13; Hoock, *Scars of Independence*, 41.

81. Marvin L. Cann, "Prelude to War: The First Battle of Ninety Six, November 19–21, 1775," *South Carolina Historical Magazine* 76, no. 4 (October 1975): 207–11; Lambert, *South Carolina Loyalists*, 44–45.

82. John Richard Alden, *The South in the Revolution, 1763–1789* (Baton Rouge: Louisiana State University Press, 1957), 196–98; Christopher Hibbert, *Redcoats and Rebels: The American Revolution through British Eyes* (New York: Avon Books, 1990), 103; Don Higginbotham, *The War of American Independence: Military Attitudes, Policies, and Practice, 1763–1789* (Boston, MA: Northeastern University Press, 1983), 135.

83. Smith, *Loyalists and Redcoats*, ix.

who prodded British commanders into allowing them to raise troops at their own expense.[84]

British officers had several reasons for their reluctance to form Loyalist regiments. Americans were unfamiliar with the doctrines of European warfare that governed the British army's operations. Furthermore, during the French and Indian War (1754–1763), many colonists had fought alongside the British and failed to impress regular officers, who complained that the American soldiers lacked discipline and were unreliable in battle. This mistrust of colonial troops persisted more than a decade later. If the Loyalists were to be made into reliable soldiers, British officials believed it would take at least a year of training.[85]

General Howe, who replaced Gage as commander of the British army in America, followed his predecessor's example in neglecting the Loyalists. Howe expected that his large force of British regulars and German auxiliaries would quickly defeat the Revolutionaries, eliminating any need to begin the lengthy process of recruiting, equipping, and training Loyalists. When the Continental Congress refused to renounce independence despite a string of British battlefield victories, Howe had no plan for utilizing the Loyalists; the most favorable opportunity for recruiting, at the height of British success, had passed. The Loyalists' willingness to support the British waned as some were angered by the army's plundering of their property during Howe's march across New Jersey. Meanwhile, Washington's victories at Trenton in December 1776 and Princeton in January 1777, followed by the British army's withdrawal from most of New Jersey, undermined many Loyalists' confidence in an eventual British victory. After six months, Howe had done little to take advantage of Loyalist support other than forming several provincial regiments. Nevertheless, he criticized the Loyalists for not doing enough to assist him.[86] However, the lack of Loyalist support "resulted not from a want of Loyalist enthusiasm" but from the failure of Howe and the British government to formulate and carry out plans for employing Loyalists.[87]

Lord Germain, Howe's civilian superior in the king's cabinet, pressed the general to make greater use of Loyalists. To placate Germain, Howe created additional provincial regiments without giving serious consideration to how he would use them. In addition to the New York Volunteers, New Jersey Volunteers, Queen's Rangers, and Oliver DeLancey's brigade formed earlier, Howe approved the creation of the King's American Regiment, the Loyal American Regiment, the Prince of Wales American Regiment, and other units. Trained, equipped, and disciplined like regiments of the British regular army, these troops served throughout the war from New England to

---

84. Smith, *Loyalists and Redcoats*, 11; Chopra, *Choosing Sides*, 29, 30.

85. Smith, *Loyalists and Redcoats*, 33, 35.

86. Chopra, *Choosing Sides*, 30; Smith, *Loyalists and Redcoats*, 37, 42–43.

87. Smith, *Loyalists and Redcoats*, 11.

Florida. Experienced provincial regiments soon proved themselves equal to their British counterparts in battle.[88]

In 1778 France entered the war as an ally of the United States, greatly straining British resources and forcing the government to reconsider how to make the best use of Loyalists. Germain ordered Clinton, who had replaced Howe as commander-in-chief, to encourage enlistment in the provincial regiments. Clinton adopted a policy of offering cash bounties to Loyalist recruits, providing funds for the troops' medical care, and promising one year's pay for officers disabled by wounds. These reforms led to an almost 20 percent increase of enlistments in 1779 compared to the previous year. Germain hoped to make up for any shortage in the number of provincial troops by relying on assistance from a Loyalist militia, men who performed short-term military service in the vicinity of their homes. He intended to focus military operations in the southern states and believed the Loyalists there could take responsibility for holding territory, freeing the British army to operate against the Revolutionaries' main forces.[89]

The major British effort to establish an effective Loyalist militia was implemented in South Carolina after the American defenders of Charleston surrendered to Clinton's army in May 1780. Clinton returned to New York shortly afterward, appointing Major Patrick Ferguson, a regular army officer, to organize the militia in the South, with overall command in the region assigned to General Cornwallis.[90] Unfortunately for the British, they failed to take full advantage of the initial outpouring of Loyalist support. Cornwallis ordered Ferguson "to take no steps whatsoever in the militia business" until the general drew up a plan to regulate the militia, delaying efforts to organize the Loyalists.[91] There were insufficient quantities of muskets to arm all of the militia soldiers, and training the men was hampered when Francis Marion's partisans and other Revolutionary irregulars attacked them when they assembled to drill.[92] Worsening the situation, American general Horatio Gates marched a new army into South Carolina, and although he was defeated in August, Cornwallis noted that reports of Gates's advance "very much intimidated our friends, encouraged

---

88. Smith, 45, 47, 48, 49.

89. Smith, 72, 73–74, 79.

90. Hoock, *Scars of Independence*, 314.

91. Patrick Ferguson to Earl Cornwallis, June 6, 1780, Charles, Earl Cornwallis Papers, Great Britain Public Record Office 30/11/2, 92, David Library of the American Revolution, microfilm.

92. R. Arthur Bowler, *Logistics and the Failure of the British Army in America, 1775–1783* (Princeton, NJ: Princeton University Press, 1975), 151–53; William Dobein James, *A Sketch of the Life of Brig. Gen. Francis Marion and a History of His Brigade from Its Rise in June 1780 until Disbanded in December, 1782* (1821; repr. Marietta, GA: Continental Book Co., 1948), 64; Richard Winn, "General Richard Winn's Notes—1780," ed. Samuel C. Williams, *South Carolina Historical and Genealogical Magazine* 43, no. 4 (October 1942): 202.

our enemies, and determined the wavering against us."[93] Ferguson's death and the death or capture of 1,000 of his militia at King's Mountain on October 7, along with the Revolutionaries' brutal treatment of the prisoners, including several executions, badly demoralized the Loyalists and undermined further British efforts to employ Loyalist militia units. The struggle between Loyalists and Revolutionaries in South Carolina devolved into a brutal, violent series of attacks and counterattacks, with both sides seeking to avenge grievances.[94] Cornwallis, in November 1780, indicated his reluctance to place any further reliance on the Loyalists by denouncing them as "dastardly and pusillanimous."[95] He either failed to realize or was unconcerned by the dangers Loyalists faced. Loyalist militia colonel Robert Gray asserted, with some exaggeration, that Loyalists in the backcountry were exposed to the full fury of the Revolutionaries and were at risk of having their throats cut while they slept.[96] "Probably the chief reason" for Cornwallis's failure to take full advantage of South Carolina's numerous Loyalists, his biographers observed, was his "distaste for the matter, which admitted of no soldierly approach." Cornwallis believed the key to British success was victory on the battlefield, not the administrative tasks required to organize Loyalists.[97]

On those rare occasions when the Loyalist militia did receive adequate support from the British, it proved to be an effective force. The best example is the British occupation of Wilmington, North Carolina, from January to November 1781. After 300 British troops occupied the town, their commander, Major James Craig, called upon Loyalists in the area to join him. Fearful of being abandoned, Loyalists waited until April to be sure the British did not leave. They then began to come forward. By summer, parties of Loyalist militia numbering as many as 500 were operating in the vicinity of Wilmington, skirmishing with the Revolutionaries and raiding inland towns. In August, a combined British-Loyalist force won a victory at Rockfish Creek and devastated rebel property in Duplin County while gathering 400 recruits, then seized New Bern. In their most famous operation, 600 Loyalists raided Hillsborough on September 12, taking 200 prisoners, including the state's governor, Thomas Burke.

---

93. Earl Cornwallis to Sir Henry Clinton, August 6, 1780, in *The American Rebellion, Sir Henry Clinton's Narrative of His Campaigns, 1775–1782, with an Appendix of Original Documents*, by Sir Henry Clinton, ed. William B. Willcox (New Haven, CT: Yale University Press, 1954), 448.

94. Hoock, *Scars of Independence*, 317–19.

95. Earl Cornwallis to General Alexander Leslie, November 12, 1780, in *Correspondence of Charles, First Marquis Cornwallis*, ed. Charles Ross (London: J. Murray, 1859), 1:69.

96. Robert M. Calhoon, "Civil, Revolutionary, or Partisan: The Loyalists and the Nature of the War for Independence," in *Tory Insurgents: The Loyalist Perception and Other Essays*, ed. Robert M. Calhoon, Timothy M. Barnes, and Robert S. Davis (Columbia: University of South Carolina Press, 2010), 213.

97. Franklin Wickwire and Mary Wickwire, *Cornwallis: The American Adventure* (Boston, MA: Houghton Mifflin, 1970), 171.

Despite their successes, the British and Loyalists were forced to evacuate Wilmington in November after Cornwallis surrendered his army at Yorktown the previous month.[98]

The success of the North Carolina Loyalist militia and the effective service of the provincial troops demonstrated that the majority of Loyalists were not passive or cowardly but willing to put their lives at risk to fight for their beliefs. If they sometimes engaged in acts of brutality against the Revolutionaries, such instances were generally in retaliation for persecution the Loyalists had suffered earlier rather than the unprovoked violence of which Loyalists have so often been accused. The Loyalists who chose to fight for king and country had to overcome obstacles not only from the Revolutionaries who implemented harsh measures against them but from the neglect, indifference, and sometimes condescension of the British government and its military officers in America.

Loyalist Clergy

Members of the Loyalist clergy conducted their battle on spiritual grounds and were also subject to intense persecution. These clerics, principally members of the Church of England, put forth many arguments based on scripture to prove that the colonists' opposition to British policy had no foundation in religious principles. They sought to counter the appeals of clerics who supported the Revolution and who insisted that resistance to King George III and Parliament was justified both by biblical texts and examples from the lives of significant figures in the Bible. Even though scripture provided a stronger case for the Loyalists' position, the Revolutionaries overcame that obstacle by silencing their opponents. Loyalist clerics were threatened, harassed, and forced from their pulpits, preventing them from effectively challenging claims that the Revolution was a divinely sanctioned undertaking.

The Declaration of Dependence

In November 1776, 547 Americans affixed their names—"at the risque of our Lives and Fortunes"—to a "Testimony of our Allegiance," an address to British authorities in New York. The signatories vowed to maintain "inviolate our loyalty to our Sovereign" despite "the strong tide of oppression and tyranny" and the "extreme difficulties and losses to which many of us have been exposed." For the Revolution represented "the most unnatural, unprovoked Rebellion, that ever disgraced the annals of Time."[99]

---

98. Gregory De Van Massey, "The British Expedition to Wilmington, January–November, 1781," *North Carolina Historical Review* 66, no. 4 (October 1989): 390, 391, 397, 401, 403–4, 407, 410.

99. "Declaration of Dependence," November 26–28, 1776, United Empire Loyalists Association of Canada, https://uelac.ca (accessed May 22, 2022).

Few Americans today have heard of the "Declaration of Dependence," as it was dubbed by the Revolutionaries, even though it included ten times the number of signatures as the July 4ᵗʰ Declaration. For that matter, most contemporary Americans would be hard-pressed to name a single Loyalist (unless perhaps Benedict Arnold is allowed). Patriot gatekeepers did their best to intimidate, excoriate, and eliminate any uncooperative voices. They did their job quite well, as attested by the relative paucity of surviving Loyalist literature and memory.

Several ministers, including the Anglican Charles Inglis, joined with businessmen, farmers, artisans, freed slaves, and members of sundry other American groups in adopting the Declaration of Dependence, and it was Loyalist clerics who shaped the most lucid arguments for choosing loyalty over liberty. They, too, loved America but were committed to peaceful protest against unjust policies rather than open rebellion against lawful authority. Many had enjoyed an elite education and were eminently equipped in logic, law, and history, as well as biblical studies. Patriot apologists certainly perceived them as a grave menace to the Revolution.[100]

Historians have identified nearly two hundred Loyalist clerics, three-fourths of whom were Anglican priests. Upon ordination, Anglican ministers were required to take an oath of loyalty to the Crown. From England, leading Methodist authorities such as John Wesley and John William Fletcher similarly urged American congregants to reject rebellion, "fear God and honour the king."[101]

Battle of the Bible

If biblical scripture is taken at face value, Loyalist interpreters clearly held the upper hand. In Romans 13:1, the apostle Paul directs: "Let every soul be subject unto the higher powers. For there is no power but of God: the powers that be are ordained of God." A second unequivocal statement is found in 1 Peter 2:17, where that apostle counseled: "Honor all men. Love the brotherhood. Fear God. Honor the King." Consequently, Patriot preachers often resorted to "creative exposition," "hasty exegesis," and "flights of fancy" in their efforts to justify revolution and sanctify republicanism.[102]

Jonathan Boucher, the erstwhile tutor of George Washington's stepson, regarded the message and life story of Jesus as incontrovertible evidence against rebellion. Jesus, wholly innocent of any crime and with all the powers of Heaven at his disposal, willingly accepted a painful and ignominious death rather than resist the temporal

---

100. Gregg L. Frazer, *God against the Revolution: The Loyalist Clergy's Case against the American Revolution* (Lawrence: University Press of Kansas, 2018), 2, 230–31.

101. Frazer, *God against the Revolution*, 28–29; Mark A. Noll, *Christians in the American Revolution* (Vancouver: Regent College Publishing, 2006), 112–16.

102. Frazer, *God against the Revolution*, 37.

authorities. As for the Patriots' much-touted prooftext, Galatians 5:1, "Stand fast, therefore, in the liberty wherewith Christ hath made us free," Boucher concluded that only with "infinite perversion and torture" could that passage be interpreted to mean anything beyond spiritual freedom from sin.[103]

Lacking New Testament support for their position, Whig apologists relied heavily upon the Old Testament, portraying America as the new Israel that God would lead out of British bondage. Republicanism was God's design, insisted Paine's *Common Sense*; the Israelites fell back into captivity only after being seduced by monarchy.

This monument, in Hamilton, Ontario, pays tribute to the Loyalists who settled in Canada after the Revolution. Contrary to the myth that most Loyalists were wealthy merchants and colonial officials, it accurately depicts the majority of Loyalists, who were members of ordinary families of farmers and artisans. United Empire Loyalist statue, Hamilton, Ontario, designed and produced by Sydney March, 1929. Photo by Saforrest, 2007.

---

103. Frazer, 55, 58–59.

Yet here again, Loyalist theologians thwarted the Patriot argument. Chapter 17 of the book of Deuteronomy delineates instructions for selecting a king, and no minister would deny the worthiness of King David, among others. King David, in fact, served as a "type," i.e., an analogous antecedent fulfilled by Jesus. Moreover, since early Christian times, biblical scholars have viewed the Old Testament principally as a symbolic foreshadowing of the New. Without New Testament authority to support political rebellion or republicanism, Loyalist ministers could logically relegate as wrong-headed any Patriot expositions of the Old.[104]

Boucher accepted that Christianity "is a suffering religion." Loyalist clergymen were not blind to problematic British policies, and many petitioned respectfully for redress. Still, the ends did not justify the means. Civil wars, which the Revolution was, appeared the most painful of all. As Charles Inglis insisted, government stood as the sole structure against "Oppression, Injustice, Violence, and Wickedness." Yet it could not succeed unless "those who rule, are honoured and obeyed." To their credit, Loyalist clergy did not respond in kind to the harassment and violence visited upon them. During the Revolution, one-fourth of Loyalist ministers left America, while another one-fifth perished. Some were physically assaulted; many more were banished, with their properties seized. The Anglican church in the thirteen colonies lost nearly half of its clergy to death or exile and was reorganized in 1785 as the independent American Episcopal Church, its connection to the British monarchy severed. In the final analysis, Patriots secured the public debate not through a superiority of argument but through an oft-unbridled militancy of method.[105]

Conclusion

The Loyalists not only lost the war against the Revolutionaries—they also lost control of its history. Frequently they were simply written out of the story of the Revolution, leaving the false impression that Americans were unified in their opposition to British rule. When Loyalists were included in historical accounts, "the dominant national narrative . . . branded the Loyalists as un-patriotic, un-American dissenters. They were effectively eliminated from public discourse, and a mantle of collective amnesia fell over the violence that Patriots had inflicted on their neighbors."[106] The contradiction of some Americans fighting for political liberty while attempting, often brutally, to silence fellow colonists, including members of the clergy, who held different political opinions, did not fit well in celebratory accounts of a struggle for freedom based on the rights of individuals.

---

104. Frazer, *God against the Revolution*, 62–63; James P. Byrd, *Sacred Scripture, Sacred War: The Bible and the American Revolution* (New York: Oxford University Press, 2013), 141.

105. Frazer, *God against the Revolution*, 25–26, 70–71, 227–28.

106. Hoock, *Scars of Independence*, 392.

The Loyalists may have failed to keep the thirteen colonies within the British Empire, but those who left as refugees influenced government affairs in their new homes. Exiles who settled in Canada and other colonies shaped imperial politics through their "commitment to liberty and humanitarian ideals."[107] "Although we cast the Loyalists as losers," historian Alan Taylor remarked, "they ultimately won the original goal of the colonial resistance: exemption from British taxation while remaining within the empire."[108]

107. Jasanoff, *Liberty's Exiles*, 12.

108. Quoted in Jasanoff, "Other Side of Revolution," 224.

Epilogue

As the origin story of the United States, the Revolution occupies a special place in the minds of Americans, evoking images of a unified people struggling to overthrow a tyrannical empire, achieving success, and going on to create an unprecedented form of representative government. The men—and, according to one myth, those who established the United States were exclusively male—who accomplished these tasks have been celebrated as another mythical entity, "the Founders." This gender-neutral term has largely replaced "Founding Fathers," which itself is relatively new, having been first used in 1916 by Warren G. Harding (who, four years later, would be elected president of the United States).[1] Politicians and opinion writers across the ideological spectrum regularly invoke the words of one, some, or all of the Founders to support

John Trumbull's well-known and widely reproduced painting of members of the Continental Congress signing the Declaration of Independence embodies many myths of the Revolution. These founders of the United States are all white men—no women, African Americans, or Indians are to be seen, even though these groups made significant contributions to achieving American independence. *Declaration of Independence, July 4th, 1776*, engraving by W. L. Ormsby, 1876, from the painting by John Trumbull. Library of Congress.

---

1. Jane Kamensky, "Two Cheers for the Nation: An American Revolution for the Revolting United States," *Reviews in American History* 47 (September 2019): 308.

their views and place themselves within the American Revolutionary tradition. In doing so, unfortunately, they appeal to yet another myth: the Founders embraced a common set of political principles. Nothing could be further from the truth; divergent views during the Revolution carried forward into the postwar era, resulting in heated debates over the Constitution and the bitter battles between Alexander Hamilton's Federalists and Thomas Jefferson's Democratic-Republicans in the 1790s. By the middle of that decade, Hamilton and Jefferson despised one another, and possibly the only point they might have agreed on was their shared animosity toward Hamilton's fellow Federalist, John Adams.

This reality is far different from that depicted in John Trumbull's painting of the signing of the Declaration of Independence, where a harmonious group of forty-seven white men, all but one of them at least nominally Protestant, are gathered to complete the task of formally establishing the new nation. While that image may have a nostalgic appeal to those Americans who yearn for a simpler—and imaginary—past of consensus and conformity, and as it reinforces the myth that American independence was the achievement of white, primarily Protestant, men, it does not capture the reality of the emerging United States existing outside the walls of Independence Hall.

Trumbull's painting does not, and cannot, explain why these men had gathered to declare independence. As we have seen, it was not as widely believed because a tyrannical British government sought to tax its American colonists into bankruptcy. On the contrary, British leaders were struggling to deal with an immense debt, largely incurred in waging a war that eliminated the French threat to the American colonies. Since the colonists had benefited from the war, British officials thought it reasonable to ask them to contribute to relieving the empire's financial burden. The taxes the British imposed were small, and Americans knew it; their concern was with the extent of Parliament's authority over the colonies, so the origins of the transatlantic dispute were political, not financial.

The painting omits any representation of many groups that supported the Revolution and made its success possible. The essays in this volume demonstrate that women, African Americans, Indians, and members of marginalized religious groups also struggled and sacrificed for the cause of independence. Whether they accompanied and assisted the Continental Army or acted as political writers, spies, and even soldiers, women were crucial to American victory. Some African Americans, Indians, and members of religious minorities likewise contributed in the hope that helping the new nation secure its freedom would bring them benefits as well. Like many written histories, Trumbull's painting creates the false impression that a small group of political leaders, ably assisted by the military skills of George Washington (the subject of another famous Trumbull painting), were almost solely responsible for establishing the United States.

Also left out of the painting, for obvious reasons, are those who opposed the Revolution: Loyalists, Indians, and African Americans. We have seen that, though often barely mentioned, especially in early histories of the Revolution, these people were major participants in the conflict. Most Indians chose to support the British because they believed doing so presented them the best chance to preserve their land and culture, just as thousands of enslaved African Americans, refuting the myth that they were satisfied with their lives in bondage, calculated that assisting the British provided a better opportunity for gaining their freedom than the Revolutionaries offered. Similarly, large numbers of Americans were convinced that the British government had done nothing to forfeit their allegiance and persisted in their commitment to the Crown. Despite often being characterized as passive, these Loyalists turned out by the thousands to fight for their beliefs. Like the Indians, they were denounced by the Revolutionaries as wantonly violent, yet the record shows that both groups were more often the victims rather than the perpetrators of violence.

British soldiers were also charged with carrying out atrocities, including the slaughter of defenseless American troops. This, too, is shown to be inaccurate, while the inhumane treatment of American prisoners of war, a well-documented subject, has received far less attention. Another refuted myth concerning the British army is that its soldiers came from the dregs of British society and were led by incompetent aristocrats whose only concept of military operations was a frontal assault made by men formed in rigid lines of battle. Instead, the Americans found themselves confronting capable, committed troops commanded by skilled officers who adapted quickly to conditions in America. As we have seen, Washington could not have succeeded against this force with the Continental Army alone—the Continentals needed the support of the militia, just as the militia could not have won without the Continental Army.

As noted in the Introduction, only a few of the most important myths surrounding the American Revolution have been addressed in this volume. However, understanding the truth about America's founding is particularly important because the subject is so frequently politicized and distorted to serve one or another agenda. As Thomas Jefferson wrote in 1789, "wherever the people are well informed they can be trusted with their own government."[2] The ability to separate myth from reality is essential, not just to historians, but to all Americans as citizens exercising the rights first obtained by the Revolution and enlarged over more than two centuries of further struggle.

---

2. Thomas Jefferson to Richard Price, January 1, 1789, Library of Congress, https://www.loc.gov/exhibits/jefferson/60.html (accessed Apr. 14, 2022).

SUGGESTED READING

This list includes many important recent works as well as several older books that remain highly influential. Although some of these volumes are no longer in print, they should be accessible through libraries or online. Journal articles are not included as they are often more difficult to access. Readers interested in exploring these topics further should consult the bibliographies of the books listed below.

General Works Addressing Myths and Lesser-Known Aspects of the Revolution

Holton, Woody. *Liberty Is Sweet: The Hidden History of the American Revolution*. New York: Simon & Schuster, 2021.

Hoock, Holger. *Scars of Independence: America's Violent Birth*. New York: Crown Publishing, 2017.

Nash, Gary B. *The Unknown American Revolution: The Unruly Birth of Democracy and the Struggle to Create America*. New York: Penguin Books, 2005.

Parkinson, Robert G. *The Common Cause: Creating Race and Nation in the American Revolution*. Chapel Hill: University of North Carolina Press, 2016.

Raphael, Ray. *Founding Myths: Stories That Hide Our Patriotic Past*. New York: New Press, 2014.

Young, Alfred F., and Gregory H. Nobles. *Whose American Revolution Was It?: Historians Interpret the Founding*. New York: New York University Press, 2011.

Taxation and the Origins of the Revolution

Bailyn, Bernard. *The Ideological Origins of the American Revolution*. Cambridge, MA: Belknap Press, 1992.

Carp, Benjamin L. *Defiance of the Patriots: The Boston Tea Party & the Making of America*. New Haven, CT: Yale University Press, 2011.

Dickerson, Oliver M. *The Navigation Acts and the American Revolution*. Philadelphia: University of Pennsylvania Press, 1951.

Morgan, Edmund S., and Helen M. Morgan. *The Stamp Act Crisis: Prologue to Revolution*. Chapel Hill: University of North Carolina Press, 1995.

Thomas, Peter D. G. *The Townshend Duties Crisis: The Second Phase of the American Revolution, 1767–1773*. New York: Oxford University Press, 1987.

The British Army

Brumwell, Stephen. *Redcoats: The British Soldier and War in the Americas, 1755–1763.* Cambridge, UK: Cambridge University Press, 2002.

Frey, Sylvia R. *The British Soldier in America.* Austin: University of Texas Press, 1981.

Hagist, Don N. *Noble Volunteers: The British Soldiers Who Fought the American Revolution.* Yardley, PA: Westholme, 2020.

O'Shaughnessy, Andrew Jackson. *The Men Who Lost America: British Leadership, the American Revolution, and the Fate of the Empire.* New Haven, CT: Yale University Press, 2014.

Spring, Matthew H. *With Zeal and Bayonets Only: The British Army on Campaign in North America, 1775–1783.* Norman: University of Oklahoma Press, 2008.

The Continental Army and the Militia

Buchanan, John. *The Road to Valley Forge: How Washington Built the Army That Won the Revolution.* Hoboken, NJ: John Wiley & Sons, 2004.

Kwasny, Mark V. *Washington's Partisan War, 1775–1783.* Kent, OH: Kent State University Press, 1996.

Martin, James Kirby, and Mark Edward Lender. *A Respectable Army: The Military Origins of the Republic, 1763–1789,* 3rd ed. Chichester, UK: John Wiley & Sons, 2015.

Royster, Charles. *A Revolutionary People at War: The Continental Army and American Character, 1775–1783.* New York: W. W. Norton, 1981.

Shy, John. *A People Numerous and Armed: Reflections on the Military Struggle for American Independence.* Ann Arbor: University of Michigan Press, 1990.

Prisoners of War

Borick, Carl P. *Relieve Us of This Burthen: American Prisoners of War in the Revolutionary South, 1780–1782.* Columbia: University of South Carolina Press, 2012.

Burrows, Edwin G. *Forgotten Patriots: The Untold Story of American Prisoners during the Revolutionary War.* New York: Basic Books, 2008.

Jones, T. Cole. *Captives of Liberty: Prisoners of War and the Politics of Vengeance in the American Revolution.* Philadelphia: University of Pennsylvania Press, 2019.

Women in the Revolution

Berkin, Carol. *Revolutionary Mothers: Women in the Struggle for America's Independence.* New York: Vintage Books, 2006.

Kerber, Linda K. *Women of the Republic: Intellect and Ideology in Revolutionary America.* Chapel Hill: University of North Carolina Press, 1997.

Mayer, Holly. *Belonging to the Army: Camp Followers and Community during the American Revolution.* Columbia: University of South Carolina Press, 1999.

Norton, Mary Beth. *Liberty's Daughters: The Revolutionary Experience of American Women, 1750–1800*. Ithaca, NY: Cornell University Press, 1996.

Oberg, Barbara B., ed. *Women in the American Revolution: Gender, Politics, and the Domestic World*. Charlottesville: University of Virginia Press, 2019.

Religion and Religious Minorities

Byrd, James P. *Sacred Scripture, Sacred War: The Bible and the American Revolution*. New York: Oxford University Press, 2017.

Carte, Katherine. *Religion and the American Revolution: An Imperial History*. Chapel Hill: University of North Carolina Press, 2021.

Farrelly, Maura Jane. *Papist Patriots: The Making of an American Catholic Identity*. New York: Oxford University Press, 2012.

Godbeer, Richard. *World of Trouble: A Philadelphia Quaker Family's Journey through the American Revolution*. New Haven, CT: Yale University Press, 2019.

Kidd, Thomas S. *God of Liberty: A Religious History of the American Revolution*. New York: Basic Books, 2010.

Rezneck, Samuel. *Unrecognized Patriots—The Jews in the American Revolution*. Westport, CT: Greenwood Publishing, 1975.

African Americans in the Revolution

Egerton, Douglas R. *Death or Liberty: African Americans and Revolutionary America*. New York: Oxford University Press, 2009.

Gilbert, Alan. *Black Patriots and Loyalists: Fighting for Emancipation in the War for Independence*. Chicago: University of Chicago Press, 2012.

Horne, Gerald. *The Counter-Revolution of 1776: Slave Resistance and the Origins of the United States of America*. New York: New York University Press, 2016.

Schama, Simon. *Rough Crossings: The Slaves, the British, and the American Revolution*. New York: Ecco Press, 2007.

Van Buskirk, Judith L. *Standing in Their Own Light: African American Patriots in the American Revolution*. Norman: University of Oklahoma Press, 2017.

Indians in the Revolution

Calloway, Colin G. *The American Revolution in Indian Country: Crisis and Diversity in Native American Communities*. Cambridge, UK: Cambridge University Press, 1995.

Dennis, Jeff W. *Patriots and Indians: Shaping Identity in Eighteenth-Century South Carolina*. Columbia: University of South Carolina Press, 2017.

Dowd, Gregory Evans. *A Spirited Resistance: The North American Indian Struggle for Unity, 1745–1815*. Baltimore, MD: Johns Hopkins University Press, 1992.

Glatthaar, Joseph T., and James Kirby Martin. *Forgotten Allies: The Oneida Indians in the American Revolution*. New York: Hill and Wang, 2006.

Schmidt, Ethan A. *Native Americans in the American Revolution: How the War Divided, Devastated, and Transformed the Early American Indian World*. Santa Barbara, CA: Praeger, 2014.

Loyalists

Brannon, Rebecca, and Joseph S. Moore, eds. *The Consequences of Loyalism: Essays in Honor of Robert M. Calhoon*. Columbia: University of South Carolina Press, 2019.

Brown, Wallace. *The King's Friends: The Composition and Motives of the American Loyalist Claimants*. Providence, RI: Brown University Press, 1965.

Chopra, Ruma. *Choosing Sides: Loyalists in Revolutionary America*. Lanham, MD: Rowman and Littlefield, 2013.

Jasanoff, Maya. *Liberty's Exiles: American Loyalists in the Revolutionary World*. New York: Alfred A. Knopf, 2011.

Piecuch, Jim. *Three Peoples, One King: Loyalists, Indians, and Slaves in the Revolutionary South, 1775–1782*. Columbia: University of South Carolina Press, 2008.

Primary Sources

At Founders Online, https://founders.archives.gov, the National Archives provides searchable access to an extensive collection of documents from American founders George Washington, Thomas Jefferson, Benjamin Franklin, John Adams, Alexander Hamilton, John Jay, and James Madison.

About the Contributors

Jeff W. Dennis is a professor of history at Southwestern Michigan College in his hometown of Dowagiac, Michigan. A graduate of Andrews University (BA, MA) and the University of Notre Dame (MA, PhD), Jeff holds more than thirty years of academy, college, and university teaching experience, including seven years in teacher education. He is author of the 2017 volume *Patriots and Indians: The South Carolina Experience*.

Don N. Hagist is Managing Editor of the *Journal of the American Revolution* (www.allthingsliberty.com). His research on the demographics and material culture of the British army in the American Revolution was a response to a scarcity of literature on that war's common British soldier and a questioning of conventional interpretations. He has published several articles and books, including *Noble Volunteers: The British Soldiers Who Fought the American Revolution* (2020), and *The Revolution's Last Men: The Soldiers behind the Photographs* (2015).

Mark Edward Lender holds a PhD in history from Rutgers University and is now Professor Emeritus of History at Kean University, from which he retired as Vice President for Academic Affairs in 2011. He is author or co-author of twelve books, including the classic *A Respectable Army* (with James Kirby Martin) and the award-winning *Fatal Sunday: George Washington, the Monmouth Campaign, and the Politics of Battle* (with Garry Stone). His latest title is *Cabal! The Plot against General Washington* (2020).

Jim Piecuch earned his BA and MA in history at the University of New Hampshire and his PhD from the College of William & Mary in Virginia. A former history professor, he is the author of seven books on the American Revolution, including *Three Peoples, One King: Loyalists, Indians, and Slaves in the Revolutionary South* and *Cool Deliberate Courage: John Eager Howard in the American Revolution* (with John Beakes), and editor of *Cavalry in the American Revolution*, and has also been involved in several public history projects.

Index